# POLITICAL ORGANIZATION OF NATIVE NORTH AMERICANS

**Ernest L. Schusky**
**Editor**

University Press
of America™

Copyright © 1980 by

**University Press of America, Inc.**™

4710 Auth Place, S.E., Washington, D.C. 20023

ISBN: 0-8191-0910-X

Library of Congress Number: 79-3715

DEDICATED TO THE MEMORY OF

D'ARCY MCNICKLE

*Congratulations to Doug.
on becoming Chairman
at Meramec!*

*Fred*

*May 28, 1980.*

# TABLE OF CONTENTS

# PREFACE

This book was conceived in 1975 when the American Anthropological Association asked members to plan symposia to celebrate the Bicentennial. The occasion was an opportune time to emphasize that the Birth of Independence for the United States meant an eventual death of independence for the Native American nations that first occupied North America.

American anthropologists always have had a special interest in Native peoples of North America because they were neighbors who offered contrasting ways of life. Comparison of differences is essential for anthropology, but the scientific interest quickly expanded to a concern for economic and political well-being. While impersonal study of different kinship systems and religious values helped build anthropological theory, anthropologists also found themselves pleading for an end to Indian poverty and a beginning of self-government in their home communities.

Thus, it was fitting to celebrate the Bicentennial by documenting the history leading to the dependency of Native Americans. Since many anthropologists had become well acquainted with the history of United States and Indian relations, I intended to show how Native independence had been lost largely through U.S. government policy; how poverty and dependence resulted from policies largely based on ignorance and a greed for land.

Since my approach focused on United States policy, I was initially disappointed when most of my colleagues explored problems from the views of the people they knew best--particular groups of Native Americans. However, I soon realized this approach is precisely what anthropologists do best; moreover, the Native American perspective is far more illuminating. Since the symposium, I have asked other anthropologists to participate to offer perspective on the entire continent.

The many books on federal-Indian relations already document the views of Congress, Presidents, and Supreme Court Justices who fashioned so much of United States policy. Such an approach fails to record what Native Americans did, and are doing, in an attempt to shape policy. For nearly two hundred years their actions and reactions were overlooked, their views never sought, and when expressed, were generally ignored. Here, Part I reexamines history to emphasize Indian political actions. It notes that even in the 1930s, when the Federal Government finally consulted Indians about policy, their opinion was scarcely recognized. Nevertheless, they have managed an important role throughout history in maintaining special rights as well as unique ways of life.

Since 1960 there has been new hope that Native Americans would have a significant voice in their future. Given the limbo of federal policy in the 1960s, the hope should have disappeared, but on the eve of the Bicentennial the nation had experienced both a militancy among Indians and a well-conceived, well-reasoned case for self-government and economic sufficiency articulated by Native Americans themselves.

The authors of Part II explore a current Indian viewpoint exemplified in communities ranging from Florida to the Northwest Territories of Canada. The work examines three issues which recur constantly in the relationship between Native Americans and their respective national governments: self-government, sovereignty, and land. For Euroamericans these topics are distinct issues. They are not so distinct in the papers that follow. I believe these issues shade into each other because the authors present a Native perspective; Indians understand that land, sovereignty, and self-government are a functional entity.

I first became aware of this difference in concepts after writing a monograph called The Right to Be Indian. It reached an Indian readership who wrote to tell me they appreciated how I defended their rights to land. I was puzzled, because I had intended to show how federal actions had guaranteed special rights to self-government. The letters reminded me of many meetings in South Dakota. When whites and Sioux gathered, they often seem to talk past each other. Invariably, whites discussed ways whereby Sioux communities could gain self-government, while the Sioux talked of their land, especially its loss. Later, land appeared again as a central issue in the books written by Native Americans such as Vine Deloria.

v

This emphasis on land loss should not be surprising if one were to view the North American continent as once one's own and now virtually lost, but Euroamerican history consistently pictures North America as an empty continent in 1492, only filled thereafter by hardy pioneers. If Native Americans are considered at all, it is not as the original occupants, but as other Americans who were accommodated by reserving some land for their use.

Needless to say, the Native American view is that the continent did indeed belong to them. This view was more or less shared by the first whites. The English settlers, especially, recognized an Indian title and regularly proceeded to transfer that title to themselves. They acquired the land largely by purchase, seldom claiming that any land was uninhabited. Time and again they carefully demonstrated by treaties that they had acquired a proper ownership in terms of Anglo-Saxon law and traditions about land.

The process started by the English colonists continued after the American Revolution. Congress reserved for itself the power to negotiate with the Native American nations and tribes, and the early treaties were always between the federal government and a Native government. Generally, the treaties were signed to specify what tracts of land were being transferred to the federal government in return for payment or other means necessary to achieve ownership. Even in the late nineteenth century, after treaties were no longer made, the federal government explicitly guaranteed land rights to Indians; equally explicitly, it devised means to acquire more of this land. One Indian aptly describes all of United States-Indian relations as a "history of land transfer." It is no wonder most Bureau of Indian Affairs paper work consists of record-keeping on land.

The history of land transfer is full of devious means for changing title from Indian to white, but the history must also show that the United States has attempted to correct some of the irregularities and unfairness. Surprisingly, Native Americans are not nearly so bitter about past injustices as they are with the end result of the many policies governing their land. These policies have resulted in a

pattern of land ownership that severely restricts
Indian communities both economically and politically.

For instance, most reservations are checkerboarded
with four types of land.  A white may own a tract
of land within a reservation with the same title
as any other white's.  A Native American may also
own a tract of land in fee simple, just as the white
does.  Another Native American may own land or a
share of land in trust.  By this title, a Native
American has some rights to land, except that ultimate ownership is in the United States government,
and the Secretary of the Interior is responsible
for its use.  Finally, a tribe itself owns land in
trust within the reservation.  As if all this were
not sufficiently complex, Native Americans sometimes
own land in trust outside the reservation, which
means reservation boundaries are not clearly fixed.

Since land in trust is "owned" by the federal government, it has the advantage of not being taxed
by state or local governments, but it has the disadvantage of being under ultimate control of the
Secretary of Interior, or in practice the Bureau
of Indian Affairs.  Thus, an Indian community is
faced with the paradox of wanting land in trust to
avoid real estate taxes, but submitting to control
by the Commissioner of Indian Affairs.  Many Native
Americans who own land in fee simple face the prospect of losing it because they cannot pay taxes.
Taxes may be low because the land is poor, but because the land is poor there is no income to pay
even minimal taxes.  To  prevent loss of the land,
the tribe often buys fee-simple lands from individual owners.  With tribal ownership, the land
becomes trust property.  I have heard Indians speak
passionately against loss of Indian land when they
have authorized a local Bureau of Indian Affairs
officer to sell tracts of their own.  The land
officer regarded them as blatant hypocrites.  But
the Indians are faced with losing their land to the
state for taxes, or taking the chance that the tribe
has enough money to purchase it.  Ironically, the
one chance of keeping the land "Indian" is to sell
it, providing tribal government can purchase it.

Land has profound symbolic value to Native Americans that whites do not understand.  The issue has

received little attention from anthropologists or other social scientists. I first became aware of its symbolism in discussions with the Sioux or Lakota who often spoke of the disappearance of their people. When I answered that census figures showed their population was increasing, they countered that parts of their reservations were continually being lost. They concluded there could be no more Indians when there was no more Indian land. Several older men told me that the original sacred Pipe given the Lakota in the Beginning was getting smaller. The Pipe shrank with the loss of land. When the land and Pipe disappeared, the Lakota would be gone. Discussions of land, and especially its loss, were always cast in emotional tones. I have heard similar tones among the Iroquois, in the Southwest, and in Alaska when land was an issue. For many Native Americans, an Indian identity is intertwined with rights to land.

This importance of a land base is part of the feelings Native Americans have about tribal sovereignty. To be sovereign is to have authority over land. From Colonial times the British recognized Native American sovereignty over their land, and the United States continued to recognize this fact. Yet, from the beginning the Euroamericans were reluctant to recognize that Indian nations had sovereign rights over them when they were on Indian land. To resolve the paradox, early treaties specified white wrongdoers would be delivered to the Colonial governments for punishment. Early in the nineteenth century the United States exerted authority even over Indians on Indian land. Native American sovereignty diminished; when Natives were made citizens in the twentieth century, many Euroamericans concluded Native Americans no longer had sovereign rights.

However, numerous Supreme Court decisions have explicitly recognized that Native tribes do have certain sovereign rights on their reservations, though the limits of this sovereignty are vaguely defined. For instance, the Supreme Court has declared the sovereign power of the Navajo is not restricted by even the Bill of Rights, but it has decided that the Suquamish tribe cannot subject non-Indians to its criminal codes. Still, the court and other federal officials are recognizing that if Indian tribes are indeed sovereign, then

they must have authority over anyone on their land.
Two justices in the Suquamish case dissented, declaring tribes did have criminal jurisdiction. While
the degree of jurisdiction remains unsettled, the
trend appears to be toward more Native control.
Carole Goldberg (1976) maintains that recent court
decisions indicate reservation governments have
sovereign rights over resident non-Indians in civil
cases, and they may exert criminal jurisdiction
given the consent of the non-Indian or the express
delegation of such power by Congress. Some reservations now post their boundaries to note that entrance constitutes consent to criminal jurisdiction.

The trend toward recognizing a greater degree of
sovereignty is even more apparent in the Report of
the American Indian Policy Review Commission, a body
recently appointed by Congress. Professor of Law,
Charles F. Wilkinson (1977), writing for the Commission, notes that tribal sovereignty was clearly
established in the case of Worcester vs. Georgia.
In the early 1960s a few cases indicated the Court
might impinge on this sovereignty, but since 1970
their decisions have "made it clear that tribal
sovereignty remains a vigorous and far-reaching
doctrine."

Wilkinson sees this sovereignty as fully established
in the treaty-making era. These agreements were
legally made contracts between governments, with the
courts interpreting the two parties as substantial
equals. The treaties have been regarded consistently
as superior to state laws and on a par with federal
statutes. Further doctrine has developed through
court decisions calling for ambiguous expressions
in treaties to be resolved in favor of the tribes,
for treaties to be interpreted as Indians likely
would have understood them, and for a liberal construction in favor of the tribes. Wilkinson (1977:
24) concludes that a "most significant by-product
of the canons of construction is the doctrine that
Indian treaties were not a grant of rights to tribes,
but from them. Thus, all sovereign powers of tribes
are retained unless expressly granted away by the
tribe in a treaty or expressly taken away from the
tribe by federal statute." The Report of the Commission recognizes that much policy, besides treaties, regulates relations with the Indian tribes.
Despite the great pressures to acquire Indian land

ix

and limit tribal government, the tribes have retained much of their sovereignty. Their government
powers have potential, and in the 1970s some tribes
began to use it. Many militant Indians today demand
an even greater use, and they have reacted strongly
to a Supreme Court decision of March 1978 that defines the tribes as "quasi sovereign." Although the
decision does limit tribal sovereignty in its criminal jurisdiction over non-members, the majority
opinion can be read as an invitation to Congress to
extend such jurisdiction.

Exercise of such sovereignty raises fears among many
whites. Tribal governments now compete vigorously
with whites for use of land and water, and especially
for government funding in a variety of areas. Yet
the greatest threat to whites is likely to be the
exercise of authority over resident non-Indians.
Native Americans have successfully taxed and regulated non-Indians operating businesses on their
reservation. The tribes' power to zone land for
economic development also affects non-Indians.
Native American regulation of hunting and fishing
has probably received greatest attention, but judged
by the minority report of the American Indian Policy
Review Commission, the area for greatest concern is
the subjection of non-Indians to Indian criminal
courts.

Lloyd Meeds, Vice Chairman of the Commission, objects vigorously to the direction of the majority
report which strongly documents a case for jurisdiction over non-members if sovereignty, or even
"quasi-sovereignty," is to have effective meaning.
He sees the question of the extent of tribal authority over non-members as one of the most important
ever asked. The Meeds dissent (1977:27), attached
to the report, notes:

> The question has profound implications in
> that the unwise exertion of such powers
> over non-Indians could have a catastrophic
> effect on whether Indian peoples will be
> left alone to make their own laws and be
> governed by them. The exercise of such
> authority would also bear upon the most
> valued political liberties and civil rights
> of those non-members who would be subjected
> to the coercive powers of tribal government.

Meeds argues further that the present authority of
the tribes has led to a situation where Native
Americans may vote for state and local officials
and yet not be subject to their jurisdiction or
taxes. Moreover, resident non-Indians may be taxed
and regulated by the tribes, but they have no vote
in the election of tribal officials. This "taxation
without representation" and representation without
taxation is contrary to American values. Meeds be-
lieves most Americans will interpret it as unjust.
Obviously, the situation is a difficult one, but
it should be recalled that Americans found it in-
tolerable that when Native Americans became citizens
they were sometimes deprived of the right to vote
in state elections. Though some states did prevent
their voting after 1924, when all Indians were made
citizens, by 1958 all states had extended the franchise to tribal members. Americans did decide that
representation without taxation was preferred to
exclusion from voting, simply because real estate
taxes could not be levied. The question of tribes
taxing non-Indians is relatively new, and American
opinion cannot be judged. United States citizens
readily recognize that they are subject to the
authority of other governments when they reside
abroad and are subject to certain foreign taxes.
They equally recognize that paying the tax does
not entitle them to vote for officials of the
country.

However, as Meeds emphasizes, Indian reservations
are not foreign countries; Congress has an authority
over reservations which it does not have over Mexico
or Canada. Yet it is not clear, as Meeds asserts,
that such authority terminates sovereignty. Congress is being asked to decide the degree and kind
of Indian sovereignty which not only stems from
past relations but also is consistent with justice
for peoples who were once fully sovereign nations,
now confined within the territorial limits of the
United States. Obviously, Congress is unlikely to
allow Indian tribes to enter into separate relations
with foreign nations, but what other limits might
be imposed are matters for debate.

While the issue of sovereignty may seem an academic
or semantic problem, it reflects the degree to which
Native American communities will be self-governing.
Meeds asserts in his dissent that tribal self-

government is legal doctrine but tribal sovereignty
is a political slogan. The dissent claims that the
Constitution provides for only two sovereigns, the
states and the federal government. Many historians
and political scientists see only the federal government as "sovereign," and a final definition can
be left to the academics. The practical issue is
the degree to which tribal governments are to have
self-government.

As some of the chapters in this book will indicate,
Native American communities still do not have as
much authority as white municipalities or counties
corresponding to reservations in size and population.
Yet treaty rights and other government actions
clearly indicate that Indians have special rights
beyond those of local governments. However, the
trust relationship to the federal government so restricts the decision-making of tribal councils that
many Indians are apathetic about tribal politics.
Land and funds in trust remain under the ultimate
authority of the Secretary of Interior. When legislation or policy changes have occurred to promote
greater self-government, the tribal councils that
have actively pursued it have received national
attention. Any attempts to include actions of non-
Indians in this self-governing process have been
especially newsworthy, as are the attempts to include treaty rights in an Indian expansion of self-
determination. It is difficult to see how Native
Americans can ever be described as self-governing
if they do not exert their rights as Indians. These
rights certainly include the ones guaranteed by
treaties, and if a tribal council is to have rights
equal to a white community, then it should be able
to regulate the actions of anyone in the community
whether Indian or non-Indian.

The issue is not unique to the United States. Canada
has experienced a parallel development. Though par-
ticulars differ, some Native Americans in the North
are also recognized as having treaty rights while
the Canadian government also claims it would like
to see all Native communities with the same privileges of self-government enjoyed by other Canadian
citizens. However, when Native Americans actively
pursue their rights, they often meet with resistance,
and their actions quickly acquire notoriety. The
isolation of many Canadian Native peoples has tended

to minimize attention to their problems until discovery of oil and other resources in the Arctic
recently spotlighted them.   The disadvantages of
dispersion are being overcome by pan-native organizations, crossing tribal as well as geographic
divisions.   Canadian Indians now have many contacts
with American Indians.   They especially watch events
in Alaska.   The Alaska Native Claims Settlement Act
is cited by Native Canadians as a precedent for adjusting their own claims, and recent events indicate
Native Canadians may exert considerable influence.
It is particularly appropriate that the present
volume contains chapters on several Canadian Eskimo
and Native groups who share a goal of self-government
with Indians in the United States.   The American
Indian Policy Review Commission (1977) could have
been speaking for the entire continent when it wrote:

> The ultimate objective of Federal-Indian
> policy must be directed toward aiding the
> tribes in achievement of fully functioning
> governments exercising primary governmental
> authority within the boundaries of the re-
> spective reservations.   This authority would
> include the power to adjudicate civil and
> criminal matters, to regulate land use, to
> regulate natural resources such as fish and
> game and water rights, to issue business
> licenses, to impose taxes, and to do any
> and all of those things which all local
> governments ... are presently doing.

Surely, such a goal can hardly be disputed either
in Canada or the United States.   Yet, given the
history of federal-Indian relations, implementation
will not be easy.   New legislation is always thought
of as an answer, but Native Americans generally fear
such a step, and rightfully so.   The Allotment Act
had disastrous effects upon their rights, and the
Indian Reorganization Act was hardly better.   Even
the 1968 Civil Rights Act seriously impinged upon
the Indian rights it was supposed to protect.   As
noted by the Policy Review Commission in its recommendation, the tribes could enjoy much more self-
government if they were simply allowed to exercise
the rights they already possess.   Thus, Congressional
action could be limited to:   redirecting funding to
insure greater tribal control, and reorganizing the
Bureau of Indian Affairs.   The goal of reorganization

should be to free the Bureau from domination by
other interests currently represented in the Department of Interior. More importantly, Congress needs
to insure that the Bureau fulfills its obligations
to guarantee tribal rights. These steps could be
taken within a simple, explicit declaration that the
goal of federal policy is to develop tribal governments to the point of exercising the same power and
having the same responsibilities as other local
American governments. To achieve such an end, Native peoples and other Americans must share in the
process. It is vital Native views be understood
by the larger society. The authors of this volume
describe that view to increase understanding among
non-Indian readers and to encourage Native Americans
to express their own views more fully. If Native
Americans are to reach the goal of self-government
most Americans see as their right, then Indians and
other Americans must join forces to secure the necessary changes.

## REFERENCES CITED

American Indian Policy Review Commission Report
    1977    Tribal Government. Washington:
            U. S. Printing Office.

Goldberg, Carole E.
    1976    A Dynamic View of Tribal Jurisdiction
            to Tax Non-Indians. The American
            Indian and the Law: A Special Issue
            of Law and Contemporary Indians.
            Duke University School of Law.

Meeds, Lloyd
    1977    Dissenting Views. Attached to: Ameri-
            can Indian Policy Review Commission
            Report. Washington: U. S. Printing
            Office.

Wilkinson, Charles F.
    1977    Concepts in Indian Law. American
            Indian Policy Review Commission
            Report. Washington: U. S. Printing
            Office.

# INTRODUCTION TO PART I

Part I reexamines Indian affairs with particular
attention to the role of Native Americans in shaping
policy, especially in the United States, because
their relationship with the federal government has
been determined in important ways by their actions
as well as reactions. Overall, as Euroamericans
became the dominant society, Indian policy became
less overtly determined by them, but their influence
has not consistently declined. Early in the twentieth century Native Americans were most at the
mercy of the larger society, but in the past fifty
years their influence often has reached considerable
proportion. It is fitting that when the United
States celebrated its Bicentennial of Independence,
Indians too were vigorously asserting their rights
toward independence.

Chapters 1 through 5 record general stages in the
chronology of the shifting power relations between
Indians and other Americans. The chronology begins
with a treaty-making era when Indian nations were
regarded as sovereign and established enduring
rights setting them apart from other groups. This
era fades into one when the federal government established more power over Indians and began defining
a special relationship for them. At the close of
the nineteenth century a popular dominant opinion
was to end the relationship and to assimilate Indians
fully into the larger society. The move failed
largely due to Native American resistance, and a
void in federal policy characterized the early twentieth century. By 1930 Native American resistance
to assimilation was so evident that the federal government responded by attempting to make Indian communities both self-sufficient and self-governing.
The policy met with only limited success because it
was primarily an action of the dominant society.
The government reacted to its own failure by revert-
ing to assimilation in the 1950s, but Native American reaction was so swift and determined that an
absence of policy marks the decade of the sixties.
Currently, Indians themselves are doing much to
shape a policy, and their influence may be coming
full circle. In the 1970s they are bargaining as
effectively as their ancestors did in the 1770s
when they were considered the equivalent of other
nations.

Chapter 1 begins the detailed examination of these various eras. It shows how Indian nations became powerful bodies taking advantage of the rivalries among the European powers. Rather than pawns of the British, French, or Spanish the indigenous nations formed new political organizations to resist and soon developed their own foreign policies. This action continued through the struggle for Independence and the War of 1812 when Native Americans capitalized on British and American conflict. As a result, the early treaties of the United States with the Indian governments continued to treat the tribes like nations, following the pattern established by Britain. Expediency in meeting tribal demands marked the legal relationship undertaken by the young United States government. These deeds of the founding fathers are often overshadowed by their words and thoughts. President Washington and his contemporaries viewed the Indian nations as inferior. Opinion varied as to whether Indians could be incorporated into the new nation or simply be left to extinction. Clearly, the political philosophy of the times would have given little power or even hope to Native Americans, but Indians did not subscribe to that philosophy. They continued to demand and win special recognition as political bodies. The discrepancy between the thought and deeds of the founding fathers caused much misunderstanding for Indians and non-Indians today. The chapter concludes that understanding the difference is an essential starting point for development of any policy.

In A Chronological Account of the Wabanaki Confederacy, authors Walker, Buesing, and Conkling record how early treaties shaped the development of federal-tribal affairs. They also describe the waxing and waning of political organization among Northeastern Indians in the face of white domination. The history begins with Passamaquoddy, Penobscot, and Maliseet becoming allies as a result of French influence. The confederacy soon developed a foreign policy involving close ties with the Iroquois. In the ensuing struggles among the Europeans and Euroamericans, the Wabanaki Confederacy used its strengths fully to win recognition as an important political body. But after independence the United States no longer needed the Wabanaki, and their fortunes faded. In the early nineteenth century, factionalism between traditionalists and progressives nearly ended the confederacy and even the tribal bodies. Yet at mid-century the Indians solved many of their problems by incorporating the factions into one political organ. Still, Indian unity declined because of continued white pressure. In the early twentieth century they hoped to persist simply as "wards" of the State of Maine. However, as their land ownership continued to erode, they formed a resistance in 1966, staging a sit-down to preserve their land base. The move expanded to legal suits including recognition of the Wabanaki as wards of the federal rather than state government. Such action revived the confederacy, and it is forming more extensive ties to include other state and urban Indian organizations. The action is among the most dramatic of contemporary Indian claims, receiving world-wide attention. Besides affecting land sales in most of Maine, the issue became an important one for New England Senators and the President. A final settlement will affect all Indians. Beyond this particular issue, the chapter illustrates the importance of the treaty-making period and how influential past Indian culture and organization is in shaping current politics.

The third chapter sheds new light on allotment policy. Most works treat the legislative details of the policy. Here, Sharlotte Neely dramatizes the tenor of the era through an examination of education policy among the Cherokee remaining in North Carolina. The case is particularly useful to illustrate how even Cherokee children resisted the severe efforts to eradicate not only Native culture but also language. Moreover, the chapter shows how even education policy was tied to the trend of acquiring ever more land from Indians. Since the aim of Cherokee education was to train the young for service jobs among the white population, they would no longer need the farms of their parents. Neely records the irony that, since elsewhere the Bureau of Indian Affairs was encouraging Indians to farm in order to "civilize" them, Cherokees sent to boardng schools entered an agricultural curriculum. The inconsistency of Bureau policy indirectly supported Cherokee resistance to assimilation. Neely's report of the end to repression introduces the influence of John Collier who redirected the course of Indian affairs in the 1930s.

3

Collier's determination to preserve Indian culture and grant tribal communities a measure of self-government culminated in the Indian Reorganization Act of 1934. Again, much has been written about the act, but most authors, attracted to its liberal philosophy, give little or no analysis of why the policy failed. D'Arcy McNickle provides new insights into the policy by exploring its failure in his chapter, The Indian New Deal as Mirror for the Future. One warning from McNickle is that a comprehensive policy like Collier's can be much distorted in the legislative process. Major provisions for transferring effective control to Indian communities simply were eliminated in passage of the legislation, partly through influence of Bureau of Indian Affairs officials. But McNickle suggests that inherent failure loomed even in Collier's original proposal. In his analysis of Navajo developments during the 1930s, McNickle details how outside control of a community is doomed to failure regardless of intentions. His examination of the sheep reduction program is most telling for the necessity of effective, local self-government. He concludes that although the policy had some positive effects, they were largely negated by post-war events. Yet today, Indian reactions to former policy lead them to demand control over their own affairs. An articulate leadership, which included McNickle, and a militant movement capitalizing on symbolic protest are laying the foundation to win the self-determinism of Collier's dream.

Margot Liberty writes of this new leadership as it is exemplified by the Northern Cheyenne and by Indian youth who demonstrated at the Custer Battlefield in June 1976. Her chapter illustrates the two-pronged attack Native Americans are making to win the rights they believe to be theirs. On the one hand they have devised their own protest strategy. Realizing they do not have the numbers to make the kinds of protests Blacks have managed, they have learned to take advantage of past injustices to gain attention from whites. Thus, Wounded Knee was appropriately occupied to remind whites that injustices to Indians still occur; the Custer Battlefield was most fitting to remind all Americans that Indians can win over injustice. Conveniently, the Little Big Horn is near the Cheyenne Reservation where the leadership is battling with a large corporation and indirectly the Bureau of Indian Affairs which co-operates with the corporation. The fight has all the characteristics of a David and Goliath combat, much like the original conflict between the 7th Cavalry and the Sioux. In addition to being the underdog, the Cheyenne have the advantage of a ready wit that captures the imagination more quickly than any of the slick advertising of the corporations. Doubtless, Cheyenne tactics will be followed by many Native peoples throughout the continent.

It is unfortunate that space does not allow a comparable analysis of Canadian and Indian relations, but the course of history in Canada parallels that of the United States. Today, the Native peoples in Canada find themselves in a similar position. In Part II several authors document the Native Canadian struggle for recognition of their rights. The second half of this book will portray what is happening across the continent as it is illustrated from a variety of Canadian reserves and United States reservations.

# CHAPTER 1

## Thoughts and Deeds of the Founding Fathers:
## The Beginning of United States and Indian Relations

Ernest L. Schusky, Southern Illinois University
Edwardsville

A major contemporary controversy between whites and
Indians concerns the interpretation of treaty rights.
At one extreme is an Indian view that the only step
necessary for the United States government is to
settle past treaty infractions; at the other end
many whites believe Indian treaties are a relic of
the past best forgotten and no longer binding.

As a first step toward reconciling these diverse
perspectives, it is useful to understand the setting
for the treaty-making era. The practice of treaty-
making was inherited from the British by the colonists who imposed a variety of innovations. By the
time the Constitution was written, it is doubtful
that the new government ever intended to treat with
Indian nations and tribes as equals. In the Articles
of Confederation, Indians had been recognized as
nations, but the Declaration of Independence refers
to them as savages. After tempers cooled, they became tribes in the one reference to them in the Constitution. This reference in the commerce clause,
specifying Congressional powers, obviously was meant
to exclude the Executive action involved in treaty-
making. Moreover, the writings of Washington, Jefferson, and others show a clear intent to improve
Indians by incorporating them as individuals into
the larger society. This intent, however, was seldom matched by deed. Instead, the early relations
with Indians are regularly governed by treaties.
Relations are consistently between sovereign bodies,
not between the federal government and individual
Indians.

The purpose of the following analysis is to establish that the men drafting the Constitution generally thought of the Indians as individuals and proposed plans for their individual welfare within the
framework of the federal government; yet, in practice, the American government drafted treaties with
Indian tribes, in fact, treating them as foreign

nations. Since the practice continued nearly a century after the Constitution, one must appreciate the validity of the Native American view that the United States intended to respect their sovereign rights.

COLONIAL AND EUROPEAN RELATIONS WITH INDIANS

This paradox between action and idealistic thought grew from a history that saw a sudden shift in the power relations between the Indian nations and colonial governments. Indeed, Indians were a dominant power over whites in the beginning of the seventeenth century. In 1622 Indians staged the first large-scale attack in Virginia. White retaliation was inconclusive, but as the settlers expanded in population, further warfare virtually eliminated the coastal tribes by 1644. In New England, the first fighting occurred in 1634; Native resistance culminated in 1676 with King Phillip's War. Defeat of the Indian coalition resulted in final termination of New England tribal sovereignty. By the close of the century, coastal Indians were decimated, enslaved, or driven into the interior.

In the interior, however, Native Americans were learning the effects of European encroachment. While a few groups like the Illinois quickly became dependent upon the French, most tribes resisted the intrusion by confederating into nations. These nations developed foreign policies that have gone largely unrecorded and unappreciated. Just as the European powers first pitted one coastal group against another in their power struggles, Native Americans now employed the same tactic. Algonkians used the French to advantage in their struggles with the Iroquois, while the Iroquois engaged British support for their cause. In the European interpretation, white powers used the red ones, but in fact it was a case of mutual exploitation, basic to most alliances.

Events among the Iroquois well illustrate what was happening among the Cherokee and Creek as well. At the end of the fourteenth century the Mohawks were using body armor and shields. They approached an enemy in concentrated bodies to shoot their arrows, tactics resembling the European pattern. But, Washburn (1975:125) reports the Mohawks converted quickly to guerrilla warfare when pitted against firearms. More importantly, they and other Iroquois developed a strategy of moving large bodies of men, based on the logistics of their agriculture, which gave them an advantage over their Algonkian enemies. To achieve this end, they had to solve their internal conflict and direct their aggression outward. The sachems in the League of the Iroquois never fully suppressed this individual violence; instead Wallace (1970:44) describes how they made use of it. Since some Mohawks would ally with the British to achieve personal gain, or a few Seneca would join the French for similar purpose, the League continually suggested the potential for throwing their weight to one side or the other. Although the Iroquois and Cherokee were the exemplars of such foreign policy on the eve of the French and Indian Wars, other groups followed suit. In 1750 Indian communities were not fully on par with the British, French, or Spanish, but their potential for shifting coalitions and upsetting balances required that they be treated as equals.

George Washington's experiences (Fitzpatrick 1931: 24-25) on the frontier in 1753 epitomize the colonists' perception of Indians. When he addressed them, it was as "brothers," and he speaks to them as equals.

> Brothers, I have called you together in Council by order of your Brother, the Governor of Virginia, to acquaint you... and deliver a Letter to the French Commandant, of very great importance to your Brothers, the English; and I dare say, to you their Friends and Allies.
>
> I was desired, Brothers, by your Brother the Governor, to call upon you, the Sachems of the Nations, to inform you of it, and to ask your Advice and Assistance to proceed to the nearest and best Road to the French.
>
> His Honour likewise desired me to apply to you for some of your young Men, to conduct and provide Provisions for us on our Way; and be a safe-guard against those French Indians who have taken up the hatchet against us. I have spoken

9

thus particularly to you Brothers, because
his Honour our Governor treats you as good
Friends and Allies; and holds you in great
Esteem.

In correspondence to other whites, Washington expresses less esteem and brotherhood for his red
allies but nevertheless underlined the necessity
of their aid. For example, a September 1756 letter
(Fitzpatrick 1931:464) to Governor Dinwiddie urges
every consideration for a war party of Cherokee and
Catawba.

Those Indians who are now coming should be
shewed all possible respect, and the greatest care taken of them, as upon them much
depends. 'Tis a critical time, they are
very humoursome, and their assistance very
necessary! One false step might not only
lose us that, but even turn them against
us. All kinds of necessary goods, etc.,
should be got for them.

Washington found himself on the frontier in the
1750s because of the population explosion in the
colonies between 1700 and 1750 when population
soared from 250,000 to 1,250,000. Land speculators
organized half a dozen companies to open lands in
western Pennsylvania and the Ohio Valley. This
search for new land was matched by the English fur
traders who were encroaching upon French domain,
not only along the Ohio, but also near the Great
Lakes. The local competition was exacerbated by
the rivalry of merchants in England and France.
In 1750, it seemed that English numbers and trade
goods would prevail, but in 1752 France exerted
itself, attacking English outposts and fortifying
its own frontier. In three years they controlled
the forks of the Ohio making life miserable for
Washington, though providing him with valuable
military experience.

Washington acquired considerable political experience as well, upon finding that his tactics, cour-
age, and determination were insufficient when un-
supported from the rear. His requests for help
often went unheeded, and his authority was generally
undermined by a lack of cohesion in Virginia, but
disunity within the colony was nothing as compared

to efforts at inter-colony cooperation. At the height of French and Indian expansion the governor of Pennsylvania was alleged to have offered the hostile forces safe passage through his colony if they would attack only the Virginia frontier (Nash 1974:264).

The failure of local forces to combat the French led England to send General James Braddock with two regiments of regulars. Just before they reached their destination, the French and Indians attacked. Braddock outnumbered his enemy, possibly three to one, yet his army was routed with tremendous loss. The victory was due largely to the guerrilla tactics developed by Indians, and the colonists learned America's first lessons for invading forces. Some of Washington's reactions are remarkably parallel to those in Vietnam two hundred years later. His recommendation that settlers be concentrated in certain selected villages sounds identical to the "strategic hamlet" planning of South Vietnam, and his observation that he would need ten militia for every Indian brings to mind Pentagon "force-ratio" estimates, while the use of Cherokee "irregulars" reminds one of CIA-recruited Montagnards.

In 1756 and 1757 the English faced the embarrassing prospect of a million and a half colonists being defeated by 70,000 French Canadians with their Indian allies. The staunch allies, however, were limited to the Algonkian. The English hoped to counter by enlisting or neutralizing the Iroquois, Creek, and Cherokee. Nash (1974:265) catches the desperation of the times by quoting Edmond Atkin, Superintendent of the Southern Indians:

> A Doubt remains not, that the prosperity of our Colonies on the Continent, will stand or fall with our Interest and favour among [the Indians]. While they are our friends, they are the Cheapest and Strongest Barrier for Protection of our Settlements; when Enemies, they are capable of ravaging in their method of War, in spite of all we can do, to render those Possessions almost useless.

The Creeks were less of a problem to Atkin than the Cherokee, but they maintained regular contacts

11

with the French, and the pro-French faction required
the English to make special efforts.  The flow of
goods to the Creeks steadily increased until 1757,
when the English blockade began to dry up French
stores.  The Cherokees drove a much harder bargain.
Though pro-English, pro-French, and neutral factions
endlessly debated, they presented a common front to
Europeans.  While the French did the best they could
to keep the Cherokee neutral, the British gave increasingly favorable trade items.  The Cherokee became particularly adept at promising large numbers
of warriors to the English but in the end sending
handfuls of mercenaries.  The practice has often
been interpreted as showing a lack of organization,
but Nash (1974:269-273) sees it as evidence of a
sophisticated realpolitic which involved not only
playing off French against English but South Caro-
linians against Virginians.

Iroquois foreign policy was even more masterful
because of their location between the major French
forces and the English.  Traditionally, they had
been enemies of the French and their Indian allies,
but as French fortunes rose, the Iroquois manipulated
their friendly ties with some French allies, and
Senecas in the West often fought alongside Frenchmen.
However, Mohawks occasionally enlisted in the English
cause as a balance.  The Iroquois Confederacy itself
maintained a steady neutrality until late in the war,
when a British victory was certain.  Today, many
historians credit the Iroquois for the outcome, but
Nash (1974:268) offers an alternate analysis:

> The evidence is much more compelling that
> the Iroquois were continually reassessing
> their own position and calculating how
> their self-interest could best be served.
> Despite English blandishments, presents,
> and even the return of previously acquired
> territory, the Iroquois refused to join the
> English side through the first four years
> of war or even to allow the English passage
> through their territory.  But when the mili-
> tary superiority of the English began to
> show itself in 1759, the Iroquois quickly
> adjusted their policy of neutrality and
> joined in reaping the benefits of victory.

The policy had some immediate benefits, but it doomed

long-term prospects for Iroquois independence. The end of the French and Indian Wars left England in complete control of all territory east of the Mississippi. Later Indian attempts to pit Spanish interests against English ones were short-lived. Events in Europe and English sea power affected the outcome as much or more than the fighting in America. At the Peace of Paris in 1763, Indian interests went unrepresented.

Indeed, the conclusion of fighting in 1760 led to a dramatic reversal in trade terms. England's staggering war debt ended gift-giving; less powder and fewer guns meant high prices. The colonies, united by the war effort, took advantage of their union to drive prices still higher. Yet land encroachment was an even more serious threat to Indian dominion; land speculators appeared throughout the interior as soon as fighting ceased. Indeed, the white threat was so obvious that a pan-Indian alliance appeared. A new religion arose stressing rejection of European ways, with the ideology soon supplemented politically by Pontiac. While the English colonists spoke of the Pontiac "conspiracy," Indians realized that to retain their homelands they would have to defend themselves without European help. Thus, most groups joined in putting an end to most of the English forts in the interior. Recognition of the Indian resistance came with the Proclamation of 1763. Prucha (1962:15-17) records that covertly the Proclamation intended to limit colonial settlement and prevent local manufacture. It was primarily an extension of Mercantilistic policy, but colonists saw it as an attempt to separate whites and Indians by drawing lines on maps in England. The King's orders to regulate trade and to prevent settlement beyond the Appalachians might have satisfied the Indians but were impossible to follow, since most colonial governors had little enthusiasm for the policy. They sympathized with landless commoners seeking a farm: more importantly they were much influenced by wealthy land speculators. Few colonists escaped the land fever, even George Washington. In a September 21, 1767 letter to his friend, William Crawford, he requests that Crawford secure a large tract of land, suggesting how restrictions on size be evaded and emphasizing he would much like "... to join you in attempting to secure some of the most valuable Lands in the

King's part which I think may be accomplished after
a while not withstanding the Proclamation that re-
strains it at present and prohibits the Settling of
them at all for I can never look upon that Proclamation in any other light (but this I say between
ourselves) than as a temporary expedient to quiet
the Minds of the Indians..." (Fitzpatrick 1931:II:
468)

Few could disagree with Washington's prophecy. The
Iroquois ceded lands south of the Ohio by the Treaty
of Fort Stanwix while Kentucky was being sized up
by speculators. In the early 1770s Indians, both
north and south, engaged in bitter warfare; the
fierceness of their resistance marked their recognition of approaching loss. None of the colonists
regarded them as equals, and the English government
would have liked them simply to cede their lands.
Following the line of least resistance, the English
continued to make treaties in order to secure land.


AMERICAN RELATIONS WITH INDIANS

This course of events was stemmed temporarily by
growing conflict between colonies and the mother
country. Lexington and Concord again converted
Native American tribes into power brokers, and the
Iroquois confederacy found itself wooed by two
opponents. English trade goods again flowed smoothly
as English hopes rose for an Iroquois auxiliary that
could isolate New England. The rebels asked only
for Iroquois neutrality. Guy Johnson, nephew of
William Johnson, spoke for the English cause as
northern superintendent. The Continental Congress
organized its own Indian Department, primarily to
keep Indians at peace. One of the earliest meetings
between Congressional representation and tribal representatives was in 1775 at Fort Pitt where Seneca,
Wyandot, Delaware, and Mingo promised neutrality.
In Mohr's opinion (1933:34) such a treaty "... was
of the greatest importance, because the frontier
was comparatively defenseless, lacking even such
necessities as powder." Particular emphasis was
placed on Iroquois neutrality or aid, and by 1777
some Iroquois were active allies for Revolutionary
forces, while others sided with England. The unity
of the League was fractured, but Iroquois statesmen
managed to maintain some order and draw concessions
from both sides. Still, the Seneca and other pro-

British Iroquois suffered grievous defeat in the
fall of 1779, while the Oneida and Tuscarora were
punished severely in 1780 by British retaliatory
raids.

In the South, the Creeks and Cherokees, along with
Choctaw and Chickasaw, quickly relearned to exploit
the differences among whites. British interests,
represented by veteran John Stuart, were quickly
advanced but countered by both South Carolina and
the Continental Congress. British trade and established contact gave them a decided advantage over
the rebels, but while the former sought active help,
the latter requested only neutrality. The choice
for the Indians was difficult and encouraged factionalism. In 1776 northern Indians finally persuaded some Cherokee to fight, leading to an American campaign that destroyed Cherokee towns on the
frontier and caused interior Cherokee to negotiate.
The Creek, under similar pressure, decided on neutrality, except for a faction led by Alexander
McGillivray, who fought alongside the British army.

In the lower Mississippi Valley, Choctaw and Chickasaw sentiment was decidedly pro-British; yet the
British agents there were ineffectual and mustered
only minor support. Moreover, their efforts were
divided. While initial planning was directed toward
an attack on the Spanish at New Orleans, George
Rogers Clark's success at Vincennes diverted attention northward. Helen Shaw (1931:144) records that
the British interpreted the victory as part of an
American move on West Florida staged from Illinois
country. Also, British generals denigrated Indians
as well as colonial loyalists, both becoming scape-
goats in defeat, so Choctaw allies were written off
after British failure against the Spanish at Mobile
in 1780. In effect, the British simply never made
good use of Indian potential.

Shaw (1931:84) records the Southern Indians were
likewise unfortunate in their choice of allies,
beginning with the French and then the English both
in the Revolution and in the War of 1812. One might
add they concluded by siding with the Confederacy
in 1860. Yet, they fared little worse than the
Iroquois and other Indians. While South Carolina
forced treaties upon the Cherokee to cede much of
their homeland, Georgia likewise proceeded against

the Creek. The Indian loss was most evident in
November, 1782 at Paris, where preliminary articles
of peace between America and England failed to mention the Indian nations.

When England ceded all land east of the Mississippi
to the United States, it abrogated Iroquois rights
guaranteed by previous treaty. The only spokesman
for the Iroquois and other tribes was the Spanish
negotiator who claimed the territory belonged to
free and independent Indian nations. John Jay's
response was, "With respect to the Indians we claim
the right of preemption; with respect to all other
nations, we claim the sovereignty over the territory" (Washburn 1975:157).

Jay was acting like the Spanish and other Europeans
who recognized Indian independence only when it was
detrimental to the opposition. In fairness to the
English, it should be noted that some of them
strongly denounced the treaty because it ignored
Indian rights. Washburn (1975:157) notes that
Benjamin Franklin's son, William, was among those
who "... denounced England's breaking of faith with
the Indians in conceding their lands without their
knowledge, but this was not the first or last peace
in which the rights of peoples not present at the
negotiations were sacrificed to the interests of
more powerful participants."

Two years later the Iroquois faced the same predicament as the Southern Indians. By treaty they ceded
much of their land in New York and Pennsylvania.
Even the two American allies, the Oneidas and Tus-
caroras, were forced to move. The commissioners
negotiating these treaties assumed the Iroquois were
a defeated people who were allowed to retain some
of their land out of American largesse. They also
conveniently assumed the Iroquois could cede by
treaty, lands occupied by Shawnee, Ojibway, Pota-
watomi, and other nations in the Midwest.

Naturally enough, these Indians denied the Iroquois
had such rights; in 1785 they formed confederacies
to prevent land cessions. Their policy established
the Ohio River as their southern boundary, although
white settlements already had appeared north of it
when Revolutionary War veterans received land grants
there. Along the Great Lakes the British continued

to occupy forts they had agreed to turn over to the
Americans. From these positions they covertly aided
the Indians. Yet it was essentially Indian tactics
and strategy that turned back General James Harmer
in 1790 from northwestern Ohio and defeated General
Arthur St. Clair in western Indiana in the American
disaster of 1791.

Parallel events occurred in the South, where Indians
achieved a degree of unity when they realized practically no outside aid was available. Between 1786
and 1790 firm resolve stopped Georgia encroachment.
In adept political maneuvering the Creeks negotiated
with Congress in a move against Georgia. Again,
short-term Indian interests were well served, but
the settlement prevented any unified effort between
northern and southern tribes.

A major advantage Native Americans enjoyed in this
period was the state of the new government. Reeling
under debt, Congress was reluctant to support military action against the Indians, though it faced
the paradox that newly opened lands in the Northwest
could help settle debts. For example, Abernethy
(1959:336) records that Virginia reserved most of
western Ohio as bounties for her Continental line.
However, the staggering problem was to achieve some
degree of unity among the former colonies if ever
a federal government was to be effective. Large
states opposed small states, and the question of
slavery opened differences between North and South.

Yet at the end of the century, Congress had to pay
attention to its western lands, because its hold
on the Mississippi Valley was tenuous. Spanish
and dissident Americans threatened to control the
river negating the advantages of Ohio River traffic
as well as Indian trade. Congress chose negotiation
with the Native American nations rather than war,
abandoning its claim to land based on conquest.
While stepping up efforts to purchase territory,
the Americans sought to incorporate Indians into
their civilization. The assimilation efforts had
some effects among the Iroquois and southern Indians,
but Native Americans in the interior gathered for
what would be their last stand.

The Shawnee, Tecumseh, led a pan-Indian political
resistance, backed by a religious movement inspired
by the Prophet. It had all the characteristics of

17

an Indian national liberation movement.  Tribal
differences were submerged, and an extraordinary
degree of unity was achieved on the basis of opposition to whites.  A dominant politico-religious
theme was that Native American land was inalienable.
Any land cessions were not only treasonable but
sacrilegious.  By 1810 Tecumseh was a major force
in the Northwest Territory.  He moved to incorporate
Choctaw, Chickasaw, and others in a pan-Indian union,
seeming on the verge of forging a powerful resistance.
However, in November, 1811, William Henry Harrison
attacked Prophetstown while Tecumseh was recruiting
in the South.  Both sides suffered major losses;
Tecumseh needed time to regroup.

Meanwhile, British and American clashes led to the
War of 1812.  The British enlisted Tecumseh's aid
and fighting broke out all along the frontier.  The
tribes hardly had time to develop any new policy
to fit the conflict nor were they any longer powerful enough to have much effect.  Most of them had
sided earlier with Tecumseh so the Indian cause
was definitely pro-British; his death in combat
in 1813 coincided with British concessions to America.  The end of overt resistance set the stage
for the Removal policy of Andrew Jackson.  It also
opened debate in intellectual circles on the eventual fate of American Indians.


THE COLONIAL WORLD VIEW OF THE INDIAN

The debate began in the Colonial period and needs
to be examined by itself, as parallel to the actual
relations traced above.  Only partly was it based
on the reality of the shifting coalitions among
colonists, the various European powers, and the
variety of Indian nations.

Eighteenth century philosophy, basic to the Constitution, provided a theme contrary to most of the
expedient steps taken to acquire Indian land.  From
the beginning the Indian as "natural man" or "noble
savage" was admired; Sheehan (1974:89-116) notes
he was even envied by many intellectuals.  In contrast, most average whites saw the Native American
as a worthless savage standing in the way of civilization.  Sea Coast intellectuals commonly were of
the former opinion while frontiersmen expressed the

18

latter view, but the issue is far more complex than this geographic division. On occasion, both thoughts were expressed by the same person; more often some compromise view of the paradox occurred.

The paradox had been preceded in the previous century by a consensus even between French and English. The newly discovered Indians were living in a state of nature, at times admired, but one that must necessarily change. Christian, civilized "man" was obliged to reveal the truth of his religion and confer the benefits of his civilization. This humanism and evangelicism allied neatly with commercial and imperial interests. The doctrine best served French purposes as Bidney (1954:323) notes:

> It was not necessary [the Jesuits] thought, to brand as criminal things that were done with an innocent intent. Thus they tried to establish a common ground between Indian standards and their own dogma and morality, and to construct a religion at the same time native and Catholic. For long they persisted in regarding evil traits as temporary and contingent upon paganism, and to the end they remained ardent advocates of the Indians.

The English on the other hand were simply not as tolerant; moreover, the bitter wars in 1622 and 1676 solidified opinion against the "savage." Pearce (1953:53) summarizes the view:

> Americans who were setting out to make a new society could find a place in it for the Indian only if he would become what they were--settled, steady, civilized. Yet somehow he would not be anything but what he was--roaming, unreliable, savage. So they concluded that they were destined to try to civilize him, in trying, to destroy him, because he could not and would not be civilized. He was to be pitied for this, and also to be censured. Pity and censure were the price Americans would have to pay for destroying the Indian.

Certainly, many colonists ascribed a complete savagery to Indians, even to the point of denying they were horticultural so as to exclude them from American life. Yet a significant number of the founding fathers did not write off the first Americans. Bidney (1954:325) objects to Pearce's conclusion that the Indian's only fate was to be extinction. He agrees they were assigned inferior status but argues that instead of forgetting them, many early Americans continued their efforts to incorporate or assimilate, or otherwise "civilize" the Indian.

It needs to be emphasized that the judgment of Indian cultures as inferior was rooted in the seventeenth century. The Indian-white conflict of the mid-eighteenth century cemented this evaluation which was further confirmed by experiences in the Revolution. Few, if any of the intellectuals, ever doubted the superiority of their culture to savage culture, but their reactions varied from benevolent paternalism to contemptuous scorn.

Cotton Mather epitomizes the latter views. From his observations he concluded (Silverman 1971:392), "That they have no family government among them; all family discipline is a stranger to them." Further, "... they are intolerably lazy: they hate work. To keep them at work would be a more grievous punishment unto them than to scourge them." Yet, Mather never quite gave up hope of Christianizing the Indian though he seemed to feel most would never be saved. In contrast, William Penn approached Indians in a brotherly fashion. It must be noted it was strictly Penn's conception of brotherhood, and Penn clearly saw himself as an older brother. An August, 1681 letter to the Indians of his colony advises them of his impending arrival.

> My Friends-There is one great God and power
> that hath made the world and all Things
> Therein, to whom you and I, and all people
> owe our well-being...
>
> This great God has written his law in our
> hearts, by which we are taught and commanded
> to love, and to help, and to do good to one
> another. Now this great God hath been
> pleased to make me concerned in your part
> of the world; and the king of this country
> where I live hath given me a great province
> Therein; but I desire to enjoy it with your

love and consent, that we may always live
together as neighbors and friends; else
what would the great God do to us ...?

Apparently, Penn saw room for Indians in his colony
and would have gladly incorporated them, but only
on his terms. He could respect them as individuals,
but he indicates no tolerance for their religious
beliefs or their aggressive ways. Thus, like Mather,
his approach was highly ethnocentric, while marked
by optimism for change. To bring such change, Penn
was convinced Indians must always be treated fairly,
and much of the rest of the above letter expresses
his resolve for fairness and justice. Still, the
letter concludes in the all-too-familiar vein of
white-Indian relations; in addition to peace, Penn
(Janney 1851:170) wants land.

I shall shortly come to see you myself,
at which time we may more largely and
freely confer and discourse of these
matters. In the mean time I have sent
my commissioners to treat with you about
land and a firm league of peace. Let me
desire you to be kind to them and to the
people, and receive the presents and
tokens which I have sent you ... [emphasis
added]

By mid-eighteenth century, conceptions of Indians
had changed little. Intermittent conflict kept
alive the notion of savagery, and continual expansion onto Indian domain was rationalized by their
"primitiveness." However, it was never possible
to dismiss them wholly as "child-like" or disdain
their presence because they so often held the balance of power. When they were not in a position to
side with one European power against another, they
were able to pit one colonial governor against an-
ther. In the French and Indian Wars the Indians
reached an apex of influence vis-à-vis Europeans, a
time when many founding fathers were maturing and
formulating conceptions of Indians. Washington's
experiences illustrate the process well.

In the French and Indian Wars he served Virginia
on the frontier, responsible for its northwest part
near the headwaters of the Ohio. He was plagued by
continual administrative problems, finding little

21

cooperation among the independent settlers, but his major headache was never knowing what Indian forces might be about to attack. In 1754 the solution he deemed most important was to enlist the aid of friendly Indians as a counterforce. This passage from an April 25, 1754 letter to Governor Dinwiddie is fairly typical of his thinking at the time.

> Perhaps it may also be thought advisable
> to invite the Cherokees, Catawbas, and
> Chickasaws to march to our assistance,
> as we are informed that six hundred
> Chippewas and Ottawas are marching down
> Scioto Creek to join the French, who are
> coming up the Ohio. In that case I would
> beg leave to recommend their being ordered
> to this place first, that a peace may be
> concluded between them and the Six Nations;
> for I am informed by several persons, that,
> as no good harmony subsists between them,
> their coming first to the Ohio may create
> great disorders, and turn out much to our
> disadvantage (Fitzpatrick 1931:I:42).

Although the southern Indians provided little relief, Washington's tone became more desperate the next year, doubtless because he received so little help from the English. To Dinwiddie on October 17, 1755, he urged all care be taken to gain Indian support in the South. He understood that "some of the Cherokees, who have been introduced to us as Sachems and Princes, by this interpreter, who shares the profits, have been no other than common Hunters, and bloodthirsty Villains!" Despite this outcome, Washington foresaw grave danger unless an alliance was made with the tribes. Even though disappointed by Indian allies, his high regard for their potential continued in the spring of 1756.

In explaining to Dinwiddie his delay on moving to Fort Cumberland, he (Fitzpatrick 1931:I:300-301) says of the Indian threat:

> However absurd it may appear, it is never-
> theless certain, that five hundred Indians
> have it more in their power to annoy the
> inhabitants, than ten times their number
> of regulars. For beside the advantageous
> way they have of fighting in the woods,

their cunning and craft are not to be
equalled, neither their activity and
indefatigable sufferings.  They prowl
about like wolves, and, like them, do
their mischief by stealth.

In the fall, he was actively recruiting, as shown
by his letter (Fitzpatrick 1931:I:486-487) to a
leading man of the Catawbas:

Capt. Johnne:  We Desire you to go to the
Cherokees, and tell them the Road is now
clear and Open; We expected them to War
last Spring, and love them So well, that
Our Governor Sent Some few men to build a
fort among them; but we are mighty Sorry
that they hearken so much to lies French
tell, as to break their promise and not
come to war, when they might have got a
great deal of honor; and kill'd a great
many of the French, whose hearts are
false, and rotten as an old Stump.  If
they Continue to Listen to What the French
Say much longer they will have great cause
to be sorry, as the French have no Match
locks, pow'd and Lead but what they got
from King George our father, before the
War began and that will soon be out; when
they will get no more, and all the French
Indians will be starving with Cold, and
must take to Bows and Arrows again for
want of Ammunition.

However, in the spring of 1757 Washington apparently
grew weary of his attempts to ally Indians.  They
promised far more than they delivered, and the few
who joined Washington often were more hindrance than
help.  Washington airs his grievance to Dinwiddie in
a May letter (Fitzpatrick 1931:II:36):

I doubt not but your Honor before this is
informed, that a party of Cherokees under
Warhatchie is come in with 4 Scalps and 2
Prisoners:  They are much dissatisfied that
the presents are not here.  Look upon Capt.
Mercers going off as a trick to evade the
promise...; and in short, they are the most
insolent, most avaricious, and most dissatisfied wretches I ever had to deal with.

Thus, in 1775, it seems Washington agreed with those colonists who felt Indians should be excluded from the fraternal struggle with England. Yet, by the close of the year they perceived an Indian threat, and it became Congressional policy to promote the neutrality of the Indian nations. By the time Washington was commander-in-chief he must have recognized that the Indian nations had again slipped into their position of power brokers. The Iroquois on the north, and the Creek and Cherokee on the south, posed a constant threat, but the British, themselves, diverted Washington's thoughts from the frontier.

## THE INDIAN IN AMERICAN INTELLECTUAL THOUGHT

However, Washington as President is once more involved with Indians. Some lack of regard becomes evident and indicates Indian policy was governed by expediency. More important matters were at hand and Indian affairs simply continued as in the past. This approach is indicated in Washington's correspondence to his Secretary of War, September 16, 1795 (Fitzpatrick 1940:34:305-306). After noting the success of a treaty with the northern tribes, Washington requested the dispatch of an agent for the southern tribes, to treat with the Creeks and Chickasaws. "It would be a pleasing circumstance not only to be enabled to say, at the meeting of Congress, that we were at Peace with all the Indian Nations, but by the mediation of the U. States, we had settled the differences between the tribes ..." Such a move would not only boost Washington's relation to Congress but confirm federal authority over the states.

Thus, relations with the tribes became an integral part of Presidential politics. It was not the only precedent established by Washington. A year later, when Washington addressed representatives of tribes in the Northwest who met with him in Philadelphia, he (Fitzpatrick 1940:35:299-300) emphasizes the nature of treaties as mutual obligations. He further notes:

> The United States, who love justice, have agreed to pay to you and your children for ever, a yearly Sum of money in Goods, for

a certain parcel of your land. By the same
Treaty, the Indian Nations mentioned Therein,
have bound themselves not to sell any of
their land, except to the United States.

Perpetual annuities did not last long, as it became
apparent that Indians would not disappear as quickly
as thought, but for nearly one hundred years the
United States would be the sole purchaser of Indian
lands, usually making annual payment for a period of
years.  Such annuities were probably intended to
insure compliance.  They also built in a dependency
on the yearly distribution, seriously disrupting
former political organization.  The United States
felt it could distribute annuities through a few
mediators.  The move reflects some ethnocentrism
(Indians must have leaders like whites do), and it
reduced expenses.  The early treaties, agreements,
and Executive Orders also began to impose a white
version of justice and morality.  Although Washington
apparently intended that Indians were to have equal
jurisdiction with whites over their respective lands,
note Washington's example:

> I shall now give you some advice respecting
> the conduct of your people, the observance
> of which, I consider of importance to their
> tranquility and peace.  There are among the
> Indians as among the Whites, Individuals
> who will steal their Neighbour's property,
> when they find the opportunity, in prefer-
> ence to acquiring property to themselves
> by honest means.  Bad White Men for example,
> will go into the Indian Country, and steal
> Horses; and bad Indians in like manner will
> go into the Settlement of the Whites, and
> steal their horses.  If the Indian Nations
> wish to deserve the friendship of the United
> States, and to prevent the white Settlers
> on the frontiers from retaliation on their
> property, the Chiefs and Warriors of the
> respective Nations must use their endeavours
> to punish such Offenders, and restore to
> the Whites, or to some Officers of the United
> States, the property they may have stolen.
> As for the Government, it will use it's
> utmost endeavours to restore to every Indian
> any property of his which may have been
> stolen by Citizens of the United States,
> and will moreover punish those who violate

the laws that have been made to prevent
such practices, whenever the fact can be
proved upon them.

While these treaty terms suggest an overt attempt
to recognize the independence of the Indian nations,
Washington's concluding remarks make it clear that
his personal view ordained a course of assimilation
as the most desirable if not the only alternative:

But, it is not enough that the United States
should furnish your Nations with an annual
quantity of Goods that you should not sell
your lands for that which could be of no
advantage to your posterity, that you should
prevent bad Indians from stealing from the
white frontier people; and that you should
live in friendship with the United States.
More than all this is required to render
your Condition comfortable. Your lands are
good. Upon these you may raise horses and
large Flocks of Cattle, by the sale of which
you may procure the conveniences and neces-
saries of life in greater abundance, and
with less trouble than you do at present.
You may also, by a little more industry
raise more Corn and other Grain, as well
for your families, as for the support of
your Stock in winter. I hope the Nations
will maturely reflect upon this subject,
and adopt what cannot fail to make them
happier. When the Government shall be
informed that they have taken this wise
course, and are sincerely desirous to be
aided in it, they may rely upon receiving
all necessary assistance.

In order that my Children [Washington
crossed out the word "Brothers"] of the
different Nations should be informed of
this advice, I request that you will explain to them what you have heard me say
(Fitzpatrick 1940:35:299-300).

Washington's lifetime marks an era when Indians went,
both figuratively and literally, from Brothers to
Children. Through the French and Indian Wars, Indian
"savages" may not have been included in a true brotherhood with Europeans, but the tribes were regarded

as equals in power and their autonomy was respected. As the Revolution began, the colonists saw Indians as useful. Their savagery was interpreted as a result of being child-like rather than being pagan or evil. They could be used, if skillfully manipulated, but they were hardly to be respected as equals. Needless to say, the Indians hardly agreed with such an interpretation. The assembled chiefs of the Wyandots, Delawares, Shawanoes, Ottawas, Chippewas, Potawatomes, Miamis, Eel River, Weeas, Kickapoos, Piankashaws, and Kaskaskias must have listened politely to Washington in Philadelphia as he exhorted them to stop being Indians, but they give no evidence of following his advice. What they had done was to secure treaties which assured them the United States intended to respect their lands and tribal sovereignty.

However, even the whites directly responsible for negotiating the treaties assumed, like Washington, that the only recourse for Indians was assimilation to the higher civilization. For instance, Washington's Secretary of War, Henry Knox, recommended in 1791 an impartial administration of justice toward Indians while at the same time calling for proper definitions and regulations for alienating their land while ensuring, "That the advantages of commerce and the blessings of civilization should be extended to them" (Drake 1873:105). Yet, Knox never developed any comprehensive policy for assimilation. Instead, he soon found himself directing Anthony Wayne's campaigns in the Northwest while supervising hostilities along the southern frontier. Since Knox was particularly fearful that oppression of Indian underdogs might mar the image of his newly independent country, he was always eager to conclude a peace treaty, providing that frontier expansion was included in the terms.

Vice-President John Adams concurred with Washington and Knox. In an evaluation of his own administration, he (Binder 1968:37) noted with pride:

> I was engaged in the most earnest, sedulous, and I must own, expensive exertion to preserve peace with the Indians, and prepare them for agriculture and civilization, through the whole of my administration. I had the inexpressible satisfaction of complete success.

27

Whether the peace policy was to benefit the Indian
as implied in the Adams statement, is somewhat du-
bious in view of Adams' earlier attitude (Binder
1968:33). Concerned about British enlistment of
Indian allies in 1775, he cautions: "The Indians
are known to conduct their Wars so entirely without
Faith and Humanity that it will bring eternal Infamy
on the Ministry throughout all Europe if they should
excite those Savages to War... To let loose those
blood Hounds to scalp Men and to butcher Women and
Children is horrid." Clearly, Adams as a protagonist
of the rights of man did not include all of mankind.
In an attack on Rousseau, Adams rationalized why
Indian claims to territory are invalid.

> Shall we say that a few handful of scatter-
> ing tribes of savages have a right of domain
> and property of a quarter of this globe cap-
> able of nourishing hundreds of millions of
> happy human beings? The Indian has a right
> to life, liberty, and property in common
> with all men; but what right to domain or
> property beyond these? Every Indian has
> a right to his wigwam, his armor, his uten-
> sils; when he had burned the woods around
> him, and planted his corn and beans ...,
> all these were his undoubtful right; but
> will you infer from this, that he had rights
> of exclusive domain and property of immense
> regions of uncultivated wilderness that he
> never saw, that he might have the exclusive
> privilege of hunting and fishing in them,
> which he himself never expected or hoped
> to enjoy (Binder 1968:40-41)?

The views of Washington, Adams, and Knox well represent emerging American thought: Indians as a race
may be equal, but they can be treated as equals
only by foregoing their primitive culture, and their
rights as owners of the land. Although the thought
is clearly expressed, no comprehensive assimilation
policy developed because of the necessity for expedient answers to matters of war and expansion.
The view is agreed to even by Franklin and Jefferson,
who might be expected to differ because of their
generally more liberal stance. Instead, they differ
only in degree of expressing greater hope for assimilation, and in an ability, at times, to evaluate
Indian life in a dispassionate and objective tone.

Thus, some of their passages are often quoted as
forerunners of cultural relativity, but elsewhere
the two reveal an ingrained ethnocentricity.
Franklin, for instance, is celebrated for his 1787
ethnography which opens:  "Savages we call them, because their Manners differ from ours, which we think
the Perfection of Civility, they think the same of
theirs."  In good Franklin form, he elaborates by a
story of Indians responding to an offer of education
by a counter offer of accepting a dozen young Virginians in order to make men of them.  Equally famous
is his high regard for Iroquois government, which
was urged as a model for the American colonies.

> It would be a very strange thing if Six
> Nations of ignorant savages should be
> capable of forming a scheme for such a
> union, and be able to execute it in such
> a manner, as that it has subsisted for
> ages, and appears indissolvable; and yet
> that a like union should be impracticable
> for ten or a dozen English colonies, to
> whom it is more necessary and must be
> more advantageous (Vogel 1974:48).

However, in between these observations Franklin
experienced direct contacts with Indians, either
as enemies or as possessors of coveted land.  In
such instances, he was far from admiration or objec-
tivity.  In a letter of August 19, 1756, for example,
he (Labaree 1963:6:487) disparages the Iroquois as
allies:

> For my own part, I make no doubt but that
> the Six Nations have privily encourag'd
> these Indians to fall upon us; they have
> taken no Step to defend us, as their Allies,
> nor to prevent the Mischief done us.  I look
> upon it as the most unfortunate Step we
> ever took, the Application made thro' Sir
> William Johnson, to these Nations to pro-
> cure us Peace.  For we tied up the Hands of
> our People till we heard the Result of that
> Application; the Affair was drawn out to
> great Length of Time; and in the mean while
> our Frontier People were continually butcher'd
> and at last either dispers'd or dispirited.
> In short I do not believe we shall ever have
> a firm Peace with the Indians till we have
> well drubb'd them.

Jefferson, likewise, was ambivalent in his perspectives on Indians. Davis (1964:204) argues that the early Virginians believed only that Indians should be exterminated, removed, or else sentimentalized while, "Few if any other than Jefferson applied the Scottish views of history and society, of moral absolutism but cultural relativism, to their red brothers" [emphasis added]. What Davis does not indicate is that Jefferson applied relativism largely for a European, intellectual audience while displaying an absolutism in his political actions and policies, as a matter of expediency. The relativism necessary for ethnography makes some appearance in Notes on the State of Virginia, but this ethnography consists of a listing of North American tribes by location and population with some speculations on Indian origins, combined with Jefferson's one excavation of a burial mound. In short, the work was so limited it can hardly be considered a forerunner of American anthropology. Perhaps a better case could be made for Jefferson, in his appeal for help in documenting Indian languages, primarily as a means for determining origins; however, little effort resulted from this interest. Instead, the best claims for his relativism lie in Jefferson's arguments that the Indians are the equals of Caucasoids. Essentially, these arguments were in response to Buffon's claims that New World species were inferior to the European. In refuting Buffon's thesis, Jefferson committed several gross ethnographic errors. Certainly, his intentions were better than his observations, though even here it is not clear what he was defending most--the Indians or his beloved continent.

Beyond doubt his relativism did not respect any right of the Indians to continue an Indian way of life. For instance, in a letter of February 18, 1803 he (Lipscomb 1905:10:362) writes:

> In truth, the ultimate point of rest and
> happiness for them (Indians) is to let
> our settlements and theirs meet and blend
> together, to intermix, and become one
> people. Incorporating themselves with
> us as citizens of the United States, this
> is what the natural progress of things
> will, of course, bring on, and it will
> be the better to promote than to retard it.

Even this view, however, is more humane than an earlier one where expediency dictated aggressive action (Lipscomb 1905:8:177):

> Constant murders committing by the Indians, and their combination threatens to be more and more extensive. I hope we shall give them a thorough drubbing this summer, and then change our tomahawk into a golden chain of friendship. The most economical as well as the most humane conduct towards them is to bribe them into peace, and to retain them in peace by eternal bribes.

Later in life, Jefferson's view is softened and a forerunner of the allotment policy is offered instead of "eternal bribes." In a consideration of Indian boundaries on December 29, 1802 he recommends for the Kaskaskians and others:

> We might agree to their laying off one hundred acres of the best soil for every person, young and old, of their tribe, we might enclose it well for them in one general inclosure, give to every family utensiles and stock sufficient for their portion of it, and give them an annuity in necessaries, on their ceding to us their whole country... (Lipscomb 1905:17:375).

Such steps were part of a general policy developed by Jefferson and expressed in detail to Congress on January 18, 1803 (Lipscomb 1905:3:489-492).

> The Indian tribes residing within the limits of the United States, have, for a considerable time, been growing more and more uneasy at the constant diminution of the territory they occupy, although affected by their own voluntary sales; and the policy has long been gaining strength with them, of refusing absolutely all further sale, on any conditions; insomuch that, at this time, it hazards their friendship, and excites dangerous jealousies and perturbations in their minds to make any overture for the purchase of the smallest portions of their land. A very few tribes only are not yet obstinately in these dispositions. In order peaceably

to counteract this policy of theirs, and
to provide an extension of territory which
the rapid increase of our numbers will call
for, two measures are deemed expedient.
First: to encourage them to abandon hunting, to apply to the raising stock, to
agriculture and domestic manufactures, and
thereby prove to themselves that less land
and labor will maintain them in this, better
than in their former mode of living. The
extensive forests necessary in the hunting
life will then become useless, and they will
see advantage in exchanging them for the
means of improving their farms and of increasing their domestic comforts. Secondly:
to multiply trading-houses among them, and
place within their reach those things which
will contribute more to their domestic com-
fort than the possession of extensive but
uncultivated wilds. Experience and reflec-
tion will develop to them the wisdom of exchanging what they can spare and we want,
for what we can spare and they want. In
leading them thus to agriculture, to manufactures, and civilization; in bringing
together their and our settlements, and in
preparing them ultimately to participate in
the benefits of our government, I trust and
believe we are acting for their greatest
good.

After noting how this policy is being pursued through
regulations over commerce, Jefferson continues:

The legislature, reflecting on the late occurrences on the Mississippi, must be sensible
how desirable it is to possess a respectable
breadth of country on that river, from our
southern limit to the Illinois at least, so
that we may present as firm a front on that
as on our eastern border. We possess what
is below the Yazoo, and can probably acquire
a certain breadth from the Illinois to the
Wabash to the Ohio; but between the Ohio
and Yazoo, the country all belongs to the
Chickasaws, the most friendly tribe within
our limits, but the most decided against
the alienation of lands. The portion of
their country most important for us is

exactly that which they do not inhabit.
Their settlements are not on the Mississippi, but in the interior country.  They
have lately shown a desire to become
agricultural, and this leads to the desire of buying implements and comforts.
In the strengthening and gratifying of
these wants, I see the only prospect of
planting on the Mississippi itself, the
means of its own safety.  Duty has required me to submit these views to the
judgment of the legislature; but as their
disclosure might embarrass and defeat
their effect, they are committed to the
special confidence of the two houses.

For the tribes east of the Mississippi, this policy
was only a prelude for authorization to dispatch
Lewis and Clark.  Jefferson already had his eye on
the West and was trying to settle remaining affairs
on the Mississippi before moving farther westward.
Certainly, Indians were not going to be allowed to
retard United States expansion.

Nevertheless, the negotiations to acquire Indian
land with their provisions for annuities or "eternal
bribes" continued through the treaty-making process.
The language of the treaties confirms the view that
two independent sovereignties were bargaining with
each other.  Indeed, as Rice (1934:81) notes:
"Habitually for nearly 100 years the nation treated
with the Indians pursuant to the constitutional
forms that were used in dealing with foreign states."

This Constitutional base was most vague, of course,
since it was limited to the commerce clause.  Gradually, Supreme Court decisions and Congressional
legislation expanded it, but for nearly fifty years,
treaty-making, supplemented by Executive Orders,
established the legal relations between the Indian
nations and the United States.  Not only did the
process indicate a relation between equals but also
the language of the treaties.  For instance, representatives of the Continental Congress first treated
with the Delaware in September, 1778.  Article II
of the treaty reads:  "That a perpetual peace and
friendship shall from henceforth take place, and
subsist between the contracting parties aforesaid,
through all succeeding generations:  and if either

33

of the parties are engaged in a just and necessary
war with any other nation or nations, that then
each shall assist the other in due proportion to
their abilities ..." The implied war is made explicit in Article VI where Delaware aid is equated
with that of a nation. "Whereas the enemies of
the United States have endeavored ... to possess
the Indians in general with an opinion, that it is
the design of the States aforesaid, to extirpate
the Indians and take possession of their country:
to obviate such false suggestion, the United States
do engage to guarantee to the aforesaid nation of
Delawares, and their heirs, all their territorial
rights in the fullest and most ample manner, as it
hath been bounded by former treaties, as long as
the said Delaware nation shall abide by, and hold
fast the chain of friendship now entered into."
In addition to respecting each other's lands, the
treaty specified a mutual respect for each other's
laws. Article IV clearly indicates Delaware sovereignty: "For the better security of the peace
and friendship now entered into by the contracting
parties, against all infractions of the same by
the citizens of either party, to the prejudice of
the other, neither party shall proceed to the in-
flection or punishments on the citizens of the
other, otherwise than by securing the offender by
imprisonment, or any other competent means, till a
fair and impartial trial can be had by judges or
juries of both parties, as near as can be to the
laws, customs and usages of the contracting parties
and natural justice." The article (Kappler 1903:
1-3) called for Congressional representatives and
deputies of the Delaware to determine the mode of
trials. While some colonial intellectuals were
denying Indian savages could possess anything like
law, other Americans, out of expediency, were
agreeing by treaty to bind United States citizens
to Delaware legal proceedings.

Shortly after the conclusion of American and English hostility, the former dealt harshly with Indian
nations in the Northwest. Two treaties in October
1784 and January 1785 begin with the United States
"giving" peace to the Indians, and then taking much
of their land. However, because of state jealousies,
the federal government had to retreat from this
position in dealing with southern Indians. Georgia
and North Carolina had agents at the Treaty of

Hopewell in November 1785; the conflict of state and federal interests allowed the Cherokee to exert their independence. Furthermore, by January 1789 the Northwestern Indians had rallied. In their unity they were treated much as equals by the Treaty of Fort Harmer. Article VIII, for instance, speaks of alliance and mutual defense, and Article IX clearly recognizes the sovereign rights of Indian nations: "If any person or persons, citizen or subjects of the United States, or any other person not being an Indian, shall presume to settle upon the lands confirmed to the said nations, he and they shall be out of the protection of the United States; and the said nations may punish him or them in such manner as they see fit." However, other articles in the treaty clearly connote United States dominance and laid the foundation for the Supreme Court's later ruling that Indian nations were domestic and dependent entities. For example, Article V specifies that individuals guilty of murder and robbery where a United States citizen is involved shall be tried by state or territorial law. No longer are Indian laws recognized in such cases, nor are Indian nations represented in the process. Moreover, while the treaty confirmed the land acquisition of earlier treaties, it explicitly prohibited future Indian land sales except to the federal government. In return for this structure, the United States explicitly rejected any claim over land remaining to the Indian nations. The article is worth examining in whole because its essence was frequently repeated in successive treaties.

> The United States of America do by these presents relinguish and quit claim to the said nations respectively, all the lands lying between the limits above described, for them the said Indians to live and hunt upon, and otherwise to occupy as they shall see fit: But the said nations, or either of them, shall not be at liberty to sell or dispose of the same, or any part thereof, to any sovereign power, except the United States; nor to the subjects or citizens of any other sovereign power, nor to the subjects or citizens of the United States.

CONCLUSION

In sum, as time passed and the power of the Indian
nations diminished, the articles of treaties conceded
more and more the power of the United States over
the Indians, and clauses or articles recognizing
this difference generally made Indian nations more
and more dependent. Yet, even as late as 1868 the
wording of treaties recognize two sovereign powers
are in the act of negotiation. For instance, the
Sioux Treaty of 1868 begins: "From this day forward
all war between the parties to this agreement shall
forever cease. The Government of the United States
desires peace, and its honor is hereby pledged to
keep it. The Indians desire peace, and they now
pledge their honor to maintain it." After defining
reservation boundaries, the treaty specifies that
this land "... is set apart for the absolute and
undisturbed use and occupation of the Indians ..."
Most other stipulations in this treaty reflect the
relative powers of the contracting parties as well
as the growing Sioux dependence on white economic
controls.

However, most treaties are between nations of une-
qual strength, and provisions regularly reflect the
inequity. The inequity in power in no way invali-
dates the treaty. Thus, one must appreciate the
contemporary view of Indians who maintain that their
past treaties should be recognized fully, and the
United States is obligated to insure that treaty
provisions are fulfilled. Realistically, since the
President and the Senate make treaties, they can
also negotiate changes or even abrogate them. Indians generally recognize such a possibility. What
they find most frustrating is an attitude among
some whites that the treaties are no longer valid
because of their age, with an implicit assumption
that the Indian nations which negotiated the treaties no longer exist, or that treaties somehow have
been abrogated by attrition because Indians have
been given the opportunity to participate in the
dominant society. To be sure, Indians are in a
unique situation because in 1924 they were all made
United States citizens, and their territories lie
within United States boundaries. Still, the United
States does recognize dual citizenship for other of
its citizens, and a number of nations are engulfed
by others. But above all, the deeds of the founding

fathers, as reflected in the treaties made with the original American nations, give Indians a forceful argument in their claims for special rights as members of their respective nations.

REFERENCES CITED

Abernethy, Thomas P.
    1959    Western Lands and the American
            Revolution. New York: Russell and
            Russell, Inc.

Bidney, David
    1954    The Idea of the Savage in North
            American Ethnohistory. Journal of
            the History of Ideas 15:322-327.

Binder, Frederick
    1968    The Color Problem in Early National
            America as Viewed by John Adams,
            Jefferson and Jackson. The Hague:
            Mouton.

Davis, Richard
    1964    Intellectual Life in Jefferson's
            Virginia, 1790-1830. Chapel Hill:
            University of North Carolina Press.

Drake, Francis S.
    1873    Life and Correspondence of Henry Knox.
            Boxton: Samuel Drake Press.

Elliot, Jonathan, ed.
    1836    The Debates in the Several State
            Conventions on the Adoption of the
            Federal Constitution. Philadelphia:
            J. B. Lippincott Co.

Fitzpatrick, John, ed.
    1931-   The Writings of George Washington.
            Washington:   U. S. Government Printing
            Office.

Hauser, Raymond E.
    1976    The Illinois Indian Tribe:   From
            Autonomy and Self-Sufficiency to
            Dependency and Depopulation.   Journal
            of the Illinois Historical Society
            69:127-138

Janney, Samuel
    1970    The Life of William Penn.   Freeport,
            New York:   Books for Libraries Press.

Kappler, Charles, ed.
    1903    Indian Affairs, Laws and Treaties,
            Vol. 2.   Document 452, 57th Congress,
            1st Session.   Washington:   U. S.
            Printing Office.

Labaree, Leonard, ed.
    1959-   The Papers of Benjamin Franklin.   New
            Haven:   Yale University Press.

Lipscomb, Andrew, ed.
    1905    The Writings of Thomas Jefferson.
            Washington:   The Thomas Jefferson
            Association.

Mohr, Walter H.
    1933    Federal Indian Relations, 1774-1788.
            Philadelphia:   University of Pennsyl-
            vania Press.

Nash, Gary B.
    1974    Red, White, and Black.   Englewood Cliffs,
            New Jersey:   Prentice-Hall.

Pearce, Roy H.
    1953    The Savages of America.   Baltimore:
            The Johns Hopkins Press.

Prucha, Francis P.
    1962    American Indian Policy in the Formative
            Years.   Cambridge:   Harvard University
            Press.

Rice, W. G.
    1934    The Position of the American Indian
            in the Law of the United States.
            Journal of Comparative Legislation
            and International Law 16:78-95.

Shaw, Helen L.
    1931    British Administration of the Southern
            Indians, 1756-1783.  Lancaster, Penn-
            sylvania:  Lancaster Press.

Sheehan, Bernard
    1974    Seeds of Extinction:  Jeffersonian
            Philosophy and the American Indian.
            New York:  W. W. Norton and Co.

Silverman, Kenneth, ed.
    1971    Selected Letters of Cotton Mater.
            Baton Rouge:  Louisiana State
            University Press.

Smyth, Albert H.
    1907    The Writings of Benjamin Franklin.
            New York:  The MacMillan Co.

Vogel, Virgil
    1974    This Country Was Ours.  New York:
            Harper and Row.

Wallace, Anthony F. C.
    1970    The Death and Rebirth of the Seneca.
            New York:  Alfred A. Knopf.

Washburn, Wilcomb
    1975    The Indian in America.  New York:
            Harper and Row.

# CHAPTER 2

## A Chronological Account of the Wabanaki Confederacy

Willard Walker, Wesleyan University
Robert Conkling, Philadelphia, Pennsylvania
Gregory Buesing, Federal Regional Council
of New England

A Native American political institution which has come to be known as "the Wabanaki Confederacy" developed in what are now the northern New England states, the Maritime Provinces, and eastern Quebec in the seventeenth and eighteenth centuries, when this entire area was part of New France. The confederacy survived the expulsion of the French in 1759, played a critical role in the American Revolution, and endured another century until its constituent parts separated, splitting into crystallized factions. For some two centuries, it would seem that the Wabanaki Confederacy preserved peace among its widely scattered constituents. It also provided mechanisms to develop and maintain political leadership, to take concerted action on matters of common concern, and to negotiate effectively with Anglo and with other Indian groups.

The history of the Native peoples of this vast area and long period can best be understood perhaps, not in terms of specific tribes or bands or of their individual leaders, but in terms of the confederacy structure and the statements and activities of its many representatives recorded under pressure of various events. It may have been confederacy policy as much as local or personal sentiment that motivated 40 to 50 St. Francis Abenakis to join Arnold's ill-fated attack on Quebec in 1775 (Allen 1831:394; Williamson 1839:444); so also with the 15 Maliseets and four Micmacs who participated in Colonel Jonathan Eddy's abortive attempt to take Fort Cumberland (Kidder 1867:78) in November of 1776. Confederacy policy may also account for the 60 Penobscots, Passamaquoddies and Maliseets who made up one-third of the force which successfully defended Machias in August of 1777, and the 30 or more Micmacs killed or captured by British sailors "after a desperate struggle" aboard the Lafayette, riding at her anchor in the Miramichi (Gesner 1847:48).

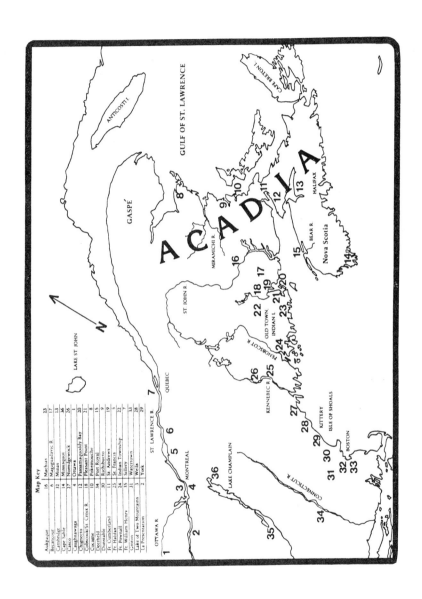

Map Key

| | | | |
|---|---|---|---|
| Auskpaque | 16 | Machias | 13 |
| Becancour | 6 | Magaguadavic R. | 17 |
| Cambridge | 32 | Minas | 13 |
| Cape Sable | 14 | Mianaquoz | 36 |
| Casco | 27 | Norridgewock | 26 |
| Caughnawaga | 4 | Ottawa | 1 |
| Chignecto | 12 | Passamaquoddy Bay | 20 |
| Cobscook/St. Croix R. | 18 | Pleasant Point | 21 |
| Cocagne | 10 | Pokemouche | 8 |
| Deerfield | 34 | Port Royal | 15 |
| Dunstable | 30 | Richibucto | 9 |
| Ft. Cumberland | 11 | St. Andrews | 19 |
| Ft. Halifax | 25 | St. Francis | 5 |
| Ft. Pownall | 24 | Indian Township | 22 |
| Ft. William Henry | 15 | Sillery | 7 |
| Groton | 31 | Watertown | 33 |
| Lake of Two Mountains | 3 | Wells | 28 |
| La Présentation | 2 | York | 29 |

These and many other episodes can best be understood in terms of decisions reached at confederacy meetings; for joint decisions of Wabanaki councils governed, to a considerable degree, Native reactions to American, British, Canadian, state and provincial policies throughout much of the northeastern part of the continent for some two centuries.

What the confederacy was, what it stood for, how it operated, and how it changed through time cannot now be reconstructed in detail. We will attempt however to sketch as best we can its origin, development and decline, something of its internal organization, its relationships with other political entities, and some of the beliefs and principles embodied in the rituals of the confederacy, articulated in the speeches of its representatives and recorded on the wampum belts preserved by its member bands until, a century ago, the confederacy broke apart, the local communities ceased to consult regularly or often with one another, and the wampums became relics of an institution that had lapsed.


THE FRENCH COLONIAL PERIOD

The far northeastern portion of North America was occupied in pre-contact times by a population speaking Eastern Algonkian languages and organized primarily in terms of kinship relations into small, local bands. Typically each band was associated with a river drainage system through which it moved seasonally, deploying up the tributaries in the fall to the interior lakes and concentrating in spring on the tidal estuaries and off-shore islands in the vicinity of the river mouth. All adult men were subsistence hunters. Relations within the bands were egalitarian; band membership was fluid; and political leadership was based on persuasiveness rather than coercion. Political leaders tended to be elder members of extended families, well versed in hunting ritual. Often, they were shamans, successful medical practitioners, who could settle disputes, collect food for the needy, and act as guardians of the corporate resources of the band, both sacred and profane and both tangible and intangible.

Early seventeenth century band chiefs must have varied considerably in their influence and authority.

43

Father Le Jeune, speaking of the Algonkians in general, wrote in 1634 that,

> They have reproached me a hundred times
> because we fear our Captains, while they
> laugh at and make sport of theirs. All
> the authority of their chief is in his
> tongue's end; for he is powerful in so far
> as he is eloquent; and even if he kills
> himself talking and, haranguing, he will
> not be obeyed unless he pleases the Savages
> (Thwaites 1897:6.243).

Membertou, a Micmac chief at Port Royal in Nova Scotia, was described by another early seventeenth century writer, Marc Lescarbot:

> He has under him a number of families whom
> he rules, not with so much authority as
> does our King over his subjects, but with
> sufficient power to harangue, advise, and
> lead them to war, to render justice to one
> who has a grievance, and like matters. He
> does not impose taxes upon the people, but
> if there are any profits from the chase he
> has a share of them, without being obliged
> to take part in it (Thwaites 1896:1.75).

Elsewhere Father Le Clercq said of a Micmac chief that:

> This man made it a point of honour to be
> always the worst dressed of his people, and
> to take care that they all were better
> clothed than he. He held it as a maxim, as
> he told me one day, that a ruler, and a great
> heart like his, ought to take more care for
> others than for himself, because, good hunter
> as he was, he always obtained easily every-
> thing which he needed for his own use, and
> that as for the rest, if he did not himself
> live well, he should find his desire in the
> affection and the hearts of his subjects
> (Le Clercq 1910:235).

European contacts in the sixteenth and early seventeenth centuries made a drastic and lasting impact on band organization. Guns, liquor, the fur trade, and new diseases were introduced. Widespread epi-

44

demics ravaged the area with consequent depopulation and deterioration of the kinship system. Competition for beaver and for access to French traders caused population movements and intraband as well as interband disputes. Subsistence hunting gave way to beaver trapping; reciprocal exchange was replaced by dependence on French traders. The band chiefs were unable to compete with their new rivals, the French priests, who had the support of French economic and political power. Conkling (1974) has detailed the efficient progress made by the French missionaries in discrediting the shamans, assuming positions of leadership in the bands, concentrating much of the population in large, permanent, hierarchically controlled settlements as at Sillery, St. Francis, and Sault de la Chaudiere, and converting the Native bands into an increasingly coherent, if not unified society, dependent upon French trade and missionary leadership, and committed to France in her developing struggle with Britain.

Large gatherings of eastern Algonkians involving members of several bands were not new. The French elaborated on a practice that had occurred earlier. Father Biard witnessed such gatherings in the second decade of the seventeenth century and described them as follows:

> Now in these assemblies, if there is some news of importance, as that their neighbors wish to make war upon them, or that they have killed someone, or that they must renew the alliance, etc., then messengers fly from all parts to make up the more general assembly, that they may avail themselves of all the confederates, which they call Ricmanen, who are generally those of the same language. Nevertheless the confederation often extends farther than the language does, and war sometimes arises against those who have the same language. In these assemblies so general, they resolve upon peace, truce, war or nothing at all, as often happens in the councils where there are several chiefs without order and subordination, whence they frequently depart more confused and disunited than when they came (Thwaites 1896:3:91).

Over the following century these early "assemblies so general" were cultivated assiduously by the French missionaries. With the addition of Catholic ritual and certain rituals perhaps borrowed from the Iroquois and Algonkian groups farther south and west, they became increasingly effective in making and enforcing decisions for an ever larger and more cohesive constituency. By the mid-seventeenth century, French missionaries were settling interband disputes brought on by the fur trade. Thus, Father Druillettes was "exceptionally successful" in his efforts to "secure intra-tribal peace" on the Kennebec in the 1640s and was instrumental in arranging peace between the Abenaki and Sokoki (Leger 1929:41-47).

The trend toward concentration in mission settlements fostered the growth of interband relationships. The inauguration of the successor to Noel Tecouerimat, the "Grand Chief" of Sillery who died in 1666, was attended by "French, Algonkins, Montagnais, Micmak, Abeneki, Etechemins, Atticamegs, Nipissings, and Hurons" (Bailey 1969:93).

Wampum certified the authenticity of delegations from distant bands as early as 1680, when Le Clercq (1910: 269) saw Micmac "ambassadors, with collars of wampum" sent to invite their allies "to take up the hatchet against another nation." Father Rale gave a fuller account of the use of wampum when he wrote from Norridgewock in 1723:

> The custom of these tribes when they write to another tribe is to send a collar or broad belt (un collier ou une large ceinture) upon which they make many figures with porcelain beads of different colors. They instruct him who bears the collar by saying to him, "This is what the collar says to such and such a tribe to such a person," and they send him away. Our savages would have difficulty in understanding what we say to them and would not be very attentive if [we] ... did not conform to their manner of thought and expression (Speck 1919:33).

In the 1670s and 1680s French diplomacy and British atrocities combined to add to the ethnic diversity of the French-oriented native population in the

Northeast and draw it together in an even more
tightly knit political network. In 1676, for example, 150 survivors of King Philip's War arrived at
Sillery. Likewise, after a battle with the British
in southern Maine a year later, many Abenaki and
Sokoki refugees fled to the Penobscot or to Canada.

> From 1681 to 1684 great numbers of Abenaki
> migrated to Sillery, so that soon the
> villages of Sillery and Sault de la
> Chaudiere comprised three hundred families,
> and another settlement sprang up on the
> banks of the St. Francis River.... By
> 1687 there were seven hundred Abenaki at
> Sillery alone, and in that year Father
> Bigot, the superior of the mission, made
> a journey to New England to induce more
> to come (Bailey 1969:31).

Farther west, the French missionaries succeeded in
converting sizable groups of Mohawks, one of which
migrated to the vicinity of Montreal and established
Caughnawaga in 1676.

From the end of King Philip's War in 1676-1677, when
the British clashed with the Sokokis, until the
American Revolution, warfare between the British
and the Wabanaki was incessant. In King William's
War (1689-1697) according to Raymond (1896:239-240),
"Every English settlement in Maine, save Wells,
York, Kittery, and the Isle of Shoals, was overrun
and probably a thousand white people killed or taken
prisoners." In Queen Anne's War (1701-1714), "Ab-
naki" under French officers "raided Casco and Wells"
in Maine (Morrison 1974:80) and Graylock and his
Missisquoi Abenakis from Lake Champlain attacked
the Connecticut River Valley towns in Massachusetts
(Day 1973:51-52). In Governor Dummer's War (1722-
1725) Graylock's raids continued (Day 1973:52), the
Maliseets and Micmacs fell on Chignecto and Port
Royal, Nova Scotia (Wallis and Wallis 1955:203),
and "French Mohawks," presumably from Caughnawaga,
raided Old Dunstable, Massachusetts (Eckstorm 1939:
226). During King George's War (1744-1748) and
again in the French and Indian War (1754-1763),
Maliseets from the St. John, led by Father Germain,
and Micmacs, led by Father Le Loutre, raided British
settlements again and again (Wallis and Wallis 1955:

202-203). The Penobscots were also drawn into the
conflict (Williamson 1846a:85-87). They were proclaimed "enemies, rebels and traitors to his Majesty"
in Massachusetts, where in 1755 the General Court
voted a bounty of Ł 40 for "every scalp of a male
Indian" and Ł 20 for "every scalp of such female
Indian or male Indian under the age of twelve years
that shall be killed and brought in as evidence of
their being killed as aforesaid" (Speck 1940:xix).
In the following year a similar proclamation was
issued in Halifax (MacDonald 1912:11-12), and the
Massachusetts bounty was raised to Ł 300 for the
scalp of any "Indian enemy" (Speck 1940:xxx). In
1760 St. Francis and its inhabitants were utterly
destroyed by Rogers' Rangers.

The Wabanaki wars with the Iroquois allies of the
British ended in 1700, however, with a treaty sub-
scribed to the following year "between all the tribes
concerned as far west as Ottawa" (Speck 1919:68;
Eckstorm 1939:214). The French missionaries and
their Mohawk converts at Caughnawaga may have played
critical roles in arranging this treaty, which seems
never to have been violated. Indeed the Five Nations
failed to act on British requests that they attack
Norridgewock in 1724 and instead sent messengers to
that village the same year (Eckstorm 1939:216-217).
The Catholic Mohawks, in fact, became active allies
of the Wabanaki after the Treaty of 1700, joining the
Deerfield raid, and later mounting their own attacks
on Old Dunstable and Groton, Massachusetts in the
1720s (Hough 1853:115; Eckstorm 1939:226).

The treaty of 1700 was surely one of the great
political achievements of Colonial times in the
Northeast since it ended forever the long series
of Algonkian-Iroquois wars and established the
basis for Native American diplomatic relations
which were to continue far into the nineteenth century. The treaty was remembered by the Five Nations
and recorded by their English speaking allies in
British Colonial documents as a "submission" by the
Algonkian tribes to the Iroquois. Oral traditions
of the Wabanaki bands tend to describe it as a "submission" of the Iroquois to the Algonkians. In
actuality it likely was a mutual agreement which,
as one version of the Passamaquoddy "Wampum Records"
suggests, was advocated by the French missionaries.

48

In any event the Treaty of 1700 set the stage for
another triumph of French and Indian diplomacy,
the creation of "the Great Council Fire," which
probably occurred in 1749. This was the year when
an Indian peace treaty is said to have been concluded
at Caughnawaga by the Wabanaki historian, Speck
(1946:359). It may also have been the year in which,
according to Iroquoian scholars, a confederacy was
established at Caughnawaga, known variously to the
western tribes as "the Seven Castles," "the Seven
Nations of Lower Canada," and the "Seven Tribes on
the River St. Lawrence" (Hodge 1907-1910:2:515).
Significantly 1749 was the year after the founding
of Father Picquet's mission at La Presentation
(Hough 1853:69). According to testimony of the
Marquis du Quesne, Picquet

> had directly rendered the [French] king
> absolute master of the national assemblies
> of four [Algonkian] nations who composed
> his first mission to the Lake of Two Moun-
> tains, with liberty to nominate all their
> chiefs at his will. He had caused all the
> chiefs of the [Iroquoian] nations which
> composed his last mission, at La Presenta-
> tion, to swear allegiance and fidelity to
> his Majesty..." (Hough 1853:82).

To the Passamaquoddies, Maliseets, and Micmacs, the
Great Council Fire was known as Búduswagan 'convention council.' The Penobscots called it either
Bé·zegowak 'those united into one' or Gizárgowak
'completely united' (Speck 1915:495). Speck's version of the Penobscot tradition of the origin of
the Great Council Fire is:

> It is supposed that the Iroquois raided
> the Wabanaki tribes so long and were
> defeated so often that the Mohawk asked
> for arbitration to secure peace. They
> then started to seek Council of the
> Ottawa, who are regarded as the most
> venerable of the eastern nations. At
> length their deliberations brought an end
> to the wars in the foundation of an alli-
> ance between the four Wabanaki tribes
> [Maliseets, Micmacs, Passamaquoddies, and]
> headed by the Penobscot, and the Mohawk
> of Caughnawaga and Oka, together with

other neighboring tribes whose fortunes were in different ways linked with those of the principals. From this time onward, still following the general tradition, the confederacy grew in importance; the four Wabanaki tribes forming themselves into an eastern member with their convention headquarters at Oldtown among the Penobscot; and the whole confederated group, embracing the Wabanaki tribes, the Mohawk and the neighboring Algonkian associates with the Ottawa at their head, appointing Caughnawaga as the Confederacy capital. Here regular meetings were held among delegates from the allied tribes where their formal relationship was maintained by series of symbolical ceremonies (Speck 1915:493).

Thus, formal and regularly recurring political relations between the Wabanaki bands and the western tribes were initiated at Caughnawaga sometime after 1700, probably in 1749, ten years before the French were expelled from Acadia. The consequences of this new relationship on Wabanaki political structure may have been profound. According to Speck (1915:494):

The effect [of this steady contact with... the Iroquois] appears clearly in the wampum procedures, the condolence, and the election of chiefs, the sending of delegates, and functions in general which characterized the internal operations of the Wabanaki confederacy, the whole fabric of which was manifestly modeled after the pattern of the Iroquoian League.

Speck (1915), Wallis and Wallis (1955:286, 223-225), and the Penobscot writer, Nicolar (1893:137-139), all agree that Wabanaki participation in the Great Council Fire at Caughnawaga brought about more structured relationships among the Wabanaki bands. Speck (1915:499-500) suggests that the Penobscots, Passamaquoddies, Maliseets, and Micmacs were organized such that each band was 'elder brother' to any band living farther east. He wrote:

The Penobscot, owing to their proximity to the western frontier seem to have been the chief medium of negotiations between the eastern group and the Iroquois. Consequently, from their village at Old Town was sent the summons to the other tribes to attend councils for war or peace with outsiders.

Conversely, the Micmacs, according to Nicolar (1893: 139), were "the last born"; and

> after the division [between older and younger brothers] was made the oldest Mik-mur present, was undressed and put into 'T'ki-nur-gann', - cradle, where he was kept tied and fed all day like the little babe, and every time the delegation met at the grand council fire this performance was repeated, which shows that the Mik-mur was once selected as the youngest of all, he must always be treated like a little baby.

Nicolar (1893:238) also states that the Micmacs were separate and distinct from the Wabanaki, by which he meant the Penobscots, Passamaquoddies, and Maliseets. This assertion is confirmed by Micmac statements reported by both Speck and the Wallises. According to Speck (1915:505-506):

> The Micmac in general seem to have less remembrance of the alliance among the four tribes than either the Penobscot, Passamaquoddy, or the Malecite. They still recognize, however, the force of their confederation with the Mohawk. The interrelation of the western Micmac of Nova Scotia, where Bear River was the capital, and their Wabanaki neighbors seems to have lapsed before 1840.... The old peace compact with the Mohawk is still a live issue [among the eastern Micmacs of Cape Breton Island, however.] The wampum documents are religiously preserved by the executive head, and each year are displayed and explained to the people, as all the Wabanaki used to do, at the tribal meetings.

The Grand Chief and Grand Council of the Cape Breton Micmacs probably date from the early days of the

Great Council Fire at Caughnawaga (Speck 1915:506;
Wallis and Wallis 1955:286). These institutions
apparently maintained formal relations with the
Wabanaki and western Micmacs until sometime prior
to 1840 and with Caughnawaga until 1872 (Speck 1915:
506-507). At least some of the western Micmac bands,
however, were clearly associated with Wabanaki councils after 1840. Gesner (1847:115-116) reports their
presence at annual meetings on Passamaquoddy Bay;
and Micmacs must have taken part in the chief raising
at Old Town in 1861, because during the ceremonies
in the council house, all "the four tribes [of the
confederacy] ranged facing each other in the form
of a rectangle" (Speck 1915:505).

In any event, while the Cape Breton Micmacs severed
their direct, formal relationship with the Wabanaki
before 1840, both they and the Wabanaki, including
the western Micmac bands, were linked through their
common participation in the councils at Caughnawaga
until after 1860.

To an eighteenth century European observer the Great
Council Fire might have seemed a peculiar blend of
French Catholic rituals and Iroquoian political symbolism, glued together with more than a trace of old
Algonkian shamanism. It was, however, a political
structure capable of mobilizing the Native bands
from Cape Breton Island to the Ottawa regardless of
linguistic or cultural incompatibilities. It was
a model or set of procedures which permitted the
Native bands from the far corners of the Northeast
to settle their differences and act in concert.


THE BRITISH COLONIAL PERIOD

When France abandoned Acadia to the British in 1759,
she left her Wabanaki allies to the mercy of the
British. The Wabanaki were quick to perceive the
gravity of their situation. An Englishman captured
by the Micmacs in 1761 recorded their analysis of
the situation:

> When they wanted to inform me that the
> French and them were in one interest,
> they said they were so, (pointing the
> same way with the forefingers of their
> right hand, and holding them parallel);

52

and when, that the English and Indians
were in opposite interests, this they
described by crossing their forefingers.
Their chief made almost a circle with his
forefinger and thumb, and pointing at the
end of his forefinger, said there was
Quebec, the middle joint of his finger
was Montreal, the joint next the hand
was Boston, the middle joint of the thumb
was Halifax, the interval betwixt his
finger and thumb was Pookmoosh [Pokemouche],
so that the Indians would soon be surrounded
[by the English] which he signified by
closing his finger and thumb (Wallis and
Wallis 1955:224).

Apparently acting on this assessment of their military position, the Penobscots surrendered at Fort
Pownall in 1760. The Passamaquoddies, Maliseets,
and Richibucto Micmacs concluded a treaty with the
British at Halifax in the same year while the remaining Micmac bands capitulated in the following
year when Chief Claude Atouash flung his hatchet
into an open grave saying, "I bury this hatchet as
a dead body that is fit only to become rotten, looking upon it as unlawful and impossible for me to
make use hereafter of this instrument of my hostilities against you" (Koren 1962:79-80). In none of
these treaties did the Wabanaki surrender their
autonomy or swear loyalty to the British Crown.
Their land was ostensibly secured by the British
Proclamation of 1763 which provided that "the several nations and tribes of the Indians with whom
we are connected ... should not be molested or dis-
turbed in the possession of such parts of our domin-
ions and territories as not having been ceded to or
purchased by us, are reserved to them ..." (Leger
1929:115). The proclamation, however, was not an
accurate expression of actual British practice or
policy. Sir William Johnson gave it as his opinion
that the Indians,

desire to be considered as allies and
Friends and such we may consider them at
reasonable expense and thereby occupy our
Posts and carry on Trade in safety untill
in a few years we shall become so formidable
throughout the country as to be able to
protect ourselves and abate the charge
(Leger 1929:114).

In 1764, only a year after the Proclamation, the Maliseets reported to Quebec authorities that white settlers were in their area taking beaver. At about the same time the Passamaquoddies wrote Governor Bernard of Massachusetts objecting to a new settlement on an island in Passamaquoddy Bay and adding the first of many requests for a priest:

> we Pray That You Would Consider and have Pittey on ouer Souls and Send us one We Should Be Glad That You Would send us a French one But if not Send us one of Youers For aney is better than none ... (Baxter 1906-1916:24:115).

On August 22, 1763, three Penobscots, representing their own people and also the Passamaquoddies, met with Governor Bernard and his Council in Boston to complain that the truckhouse on the Penobscot lacked provisions, that the weights and measures were incorrect, that the traders tried to get them drunk before trading with them, and that many Englishmen, including the soldiers of the garrison, were hunting in their territory (Baxter 1906-1916:24:116-119).

In his response the next day Bernard promised a full investigation of the trading and trapping practices, but insisted:

> The English have a right to hunt as well as you   They fairly conquered your Country in time of War   Govr Pownall built the Fort at Penobscot when you were at War with Us.  He told you that the English should hunt in that Country:  You could not then help yourselves, and should now sit down content when you are assured of our protection and friendship (Baxter 1906-1916:24:120-122).

A month later Bernard was at Fort Pownall on the Penobscot. He was addressed by Toma, who requested a priest and complained of settlers on the river and the price of the truck. Bernard's response included the following statement:

> The English have conquered this whole country; and the Indians must not prescribe to them what shall be the bounds of their settlements (Baxter 1906-1916:24:128-129).

In March of the following year, 1764, Captain Goldthwait, the commander of Fort Pownall, learned that
two of the Penobscot leaders favored a war to drive
out the British while the rest favored preserving
the peace. He was told by a certain Captain Frost
that the Indians were becoming "surly." At yet another meeting with Bernard, the Penobscots complained
the British were killing their beaver. This time
Bernard ordered surveyors to mark the limits of the
English settlements (Leger 1929:115).

In August, 1765, Bernard met in Boston with representatives of the Norridgewocks, Wawenocks, and
Arasagunticooks from the Kennebec and adjoining
coast. He was told that their constituencies were
all one family, that the beaver in their country
was "mostly killed up," and that,

> We want to have Money at the truck house
> for our Bever in order to pay our Debts at
> Quebec. Father have Mercy upon us we want
> a priest among us to Marry and to Christen
> our Children -- there is no priest at
> Wewenock, he that was there is dead...
> (Baxter 1906-1916:24-126-127).

Within a few months of this meeting, the spokesman
of the group, Nodogawerrimet, and his wife were
murdered by white trappers. Their guns, traps,
pelts, and other equipment were stolen and their
bodies burned in their wigwam. The relatives of
the victims were compensated and a reward was offered for the arrest and conviction of the murderers.
But in July of 1767 another murder was committed
near Fort Halifax on the Kennebec. "Sagamore Esak"
and 12 other Arasagunticooks wrote Bernard on July
29 "for protection and assistance" and,

> to procure Justice for the murder & robbery
> of Joseph an Indian Man, with Squaw Matty-
> Oneas & Two Daughters, Hannah aged about 14
> years & Prasawa about 4 years.... (Baxter
> 1906-1916:24:145).

Later that year a general council of the Wabanaki
Confederacy met at Penobscot, apparently to discuss
the problem of British intruders. Goldthwait wrote
Bernard from Fort Pownall that Indians had told him

that there are a great number of Indians
of different tribes now assembled on
Penobscot river; that they are determined
to maintain their right to 12 Rivers which
they claim, and that they intend soon to
pay me a visit together.... All I know
of certainty is, that there are a considerable number of Indians of different nations
such as Cape Sables [Micmacs] St. Johns
[Maliseets], Norridgewalks, Aresegunticooks
with some other Indians & some white men
now on Penobscot River, and that they have
had a Council with the Penobscots (Baxter
1906-1916:24:149-150).

Before the Council ended some of the young men
raided the settlements on the Penobscot, intimi-
dating the settlers and killing some cattle. When
Goldthwait learned, and promptly dispelled, a rumor
that France had gone to war against Britain, the
violence subsided.

Bernard instructed Goldthwait, however, to,

... tell them that if nothing but Soldiers
can keep them in order, they shall have
Soldiers enough and higher up the River
than they are at present.... Tell them
not to deceive themselves with idle stories
about a War between England & France...
(Baxter 1906-1916:14:55).

The garrison was evidently reinforced and two years
later, on July 25, 1769, some Penobscots appeared
before Governor Bernard and his deputies in Boston
to say:

We acknowledge that we have sided with your
Enemies and that they and we have been conquered, and that we are become the Subjects
of that great King George. We do now in the
name of our whole Tribe recognize it, and do
declare that we are now, and always will be,
ready to obey his call upon any duty whatever.
... We are not acquainted with Husbandry,
nor Arts, sufficient to get our living by,
and if we have not a sufficiency of Land
assigned us, for our use only, to Hunt in,
We and our Wives and our Children must perish.

Brother - We have another request to make
of you. It is a long time since we have
had any Priest among us and if we are kept
much longer without one, We shall become
like wild Beasts.... We are obliged to go
a great Journey to St. John's River for a
Priest to Baptize our Children and carry
our Families with us. We pray that our
Father the great King would pity us and
suffer us to have a Priest, a good man,
of our own profession to reside among us,
that we and our Wives and our Children may
worship God in the way that we have been
taught, which may save us from Eternal
death. It is too late for us at this time
of life to learn a new Religion. Those
who come after us may follow their own in-
clinations.... (Baxter 1906-1916:24:159).

It is not certain that this submission was endorsed
or honored by the Penobscot political authorities
or the majority of their constituents, who were to
rise against King George six years later as allies
of the emergent United States.


THE WAR FOR INDEPENDENCE

The conflict between Britain and her American colonies promised an end to the impotence of the Wabanaki
because it gave them the balance of power between
the Whigs in Massachusetts and the British loyalists
in Nova Scotia. Both sides sought the aid or, failing that, the neutrality of the Wabanaki and were
willing to make many concessions to achieve that end.

As early as March, 1775, the New Englanders received
intelligence from Canada that the Caughnawagas "say
they have been repeetedly applyed to and requested
to Join with the Kings Troops to fight Boston, but
have peremptorily refused, and still intend to re-
fuse" (Baxter 1906-1916:14:240). In August the
British Governor of Canada, Sir Guy Carlton, wrote
that "Many of the [Canadian] Indians have gone over
to [the Americans]" (Hough 1853:186).

During the summer the General Assembly of Nova
Scotia required special license to transport gun-
powder along the coast, intending to end supplies

to the rebels, but the move also jeopardized the
subsistence economy of the Wabanaki hunters (Kidder
1867:167). To mollify them, Governor Legge held
two conferences at Halifax, attended primarily by
Micmacs. He issued ammunition, provisions, and
clothing and urged the Indians to "take up Arms &
oppose the Rebels & harass their back settlements
..." (Kidder 1867:167). The Micmacs accepted the
provisions but failed to attack the rebels.

In April, 1775, a British sloop-of-war arrived at
Penobscot, took and dismantled Fort Pownall, and
carried away the guns and ammunition (Williamson
1839:417-418), thus destroying the Penobscot trade
in violation of the Penobscot treaties. The Provincial Congress of Massachusetts was quick to capi-
talize on this situation, writing the Penobscots,
their "Friends and good Brothers" on May 15 that,

> our enemies ... have laid deep plots to take
> away our liberty & your liberty ... to make
> you & us their servants & let us have nothing
> to eat, drink or wear but what they say we
> shall and prevent us from having guns & pow-
> der to use and kill our Deer and wolves &
> other game, or to send to you for you to
> kill your game with and to get skins & fur
> to trade with us for what you want. But
> we hope soon to be able to supply you with
> both guns & powder of our own making (Kidder
> 1867:51).

On the strength of this letter, Joseph Orono advocated war, telling the Penobscots that,

> Our white brothers tell us .... Their
> great sagamore is coming to bind them in
> chains, to kill them. We must fight him
> .... For should he bind them in bonds,
> next he will treat us as bears. Indians'
> liberties and lands his proud spirit will
> tear away from them. Help his ill-treated
> sons; they will return good for good, and
> the law of love run through the hearts of
> their children and ours, when we are dead
> (Williamson 1846a:88).

In June Orono and three other Penobscots appeared
in Watertown before the Provincial Congress which

promised to set up a truckhouse at Fort Pownall and
undertook to,

> strictly forbid any person or persons what-
> soever from trespassing or making waste upon
> any of the lands and territories or posses-
> sions ... now claimed by our brethren the
> Indians of the Penobscot tribe.... We thank
> our brethren of the Penobscot Tribe for their
> generous offers of friendship and assistance
> in our present war with our brethren in
> Great Britain (Kidder 1867:53).

News of these concessions travelled rapidly through-
out the Confederacy. Paul Higgins, chief of the
Norridgewocks and Pigwackets, offered his support
to George Washington in Cambridge that same summer.
A letter from Ambrose St. Aubin Bear and Pierre
Tomah of the Maliseets, dictated in behalf of "ye
St Johns Tribe" and also "the Micamac Tribe," reached
the Provincial Congress in October, reading in part:

> We heartily join with our brethren the
> Penobscot Indians in every thing that they
> have or shall agree with our Brethren of
> the Colony of the Massachusetts and are
> resolved to stand together & oppose the
> People of Old England that are endeavouring
> to take yours and our Lands & Libertys
> from us.
>
> We are brothers of one father & one God
> made us all, & we will stand by you as
> long as the Almighty will give us strength,
> & we hope you will do the same for us.
> We have nowhere to look too for assistance
> but to you & we desire that you would help
> us to a Priest that he may pray with us to
> God Almighty.
>
> We have no place to go to but to Penobscot
> for support & we desire you would provide
> Amunition Provisions & Goods for us there,
> and we will come in there, & give you our
> fur, & skins & take our support from you
> in return and will be thankful to you for
> the Kindness. Brothers We pray God to
> Bless you & Prosper you & strengthen &
> Lengthen this New Chain with us (Kidder
> 1867:55).

Wabanaki speeches were translated into action before
the end of 1775. In October, enroute for Quebec,
Arnold found a birchbark map showing the route to
St. Lawrence; on November 4, he received a letter
from George Washington urging "that you consider
yourselves as marching not through an enemy's country, but that of your friends and brethren: for
such the inhabitants of Canada and the Indian nations,
have approved themselves in this unhappy contest..."
(Williamson 1839:442). Still later some 40-50 Abenakis appeared in time to join his attack on Quebec.

East of the Penobscot, the Wabanaki were in an economic bind. The Americans failed to supply them;
and British supplies were contingent on their loyalty.
In February, 1776, Washington gave a Maliseet-Passa-
maquoddy delegation a letter and "Chain of Friendship" to be circulated among all the Wabanaki bands
(Kidder 1867:57-59). The letter evidently promised
truckhouses and indicated that the Indians might
remain neutral, if they wished, but invited their
active participation in the war. On receipt of this
letter, in the spring of 1776, the Maliseets plun-
dered Tory settlers on the St. John (Kidder 1867:
65-66), and three Micmac chiefs told John Allan in
June that,

> Genl Washington's letter had given uni-
> versal satisfaction, they adored him as a
> Saint for the reason that though he was
> harrassed with war himself still he tells
> us (says they) "to be at peace & if we
> want help he will grant it and defend us,
> that for this their incessant prayers were
> for his success." - They further told me
> they had turned out one of their chiefs
> because they had spoken disrespectfully of
> Genl Washington [and] they expected a truck-
> house would soon be erected on their shore
> (Kidder 1867:169-170).

In the same month Captain Smith, the truckmaster at
Machias, wrote the provisional congress complaining
that,

> ... the Numbers of [the Indians] far Exceed
> my Expectations, and the Offers they have
> from the Factors of Nova Scotia causes them
> to be very troublesome. The sum of 400 ₤

My granted by your Honors to supply at
least One Thousand Men Exclusive of their
Familys, is but small, your honors cant
Expect I can satisfy them & keep Friends
with that sum... (Kidder 1867:60).

In the same letter Smith noted that the Indians had
learned of Arnold's defeat at Quebec, which caused
some doubt as to the Americans' ability to prosecute
the war.

Seven Micmacs and three Maliseets travelled to
Watertown in July to respond to Washington's letter.
Ambrose St. Aubin Bear requested a "Truckhouse" and
"a Father or a French Priest." "The St. John's and
Mickmac Tribes," he said, "are all one people and
of one Tongue and one Heart.... The Captains that
are come up with me and all our people are all one
as Boston, Our Eyes and our Ears will not turn to
the other side of the Water to see or hear what they
do..." (Baxter 1906-1916:24:165-170). Bear made no
commitment to engage in hostilities; Governor Bowdoin's response was:

> ... [we] will do all in our power to protect
> you from [your Enemies] - We do not however
> ask you to join us in the War, unless it is
> your free choice to do so... (Baxter 1906-
> 1916:24:173).

The next day Bear stated that "we ... will join in
the War on your side," provided that military supplies be made available on the St. John, and indicated that three chiefs from different villages were
ready to join Washington's army in New York (Baxter
1906-1916:24:177). In the subsequent discussion he
qualified his statment, emphasizing that, while he
and his delegation were personally committing themselves to fight, they had no authority to commit
their constituencies without consultation and rati-
fication of the agreement by their people at home.
Thereupon, Bowdoin pressed for the number of each
delegate's constituency, the number of men willing
to fight, and the number of people in the villages
not represented. The talks were not resumed until
July 16 when Bowdoin had received an authorization
from Washington to recruit St. Johns (Maliseet) and
Micmac Indians in the service of the United States.
Then he suggested to the delegation that a regiment

be created consisting of 250 colonists and 500 Indians (Baxter 1906-1916:24:180-185). To raise such a
regiment would be to deprive all the Wabanaki bands
of the men and arms needed both for defense of their
own territories and for the winter's hunt. Yet, on
July 19, under pressure from Bowdoin, while protesting
they lacked authority to bind their constituencies,
the delegates signed the Treaty of Watertown providing for the regiment (Baxter 1906-1916:24:192-193).

After their departure Bowdoin explained why he had
pressed for the military alliance and the regiment
in a letter to his council:

> The most effectual means of Securing the
> Eastern Parts of the Colony from an inland-
> Attack ... is to engage the ... Eastern
> Indians to engage heartily in the war,
> agreeable to Genl Washington's Request...
> and enlist them into the Service without
> delay ... which would answer the double
> purpose of assisting him, and securing
> our Eastern Frontiers, which otherwise
> may be in great danger of being broken
> by these same Indians (Baxter 1906-1916:
> 14:361-362).

The treaty of Watertown was probably never ratified
by the Micmacs. When a Massachusetts agent asked
the Penobscots in August to send troops to New York,
he was told that the young men might be needed to
defend their own territory.

In September John Allan, who later became Washington's agent on the eastern frontier, was informed
by Micmacs at Cocagne that the delegates at Watertown had no authority to conclude a treaty. They
were sympathetic to the Americans but could not un-
dertake a war without assurance of supplies. They
intended to abide by the terms of Washington's letter permitting them the option of friendly neutrality
(Kidder 1867:171-175).

The Maliseets, being farther than the Micmacs from
the British garrisons and nearer to the American
truckhouse at Machias, were more enthusiastic in
the American cause. Although they never sent a
regiment to the New York campaign, Washington's
letter had set them to "Plundering all People they

think are Torys" on the St. John (Kidder 1867:65).
Fifteen Maliseets and four Micmacs joined Eddy's
attack on Fort Cumberland in November (Kidder 1867:
78).

George Washington promised a truckhouse on the St.
John in a letter to the Maliseets and Passamaquoddies
written on December 24, 1776, the day he crossed the
Delaware (Kidder 1867:59). The truckhouse was established in late January, but its prices were exhorbi-
tant and it failed to extend winter credit. John
Allan was appointed "Superintendant of the Eastern
Indians and Colonel of Infantry" by Congress in
January, 1777, charged with responsibility for treating with the Indians "Eastward & Northward of Connecticut River, making no exceptions in what Nation
or Country the Indians resorted" (Kidder 1867:311).
Allan set off for the St. John and conferred with
the Maliseets in June, reporting that,

> They are naked & in great want of Provision,
> notwithstanding they Persevere, and only in
> distress will Purchase from the adherants of
> Great Brittain (Kidder 1867:193).

Allan concluded a treaty in 1777 at Aukpaque with
the Maliseets and Passamaquoddies which promised
adequate supplies, trade without "imposition," payment for military service, a priest, and the exclusive right to hunt beaver, in return for which the
Indians, "in the vicinity of the States should immediately withdraw and assist in the defense of the
country" (Kidder 1867:311-312; 186-196). The treaty
was barely concluded before the British occupied
the St. John valley in force. Allan was forced to
retreat to Machias with nearly 500 Maliseet allies
(Kidder 1867:110-117). Allan's secretary, Lewis
Delesdenier, described the Maliseet retreat from
the St. John:

> It is incredible what difficulties the
> Indians undergo in this troublesome time,
> where so many families are obliged to fly
> with precipitation rather than become
> friends to the Tyrant of Britain, some
> backing their aged parents, others their
> maimed and decrepid brethren, the old women
> leading the young children, mothers carrying
> their infants, together with great loads of

baggage. As to the canoes, the men make
it a play to convey them across (Kidder
1867:117).

At Machias on August 14-16, the Maliseets and Passamaquoddies, some Penobscots, and the Machias volun-
teers repelled an attack by four British naval ves-
sels and a detachment of marines, thwarting British
designs on the eastern front (Kidder 1867:126-129,
203-208). According to Allan,

> none Deserve Greater Applause than our
> Indian Friends. For the Difft Officers
> at the Several attacks assure me, that
> no person Behaved more gallantly, Exposing
> themselves openly to the fire of the cannon
> & small arms ... (Kidder 1867:208).

France's entry into the war early in 1778 ensured
the continued loyalty of the Wabanaki to the American
cause; even the "civil chiefs" and "Warriors" of the
Micmacs declared themselves "ready when called upon
to take up the Hatchet" in July of 1778 (Kidder,
1867:250-251). But as the war dragged on, problems
involving trade, lack of pay for military service,
trespass on hunting territories, and the lack of
priests continued; a plan for the invasion of Nova
Scotia was continually deferred; and Michael Frank-
line, Allan's British counterpart, with the aid of
a Catholic priest, Father Bourg, succeeded in negotiating a treaty of peace in September, 1778, with
two pro-British Maliseet chiefs and Micmac representatives from Richibucto, Miramichi, Chignecto,
and Minas. British pressure on the Wabanaki intensified as American support continued to be deferred. On April 30, 1779, John Neptune of the
Penobscots showed John Preble, Allan's representative,
three strings of wampum, apparently from the Five
Nations, staunch allies of the British. They re-
cited them to him, together with a fourth and larger
belt of wampum which called upon the Penobscots, St.
Johns, and Micmacs to sever relations with the Americans. The Wampum also forecast an invasion of
Maine and destruction of the white settlements by
an army of Canadian Indians "coming across the Woods
as soon as the Leaves are as big as our Nails"
(Kidder 1867:263-264). The Indians in and around
Machias remained firm, but no supplies reached them
in 1780. They barely survived the winter on "fish,

parched corn, and seals' meat" (Kidder 1867:17). In the summer of 1781 no provisions arrived for them. At the end of October the Maliseets were forced to return to the St. John rather than starve at Machias in the service of the United States.

In the spring of 1783 John Allan appeared before a Congressional Committee in Philadelphia to explain that the eastern Indians had been instrumental in holding the territory eastward of Penobscot for the United States and that he had made certain assurances to these Indians including the exclusive right to the beaver hunt. He urged Congress to fulfill these promises.

Mentioning specifically the Penobscots, Passamaquoddies, St. Johns, Micmacs, and several from Canada, he said:

> These Indians, particularly St. Johns and Passamaquoddy are very tenacious of their liberties; delegacious and subtle people and may be very dangerous if not attended to; their zeal in the cause and their virtue in persevering through many difficulties throughout the war with the attachments and affections the subscriber has experienced himselfe commands his attention as well personal as official in fulfilling as much as possible the engagements made (Papers of the Continental Congress, roll 163:149 II:561-562, May 24, 1783).

THE AMERICAN COLONIAL PERIOD

The American Revolution ended with the Treaty of Paris in September, 1783. Since the Wabanaki allies of the Americans and French were not consulted, their interests were not represented. The treaty provided for a boundary between Nova Scotia and Massachusetts at the St. Croix River, but the British and Americans had conflicting notions as to which of two rivers was the St. Croix. Even before the treaty was signed, British settlers appeared on unceded Passamaquoddy land to build the town of St. Andrews on the site of a Passamaquoddy summer campground and to cut timber for export. The Passamaquoddies objected repeatedly to this intrusion, which violated not only their

wartime agreements with the Americans and the Proclamation of 1763, but also the Treaty of Paris itself, for in their view the river called St. Croix
by the French was not the river at St. Andrews, but
another river, the Magagaudavic farther east (Kidder
1867:306).

In November of 1783 Allan met with representatives
of the Passamaquoddies, Penobscots, Maliseets, and
Micmacs on what the British claimed was, and what
is now known as, the St. Croix River, to discuss
the British settlement at St. Andrews.  Nicholas
Hawwawas of the Maliseets, holding a wampum belt,
spoke for the Maliseets and Micmacs, and doubtless
for the others as well:

> ... A number of people have come among us
> whom we don't know and taken our lands and
> streams.  You say it is peace with America
> and England, but we don't hear anything is
> done for us, no mention made of the Indians
> in this country.  We have been fighting for
> you and secured for America all the lands
> on this eastward country to the River St.
> Croix and always been ready to take up the
> hatchet when you call.  You promised to
> secure for us our hunting grounds....  How
> must we live now, we know nothing but hunting,
> you white men can live other ways.  It is
> said Magagaudawick, called by the French St.
> Croix (the Easterly River Passamaquoddy),
> is the line between you and the English.  We
> wish the line had been further east.  [We all]
> are willing to submit and take our chances on
> the lakes and streams above Passamaquoddy;
> but now the refugees as you call them, have
> come twenty miles westward of the river and
> say they will go to Cobscook (the westerly
> branch).  Why don't you drive them away.
> We are ready and willing to assist you, as
> we have been for America during the wars
> though we want to live with them in peace....

> Brother you remember when we came from St.
> Johns and followed you we had plenty of
> everything for the comfort of our families.
> You see the situation we are now in and the
> distress of our families.  All this we will
> submit to if we can be sure to have our

hunting secured. We cannot sleep or rest,
our women and children are crying about
us, all our villages are distressed, we
cannot sit down easy in any one place, our
old homes are forsaken and like a deer pursued by the hunters leave us no place of
rest.

Brother we will not detain you much longer,
but will conclude what we have to say. As
we have all the war acted on the part of
America so we expect you will see justice
done us. That we may enjoy our privileges
which we have been fighting for as the
other Americans, this is the view of all
the Indians through the country; we shall
all be upon our guard this winter and consult for our own safety. We will wait to
know what is done, until next spring. If
nothing appears for us, necessity will compel us to take care of ourselves, our women
and children.

Brother the belt we have delivered you is
for the great council of America as a token
of our love and friendship. We desire that
they may look upon us as their brothers,
that they will support us in our rights,
that they will prevent their own people
from disturbing and molesting us in our
own hunts.

With this belt also we salute the King of
France, our ancient Father who first instructed us in the Christian religion. We
hope that he will not forget us but as soon
as he can send a reverend father which we
are now much in want of .... (Papers of the
Continental Congress roll 71:58:59, Dec. 25,
1783).

Allan left with the text of Hawwawas' speech and
reported to Governor Hancock of Massachusetts in
December. He also wrote the President of Congress,
pleading that something be done to secure the hunting territories. In another letter written on
February 10, 1784, to Elbridge Gerry in Annapolis,
he said that,

> Should the Massachusets give this [the
> St. Croix drainage] up, I feel myself
> bound by duty to claim the lands left
> out, as far as Old St. Croix as the pro-
> perty of the Indians who have fought &
> bled for it (Allan to Gerry, Feb. 10, 1784).

No action was taken on Allan's recommendations, however; and on March 5, 1784, Allan's authority to
deal with the Eastern Indians was revoked by Congress
(Papers of the Continental Congress, roll 13:35:510).
Ten years later, Allan was to write that from this
time on, "It does not appear that any notice has been
taken of [the Indians living] Eastward of Penobscot"
(Kidder 1867:314).

Farthur west, however, Massachusetts' representative,
Benjamin Lincoln, tried and failed to get the Penob-
scots to cede more land in 1784 and again in 1786.
He reported difficulty in convincing them of,

> their real situation ... that they [had]
> voluntarily surrendered their whole right
> to us in the administration of Governor
> Pownal -- this they did and have no right
> to any Lands but an implyed right under
> the doings of the Provincial Congress in
> 1775 (Lincoln to Governor John Hancock
> March 4, 1788).

A treaty was finally concluded between Massachusetts
and the eastern Indians in 1794 and a separate treaty
with the Penobscots in 1796. Three Massachusetts
representatives, including John Allan, negotiated
the 1794 treaty on Passamaquoddy Bay with 40 Indians
"comprehending principle characters of the Malli-
sheete, Passamaq. & Micmac Tribes, & some belonging
Canada" (Campbell, Allan, and Stillman 1794:1). The
solidarity of the several Wabanaki delegations is
indicated by the fact that,

> The Chiefs of Passamaquody & Merrisheets
> Tribes, delivered their speeches alternately.
> No distinction was observed, nor woud they
> allow any settlement, wherein they were not
> equally concerned, as well more residing in
> the Micmac Country & Confines of Canada
> (Campbell, Allan, and Stillman 1794:2).

After the conference at Passamaquoddy Bay,

> a large Council of the several Tribes have
> met at a distant Village, and in a solemn
> manner, Confirmed what had been done at
> Passamaquody, which proceedings were com-
> municated accompanyed with strings of
> Wampum (Campbell, Allan, and Stillman
> 1794:2).

By this treaty the Passamaquoddies ceded all their
territory within the United States with the exception of some 27,000 acres. The Penobscots ceded
their lands, excepting certain islands, in the
treaties of 1796 and 1818 with Massachusetts and in
a nontreaty sale of land to the State of Maine in
1833. By the end of the eighteenth century Wabanaki
claims to hunting territories in the United States,
their beaver, their access to the coast, and their
ability to negotiate effectively had evaporated.
Their mutual political ties remained, however, although they were now divided by an international
boundary and the Penobscots had signed a separate
treaty with Massachusetts. Even their relationships
with the Great Council Fire remained intact. Despite the pressures of contending Anglo forces during
the war, the Wabanaki peoples and those represented
at Caughnawaga had preserved their political institutions and harmonious relationships. Only George
Washington's "chain of friendship" seemed tarnished.


CUTTING THE POLES AND THROWING DOWN THE BELTS

The Wabanaki Confederacy began to unravel only when
its constituents themselves split into polarized
factions in adjusting to conflicting external pressures in the nineteenth century. The crystallization
of these factions proceeded slowly but inexorably,
as the century unfolded, at least among the Passamaquoddies and the Penobscots. The confederacy assembled on several occasions attempting to reunite
the factions. At various times and in quite different ways the Catholic Church, the State of Maine,
and the Great Council Fire also tried to restore
political unity. These attempts only served to
exacerbate the centrifugal forces that emerged in
the 1820s and 1830s as a consequence of the shrink-
ing land base, the decline of the hunting economy,

and most importantly perhaps, the dilemma posed by continuous pressures to conform to the dictates of a powerful Church and to the conflicting demands of an equally powerful State.

The Passamaquoddy factions had their origins in a dispute over public education in the 1820s while Francis Joseph Neptune, the shaman who fired the first shot at the Battle of Machias in 1777, was still chief. In 1821, the year after Maine became a state, a Protestant missionary, Elijah Kellogg, appeared at Pleasant Point and offered to establish a school with English classes. The school was established, with funding from both the state and federal government, but the priest and many Indians were suspicious of Kellogg's motives, particularly since he incorporated certain Protestant prayers and psalms into his English classes. Francis Joseph Neptune, the old chief, favored the English classes, but a church-oriented group on the reservation succeeded in having the state and federal funds diverted in 1829 to the priest who allocated the money to the teaching of Latin.

After Neptune's death in 1833 or 1834, his son, John Francis, was raised as the new life chief of the Passamaquoddies. Doubtless, the traditional forms for raising a chief in the Wabanaki Confederacy were observed and delegations from other bands were present. John Francis proved to be, like his father, an advocate of progressive education and of preserving the Native political institutions, including life tenure for chiefs. His council, however, seems to have been composed largely of members of the anti-Kellogg party, which looked for leadership to the Church. Early in the summer of 1838 John Francis broke with his council,

> threw down his belt and medals, the signs of his office, and said, You have me for governor no longer. Very quick, he brings all old writings from General Washington and papers from the State, and fling them down too, very hard (Sabbatis Neptune's account, as told to Williamson 1846b:96).

Francis later reconsidered and reclaimed his life chieftaincy but not until the Church Party had consolidated. A July, 1842 meeting to settle the dispute resulted in a fight during which "the liberty pole" was cut down. No doubt, it was the chief's pole, traditionally erected when a new chief was "raised up" (Speck 1915:503-504) and apparently cut down only at his death or resignation.

In 1844 a new chief was elected unanimously by 68 votes, but the traditional (John Francis) party boycotted the election refusing to acknowledge the new chief. Finally in 1848 at a confederacy meeting, with Penobscot and Maliseet delegates present, it was decided that each faction should have its own chief. The church party then withdrew from the village at Pleasant Point, its members going up river. Ultimately the two parties agreed to petition the state "to build a village for the new [church] party on the northern shore of the Schoodic lakes" (Vetromile 1866:119).

Perhaps prompted by this petition, Governor Hubbard of Maine wrote to the Passamaquoddies in January of 1852, saying they must cultivate the land, since "Your game is gone," and that their traditional political institutions were outmoded. He advised them to "let your present chief be your chief as long as he lives.... then if you think best, you can elect a new chief for a shorter time." He also asked them to elect by majority vote a single representative to attend the state legislature, without voting privileges, each year. He recommended the advice of the priest and of the state's agent to the Passamaquoddies, but not that of the Canadian Indians who,

> are no better than you are. They have
> difficulties amongst themselves....
> They are controlled by the British
> government, and their interests are
> different from yours and from ours.
> They now come into our state and kill
> your moose because their British Fathers
> will not let them kill their own moose,
> and their moose are almost gone...
> (Hubbard 1852).

Later in 1852 the two factions reconciled their differences in a formal treaty, signed by 133 Passamaquoddy men at Pleasant Point (Vetromile 1866:119). The treaty pledged mutual friendship and forgiveness, validated each of the factions and their officials, and provided for a representative to the state legislature to be elected annually from the Old Party at Pleasant Point and in alternate years from the New, or Church Party at Indian Township. The treaty was confirmed when the members of both parties entered the church and took "an oath on the missal upon the altar and separated in peace" (Vetromile 1866:119). Thus the two parties became politically and geographically distinct bands by mutual consent, each recognized by the Church, the State, and the Wabanaki Confederacy. Despite Governor Hubbard's advice to the contrary, they continued to consult with Canadian Indians. Thus Passamaquoddy representatives were involved together with Maliseet and Micmac representatives from Canada in raising the last Penobscot life chief in 1861 (Speck 1915: 504), and in about 1870 Joe Lola and Captain Sapiel Selmore, the last keeper of the Passamaquoddy wampums, attended the Great Council Fire at Caughnawaga (Speck 1915:498). Even as late as the 1890s, when Mrs. W. W. Brown described a chief raising by the Church-oriented band at Indian Township, "a stand held the tribal wampum" together with "the silver gorgets, and the chief's hat," and it was still "usual" to read the wampum and "customary to invite friends from neighboring tribes to attend the festivities" (Brown 1892:58-59). Ironically, Brown's account of Passamaquoddy political activity and participation at confederacy meetings appeared in the same year, 1892, that the Maine State Supreme Court found, in the case of State v Newell, that,

> Though these Indians are still spoken of as the "Passamaquoddy Tribe", and perhaps consider themselves a tribe, they have for many years been without a tribal organization in any political sense. They cannot make war or peace, cannot make treaties; cannot make laws; cannot punish crime; cannot administer even civil justice among themselves.... They are as completely subject to the State as any other inhabitants can be... (O'Toole and Tureen 1971:17).

The segmentation of the Penobscots paralleled that of the Passamaquoddies in many ways. Factions seem to have developed soon after the death of the Revolutionary period chief, Joseph Orono, in 1801.

In 1816 according to Williamson (1832:495), "The parties... were so sanguine and violent after they lost their chief, that they could not for many months agree upon a successor." After the priest "interposed his influence," however, they finally settled on John Aitteon from up river as Governor and John Neptune from a coastal family as Lt. Governor (Williamson 1832:495). For reasons that are far from clear, but which undoubtedly include the sale of Penobscot land in 1833 and the sexual adventures and other improprieties of John Neptune, both men were impeached at a meeting at Old Town in 1838 attended by 21 Passamaquoddy and 12 Maliseet delegates (Williamson 1846b:94). The impeachment occurred only a few weeks after John Francis "threw down his belt" at Pleasant Point and split with his council. Perhaps for this reason the Passamaquoddy delegates were all members of, or sympathetic to, the Church party. One of them, Sabbatis Neptune, publicly advocated the impeachment of Lt. Governor John Neptune, accusing him of excessive drinking, shamanistic practices unbecoming a Catholic, adultery, and failing to provide for his illegitimate children (Williamson 1846b:97-98). A new and more reputable Governor and Lt. Governor were raised with a majority of Penobscot votes, about half the Maliseet votes, and the unanimous support of the church-oriented delegation from Passamaquoddy. Several "Tarratines" (Williamson's designation for Penobscots) abstained, choosing "by their absence to avoid the controversy." Since the impeachment was unprecedented, the new officials were not acknowledged by Aitteon, Neptune, or their supporters (Williamson 1846b:96-99).

Two flags flew from two chiefs' poles on Indian Island that day. Each flag had as its central figure "a large red crucifix, cut from scarlet broadcloth, the perpendicular piece being four or five feet in length, and four inches in breadth, and the horizontal cross-piece, towards the top, two feet long or more;" but only the Aitteon-Neptune flag had a crucifix with the two horizontal bars of the Cross of Loraine (Williamson 1846b:96; for a conflicting account, see Eckstorm 1945:161). The tension engendered by the impeachment prompted Governor Kent of Maine to send a "monitory letter" in which, according to Clara Neptune's testimony given long after, he threatened to send in troops in the event of disorder (Eckstorm 1945:172-173).

After their impeachment Aitteon and Neptune strengthened their party by establishing a coalition with a
group which favored public education and included
Joe Polis, Thoreau's guide in The Maine Woods. Thus
the Penobscot parties, at least by the 1840s, were
divided over the same issues as the Passamaquoddy
parties--the traditionalists tending to stand by the
treaties, to rely upon the state, and to favor public
education and life tenure for chiefs, while the "new"
parties stood by the Catholic Church, relied upon
the priests, and favored church control of the schools
and the option of deposing chiefs for cause. Both
parties, of course, had their roots in the eighteenth
century alliance with France whose clergy and civil
officials had acted in concert. The traditionalist
parties emphasized their treaty relationships with
the State of Maine which had taken over France's
secular relationship to the Wabanaki. The "new"
parties in contrast stressed their religious affiliation with the Catholic Church which had continued
in the role of the early French missionaries. The
polarization of the parties and the collapse of the
confederacy occurred in the context of enforced dependence on an American society whose Catholic clergy
and secular officials frequently worked at cross
purposes. By so doing they divided the native communities.

After the impeachment in 1838 the church party of
the Penobscots evidently appealed to the Great
Council Fire for support. If so, they may have
succeeded only in causing the end of the State
party's association with the Great Council Fire
because the last State party delegation from Penobscot left Caughnawaga in 1840, according to the
traditionalist Penobscot historian, Joseph Nicolar.
He pointedly ignored the continued participation
of the Church party when he wrote, in 1893, that
"the last visit made from the east was only fifty-
three years ago, and some of the young men that
went with the old men on that last visit are still
living" (Nicolar 1893:138).

About 1850 Bishop Fitzpatrick of the Boston Diocese
attempted to mediate the Penobscot dispute. Both
parties were to be abolished; both governors were
to resign; and both chiefs' poles were to be cut.

When the pole-cutters had cut the church party pole
and were preparing to cut that of the traditionalists, they were prevented from doing so by adherents
of the Aitteen-Neptune party, who ran to the pole
to shield it with their bodies. To avert bloodshed
the Bishop recalled the pole-cutters, but he excom-
municated three of those who had defended the pole
(Eckstorm 1946:160, 170). After this episode the
members of the Church Party were evidently so harassed by the Traditionalists that they appealed to
the state for protection. Governor Hubbard, ever
ready with advice for Indians, instructed his agent
to tell Aitteon and Neptune to treat their political
opponents with kindness and forbearance and also
told him to say:

> So long as they are peaceable amongst them-
> selves, they will be permitted to control
> their own social and civil affairs, and to
> live as we do, under a republican form of
> government, managed by themselves, and con-
> trolled by their own majority; But you will
> say to them, at the same time that they are
> answerable to our criminal laws, and that
> every crime committed, every breach of the
> peace will and must be tried and punished
> severely by our laws (Hubbard to Staples,
> July 30, 1851).

In the same letter Governor Hubbard threatened to
end the annual treaty payments to the Penobscots if
they continued to be wasted "in useless festivities,"
i.e., in support of confederacy meetings and other
political or quasi-political meetings at Old Town.
Thus the governor of Maine was, in 1851, prepared
to violate the terms of the treaty of 1818 between
Massachusetts and the Penobscots, which Maine had
undertaken to uphold when it became a state in 1820.
He also asserted that state laws would be applied
to Penobscots on their own land and that the Penobscots would be permitted to govern themselves only,
"So long as they are peaceable amongst themselves."

The Church Party continued, nonetheless, to be
harassed. In the mid-1850s Father John Bapst left
Old Town for Passamaquoddy, and the Church Party
left also on his advice; some groups emigrated to
Caughnawaga, others to St. Francis (Vetromile 1866,

as quoted by Eckstorm 1946:162fn.). Some 10 or 12 families returned the next year, however, after an unhappy winter at Caughnawaga. This group may have been largely responsible for the final break between the Penobscot Church Party and the Great Council Fire, which occurred when Attean Orson, the last Penobscot delegate to Caughnawaga, returned in 1862 and laid the wampum on the table in the council house at Old Town. In the ensuing discussion, Nick Socka-besin suddenly took the belt from the table and threw it out the door. No one moved to raise it from the dust; thenceforth all connections with the Great Council Fire were severed (Speck 1915:498). In breaking with Caughnawaga, the Church Party aligned itself more closely with the Aitteon-Neptune party which had severed its ties in 1840.

In any event the Penobscots' dispute was resolved in 1866, and both parties were perpetuated when the Maine legislature passed a bill providing that lead-ers of the two parties would hold office in alter-nate years (Eckstorm 1945:159; Snow 1978:145). Penobscot tribal government operated under this unique political arrangement until both parties were abolished in 1931.

By the 1860s both the Penobscot and the Passamaquoddy factions were reconciled. The Passamaquoddies re-sided in two politically and geographically distinct reservation communities with the approval of both church and state, while the Penobscots lived, for the most part, in a single reservation community but with two sets of officials each holding office in alternate years, an arrangement approved by both church and state. The Penobscots had severed all ties with Caughnawaga, and the Passamaquoddies allowed their connection to lapse after 1870.

Old political forms and symbols lingered on into the twentieth century, but the Penobscot chief raising in 1910 was a pale shadow of the gorgeous and intri-cate rituals of earlier times (Speck 1940:240-245). Poverty and dependency had taken their inevitable toll. By 1936 only two dance song leaders remained among the Penobscots, one of whom at age 85 was re-duced to dancing in the streets and singing sacred songs for the Whiteman's pennies. The Wabanaki were destitute, degraded, and divided. The wampums were lost and Native leadership aspired only to preserve

the Indians' special status as wards of the state,
insulating themselves from federal intervention.
To this end 64 Passamaquoddies and some Penobscots
petitioned Governor Milliken of Maine in 1920 to
use his influence against the extension of citizenship to Indians born in the United States. "We are
wards of the State of Maine," they insisted,

> and we want the Passamaquoddy Tribe to
> remain as a relic of the State. Once, we
> received kind advice from Hon. James G.
> Blain.... He advised us to stay in the
> wigwam. By so doing the Government will
> always help us. We are satisfied with
> our lot as Indians (Anonymous Feb. 29,
> 1920).

## REVITALIZATION AND THE FEDERAL TRUST RELATIONSHIP

By the 1950s over 6,000 acres of the land reserved
to the Passamaquoddies by the treaty of 1794 had
been alienated without their consent and without
compensation. However, the erosion of the land
base stopped in 1966 after a white entrepreneur won
a deed to some Indian Township land in a poker game
with another white man. He attempted to build summer camps on his new property and to force three
Indian families to move. The Passamaquoddies halted
construction with a sit-in, and several were arrested
and charged with trespassing in state district court.
Their defense was based on the treaty of 1794, which
reserved to the Passamaquoddies 23,000 acres of
Indian Township (McLaughlin 1977:72; Taylor 1977:17).
The case was dismissed on technical grounds, but
since that time no Maine Indian land has been alienated, and the Wabanaki have taken a series of legal
actions in the federal courts to regain title to
lost land and to establish their right to federal
protection and services as provided for Indian tribes
by the Commerce Clause of the Constitution of the
United States. In January, 1975, Judge Gignoux'
court found that the "Indian Non-Intercourse Act ...
is applicable to the Passamaquoddy Indian Tribe; and
that the Act establishes a trust relationship between the United States and the Tribe (McLaughlin
1977:78; Taylor 1977:18). This opinion was upheld
unanimously by the U. S. Court of Appeals in Boston
in December, 1975. Since the deadline for appeal

to the U. S. Supreme Court has passed, this decision
is now the law of the land.  It extends to the Passamaquoddies, Penobscots, and other New England
tribes the same benefits enjoyed by western tribes
as "wards" of the federal government.  Significantly,
Judge Gignoux also ordered the United States Department of Justice to file a protective suit on behalf
of the Passamaquoddies and Penobscots and against
the State of Maine and other land owners so the
courts might determine whether, as attorneys for
the Maine Indians contend, the Passamaquoddy and
Penobscot land transactions violate the Indian Non-
Intercourse Act of 1790.  If so, and if there is no
out-of-court settlement, the eastern half of the
State of Maine, some 10,000,000 acres, may be awarded
to the Indians.  This step would make the non-Indian
residents subject to damage suits and "ejectment
actions" (Taylor 1977:20).  Ironically, the legal
actions which began in 1966 with the defense of
Indian "trespassers" by appeal to the treaty of
1794 may soon develop into a case against white
"trespassers" based on the fact that the land transaction negotiated in the treaty of 1794 was invali-
dated by a prior act of Congress, the Non-Intercourse
Act of 1790.

At any rate the old reliance on the state and the
church which polarized the confederacy in the nineteenth century has given way to a new reliance on
federal courts and the federal departments of Justice and the Interior.  The current Wabanaki leaders
have learned to deal with legal counsel, the news
media, and a wide variety of foundations and federal
agencies (Willard 1976).  Parallel developments have
taken place in Canada where the Micmacs and Maliseets
are preparing claims for aboriginal lands in Nova
Scotia and New Brunswick.

In the process of asserting their claims to land and
to an historic ethnic identity, the Wabanaki communities have rediscovered one another and have begun
to develop new institutions to deal with common
problems.  To give just one example a meeting was
held in August, 1977, at Indian Island on the Penobscot.  Delegations were expected from the three
Maine reservations, from the Southern Maine Indian
Association, the Central Maine Indian Association,
the Association of Aroostook Indians, the Wabanaki
Corporation, the Abenaki Council of Vermont, the

New Hampshire Indian Nation, Inc., from a number of
southern New England Indian organizations including
the Boston Indian Council (the largest Micmac organization in the United States), and from many more in
Canada.  A delegation from the Confederation of Indians of Quebec represented the Abenakis of St.
Francis, Odanak, and Becancour, the Micmacs of Res-
tigouche and Maria, the Hurons of Lorette, and the
Mohawks of Caughnawaga, St. Regis, and Oka.  Other
Micmac bands, including those of Nova Scotia and
Cape Breton Island, and the six St. John River bands
of Maliseets were represented by a delegation from
the Union of New Brunswick Indians.

At this meeting there was no reading of wampums and
no flag with a red crucifix, but a moose-meat stew
and even a "greeting" dance were planned.  The delegations came by car and by airplane, rather than
canoe.  Their business was to construct new institutions that express the sense of Wabanaki unity
which has smouldered for more than a century, since
John Francis threw down his belt at Passamaquoddy
and Nick Sockabesin threw the wampum out the door
of the council house at Indian Island.

REFERENCES CITED

Allan, John
        1784    To Elbridge Gerry, February 10.  Samuel
                Adams Papers.  New York Public Library,
                Manuscript Division.

Allen, William
        1831    "A Journal of the expedition to Quebec
                in 1775," Collections of the Maine
                Historical Society 1:387-416.

Anonymous
        1920    "File protest being made citizens U.S.,"
                Portland Sunday Telegram.  February 29.

Bailey, Alfred G.
        1969    The Conflict of European and Eastern
                Algonkian Cultures.  Toronto:  Uni-
                versity of Toronto Press.

Baxter, James P.
     1906-    Documentary History of the State of
     1916     Maine. Maine Historical Society, Series
              2, vols. 12, 14, and 24.

Brown, Mrs. W. W.
     1892     "Chief-making among the Passamaquoddy
              Indians," Journal of American Folklore
              5:57-59.

Campbell, John, John Allan, and George Stillman
     1794     To Governor and Council of Massachusetts.
              Report on treaty with Passamaquoddies
              and others connected with them, Pine
              Tree Legal Assistance, Inc., Indian
              Unit, Calais, Maine. (Microfilm)

Conkling, Robert
     1974     "Legitimacy and conversion in social
              change: the case of French missionaries
              and the northeastern Algonkian, Ethno-
              history 21:1:1-24.

[Continental Congress]
National Archives
              Papers of the Continental Congress,
              Microfilm edition.

Day, Gordon M.
     1973     "Missisquoi:  a new look at an old
              village," Man in the Northeast 6:51-56.

Eckstorm, Fannie H.
     1939     "Who was Paugus?"  New England
              Quarterly 12:2:203-226.

     1945     Old John Neptune and Other Maine Indian
              Shamans.  Portland.

Gesner, Abraham
     1847     New Brunswick with notes for Emigrants.
              Comprehending the early history an
              account of the Indians, settlement,
              topography, statistics, natural his-
              tory, etc.  London:  Simmonds & Ward.
              388 pp.

Hodge, Frederick W. (ed.)
    1907-    Handbook of American Indians North
    1910     of Mexico. Smithsonian Institution,
             Bureau of American Ethnology, Bull.
             30, 2 vols.

Hough, Frederick
    1853     A History of St. Lawrence and Franklin
             Counties. Albany.

Hubbard, Gov. John
    1851     To Isaac Staples, July 30. Augusta:
             Maine State Library 4:213-214.

    1852     "To our Brethren the Passamaquoddy
             tribe of Indians," January. Augusta:
             Maine State Library 4:222-226.

Kidder, Frederick
    1859     "The Abenaki Indians: their treaties
             of 1713 and 1717 and a vocabulary; with
             a historical introduction." Maine
             Historical Society Collection, Series
             1, 6:229-263.

    1867     Military operations in eastern Maine
             and Nova Scotia during the Revolution,
             chiefly compiled from the journals and
             letters of Colonel John Allan, with
             notes and a memoir of Col. John Allan.
             Albany. (Reprinted 1971 by Krauss
             Reprint Co., New York.)

Koren, Henry J.
    1962     Knaves or Knights? A History of the
             Spiritan Missionaries in Acadia and
             North America, 1732-1839. Pittsburgh:
             Duquesne University Press.

Le Clercq, G.
    1910     New Relation of Gaspesia, W. F. Ganong,
             ed. Champlain Society, vol. 5.

Leger, Sister Mary Celeste
    1929     The Catholic Indian Missions in Maine
             1611-1820. Washington, D.C.: Catholic
             University of America.

Lincoln, Benjamin
    1788    To Gov. John Hancock, March 4. New-
           berry Library, Chicago.

MacDonald, J. S.
    1912    "Memoire of Lt. Gov. Michael Frankline,"
           Nova Scotia Historical Society, vol.
           16.

McLaughlin, Robert
    1977    "Giving it back to the Indians,"
           The Atlantic Monthly 239:2:70-74, 78,
           82, 84-85.

Morrison, Kenneth M.
    1974    "Sebastien Racle and Norridgewock,
           1724: the Eckstorm conspiracy thesis
           reconsidered," Maine Historical Society
           Quarterly 14:2:76-97.

Nicolar, Joseph
    1893    The Life and Traditions of the Red
           Man. Bangor.

O'Toole, Francis J., and Thomas N. Tureen
    1971    "State Power and the Passamaquoddy
           tribe: 'a gross national hypocrisy?'"
           Maine Law Review 23:1:1-39. Portland.

Raymond, William O.
    1896    "The Old Meductic Fort," New Brunswick
           Historical Society Collection 1:221-
           272.

Snow, Dean R.
    1978    "Eastern Abenaki," Handbook of North
           American Indians, vol. 15, pp. 137-147.
           B. Trigger, volume editor; W. Sturte-
           vant, general editor. Washington, D.C.:
           Smithsonian Institution, Office of
           Anthropology.

Speck, Frank G.
    1915    "Eastern Algonkian Wabanaki Confederacy,"
           American Anthropologist, New series
           17:492-508.

1919      "The Functions of wampum among the
          eastern Algonkian," Memoirs, American
          Anthropological Association, New
          series, vol. 6, no. 1. (Reprinted
          1964 by Krauss Reprint Corporation.)

1940      Penobscot Man:  the Life History of a
          Forest Tribe in Maine.  Philadelphia:
          University of Pennsylvania Press.

Speck, Frank G. and Wendell S. Hadlock
    1946  "A Report of tribal boundaries and
          hunting areas of the Malecite Indians
          of New Brunswick," American Anthro-
          pologist, New series, 48:355-374.

Taylor, Stuart
    1977  "Indians on the Lawpath," The New
          Republic, 176:18:16-21.

Thwaites, Reuben Gold, ed.
    1897  Jesuit Relations and Allied Documents:
          Travels and Explorations of the Jesuit
          Missionaries in New France, 1610-1791.
          Cleveland.

Vetromile, Eugene
    1866  The Abnakis and Their History.  New
          York.

Wallis, Wilson D., and Ruth S. Wallis
    1955  The Micmac Indians of Eastern Canada.
          Minneapolis:  University of Minnesota
          Press.

Willard, Lawrence F.
    1976  "Passamaquoddy uprising," Yankee 40:
          10:82-87, 162-164, 167-169.

Williamson, William D.
    1832  History of the State of Maine, vol. 1.
          Hallowell.

    1839  History of the State of Maine, vol. 2.
          Freeport.

1846a   "Notice of Orono, a chief at Penobscot,"
Massachusetts Historical Society
Collection, series 3, 9:82-91 (1846).

1846b   "Indian tribes in New England,"
Massachusetts Historical Society
Collection, series 3, 9:92-100
(1846).

CHAPTER 3


The Forced Acculturation of the Eastern Cherokees:
  Bureau of Indian Affairs Schools, 1892-1933[1]

  Sharlotte Neely, Northern Kentucky University


The Eastern Band of Cherokee Indians live on a federal reservation in the mountains of southwestern
North Carolina, scattered over a rugged four-county
area. They are the descendants of Cherokees who
escaped the 1838 Removal to Indian Territory. Originally a small group of about one thousand people
living relatively isolated lives, the Eastern Cherokees had experienced great changes in their culture
by the end of the nineteenth century. At that time
many whites, some claiming minimal Cherokee ancestry,
moved onto the reservation. This innovation, along
with the arrival of formal education, accelerated
acculturation. A trend toward an even harsher system of forced culture change began formally in 1892,
when the Bureau of Indian Affairs took control of
the Cherokee schools, originally founded in 1881 by
the Society of Friends. The era of strict B.I.A.
control thus began in 1892 and extended to 1933; its
effects are still felt.


GENERAL POLICY AND EDUCATION

Ironically, this repressive era is sandwiched between
two progressive periods which demonstrated some concern for Indian culture. These periods were the
"Quaker Policy" of President Ulysses S. Grant and
the "Indian New Deal" of President Franklin D. Roosevelt (Neely 1975; Weeks 1976). The Society of Friends
themselves described the "Quaker Policy" as one of
"educating instead of exterminating Indians" (Quaker
Collection 1883). Although following an acculturation
policy, the Quakers demonstrated some tolerance for
Cherokee culture. Attendance at the Quaker schools
was not compulsory. One of the superintendents for
Quaker education emphasized that someone in his
office needed to visit with the Indians in their
homes and consult with them as he had done (Quaker
Collection 1882). The Quakers' emphasis on practi-
cality meant that among the Eastern Cherokees they

worked, beyond their role as educators, to remove fraudulent financial claims against Indian individuals and to have promised government funds awarded to the Cherokees. The Quakers even employed a few Indian teachers. By 1892, however, the "Quaker Policy" was waning in popularity among federal officials at the national level. The corruption of a local Quaker official in the Eastern Cherokee area was used to transfer operation of the schools to the federal government and the Bureau of Indian Affairs. Soon afterward, a policy of forced acculturation developed, largely implemented through the schools where attendance was made compulsory.

In many ways this era of initial B.I.A. control was dismal. It is true that by this period the Native American population in the United States was finally beginning to increase again, but diseases still plagued Indian areas. The Cherokees were often hit hard by bouts of influenza. Shortly before 1920 the swine flu epidemic engulfed the Cherokee area taking many lives. About the same time, a whooping cough epidemic struck Chilocco Boarding School in Oklahoma, and an unnamed disease killed many Indian students at Haskell Boarding School in Kansas. Letters to and from the superintendent at Cherokee mention tuberculosis as well.

As late as 1930, Cherokee Indians were not being allowed to vote by the State of North Carolina, although in the Cherokee area itself, one county permitted resident Cherokees to vote, while neighboring counties refused (Annual Report of the Commissioner of Indian Affairs, 1931). Cherokees were having problems with land taxes as well. In 1925 one U.S. District Court judge ruled that the act of 1924, making Indians United States citizens, exempted reservation land from taxation. The next year, however, the local counties again tried to tax reservation land. In the ensuing court case, a different judge ruled that Indian land could be taxed. By 1931 the Cherokee case was on its way to the U.S. Supreme Court, still unsettled. Some Indian families, unable to pay their taxes, lost their land. More land would have been lost, but the Tribal Council sometimes was able to pay the back taxes:

It seems that the Eastern Band of Cherokee
Indians through its council seeks to pay
the taxes of lands in Graham County owned
by the individual members of the Band.
These Indians have fallen behind in their
tax payments and are unable to pay same...
it now becomes necessary to act or the
Indians will in all probability lose their
lands.... The tribe has a sufficient amount
[$300] to take care of the taxes involved
and there is no question of its desire to
do so (Annual Report of the Commissioner of
Indian Affairs, 1931).

During this era threats of land allotment, under the
Dawes Act, haunted the Eastern Cherokees. Local
whites understood the issues poorly, and the Asheville Times, a regional newspaper for western North
Carolina, asked in May, 1923: "Are the Cherokees
united in their opinion that the land should be
allotted to them directly [as private property]?"
Eastern Cherokees living out of state and anyone
who believed they might have any Indian blood wrote
to the superintendent to ask for a share of money
or land. Eastern Cherokees justifiably felt insecure about their futures, with allotment hanging
over them. In 1931 the superintendent wrote about
a Cherokee man in the Snowbird community who was:

... wondering now if it is safe to go ahead
and improve the holding with the view of
having his allotment made out of this tract
and covering the land which he will improve,
provided, of course, allotments are ever
made (Annual Report of the Commissioner of
Indian Affairs, 1931).

Needless to say, the era was not made any less dismal by the Great Depression of the 1930s or even
World War I when some Cherokees were drafted although
not then United States citizens.

Land disputes, due to overpopulation and threat of
allotment, increased on the Cherokee reservation.
More and more individuals of minimal Cherokee blood,
or none at all, were challenged by the Tribal Council when they attempted to enroll as Eastern Cherokees.

It was also an era of job discrimination against
Indians, of the first attempts to persuade Indians
to migrate to urban areas, of denied rights and con-
fusing legal problems, of economic disaster, and of
diseases. This time of forced acculturation, much
of it accomplished through the educational system,
is the focus of this chapter. The end result of
this repressive policy was the loss of much traditional Cherokee culture and the emotional scarring
of many individuals; yet Cherokees managed to retain
a remarkable part of their society and culture despite the pressure.


EDUCATION AS INTENSE ACCULTURATION

Journalist Virginia Young, of Woman's Progress,
visited the Qualla Boundary in 1894. Her article
about the Cherokees provides a vivid picture of
the training given Indians at the turn of the century. She found the school situated: "On a green
plateau, about which winds the current of the river,
called in their musical tongue 'Oconeeloughky'
[Oconaluftee]" (Young 1894:171). The students were
engaged in vocational duties much like those conducted in the previous Quaker era. In fact, she
found Henry W. and Anna M. Spray, holdovers from
the last corrupt years of the Quaker era, in charge
at the school. Amid pictures of Bible scenes, an
organ, and their own "Indian Brass Band" the students worked:

> These girls were taught to sew, mend, darn
> and use sewing machines. They were also
> instructed in laundry work and cookery, and
> turned out such accomplished mistresses of
> these arts that the demands for them as
> house servants at Asheville and other
> neighboring towns, could not be supplied....
> Everything about the premises indicated
> thrift and discipline. There was a farm
> attached to the school, and on this good
> crops of corn and peas were growing, while
> vegetables were raised in abundance for
> the school and some to sell. They also
> sold fine butter and honey (Young 1894:
> 172).

This pattern in education persisted for the next

four decades, with Indian girls being trained for "careers" as maids to white families. Boys were taught the same farm work they performed at home. The main achievements of this early period were in construction and improvement of school facilities. No curriculum improvements occurred until the "Indian New Deal" of John Collier.

Throughout the era no high school existed on the reservation, and the state discouraged Cherokees from attending public high schools (Owl 1929:157-158). During some periods it was even illegal for Indians to attend white public schools. Usually Cherokee students attended one of the five local Cherokee day schools through the fourth grade, or entered boarding school immediately if they lived more than one and a half miles from a day school. They could also attend the boarding school at Yellow Hill, one of the Cherokee townships, through the ninth grade. Then they would be sent out-of-state to high school, usually at Chilocco in Oklahoma, Haskell in Kansas, Carlisle in Pennsylvania, or Hampton in Virginia. At Haskell, students were asked to attend for at least four years. Compulsory education laws offered little alternative to this system for younger students. Some students ran away, but truant officers brought many of the run-aways back to school. Henry M. Owl (1929:160), himself an Eastern Cherokee, describes an habitual runaway of the 1920s who was supervised all day and chained to his dormitory bed at night to prevent a future escape. The child still managed to get away, dragging the bedstead to which he was chained. A 1918 letter from the local Bureau of Indian Affairs superintendent to the Commissioner of Indian Affairs described "one of the most troublesome Indian families we have on the reservation" when he wrote:

> We have had considerable trouble keeping a small boy of his [a Cherokee man's] in school. When the policeman goes to get the boy the whole family have been known to stand him [the policeman] off with drawn knives (Annual Report of the Commissioner of Indian Affairs 1918).

Such descriptions clearly reveal the Cherokees were less than satisfied with the education of their children.

Some Cherokee students even ran away from the distant out-of-state boarding schools. In 1920 a Cherokee boy in his teens left Haskell Institute and joined the army rather than run the risk of being returned to Kansas. Once in the army, he wrote both the director at Haskell and the Eastern Cherokee Agency superintendent to complain about the educational system he had experienced. The director at Haskell decided the boy was "drunk as a Lord" when he wrote the letter and ignored the complaint. The letter is one of the few from this era in which Cherokees themselves openly criticized the educational system imposed upon them. Since most of the letters preserved are written to superintendents or school directors asking for advances of money, permission to return home, or similar requests, they are necessarily lacking in criticisms. The letter from this particular runaway is informative:

> I am in Fort Logan near Denver Colo. I am
> a man now in the U.S. Army. Don't forget
> that Old Man. I am a fighting man from
> North Carolina. What do you think of me
> Jack. I am all right. I am in to make a
> real man out of me. I'll say so. And
> learn a real trade. What the hell can a
> guy learn in Haskell. I am [in] for three
> years. I think I'll know something [by]
> that time. I am going to know something
> to[o] let me tell you old boy. I [wanted]
> to go to work last spring in Haskell so
> they won't let me go.... I could not stay
> any longer. I had to go.... I did it for
> real cause. Not to be out of school don't
> think that. I am not in the army to keep
> out from work. I am in to learn a real man
> trade. Not to be a farmer all the time.
> I can do farm work any time in my sleep.
> Can't I. I am a farmer son from North
> Carolina.... Tell my sisters I am in the
> U.S. Army in Fort Logan, Colo. I am not
> in H.I. any more. I've pass my time there
> .... I don't ever be home for a long time
> ... (Correspondence, Eastern Cherokee Agency
> File, Federal Archives and Records Center,
> July 10, 1920).

The letter says much about boarding school education.

It clearly implies, for example, that even the discipline and routine of the military did not seem as bad as life at Haskell. It also points to a problem many Eastern Indians must have experienced at Western boarding schools. These boarding schools, housing large numbers of Indian students from the Plains area, were committed to "civilizing" Indians by replacing a hunting lifestyle with that of the farmer. The vocational work centered around instruction in farming. Any Cherokee boy would have had lifelong experience in it. His education at Haskell, therefore, was lacking in new knowledge. The above letter is also interesting in that, despite its anger, there are still concerned references to family. Boarding school education broke up families temporarily, but students and their kinsmen continually made efforts to remain in touch and ultimately to be reunited.

Another student letter demonstrates still further the importance of the Cherokee family. In 1920 the director at Chilocco wrote to the superintendent on the Cherokee reservation about an Eastern Cherokee boy who:

> ... came to me a day or so ago feeling very badly, saying that he had received word from home that his mother was in very poor health and needed some money to buy things to eat (Correspondence, Eastern Cherokee Agency File, Federal Archives and Records Center, April 30, 1920).

A week later the reply was written by the superintendent who explained that the boy's:

> ... mother died on Monday May 3rd and the funeral was held the following day. With the assistance of the [Cherokee boarding] school she was given a decent burial. The father is able to work and I see no reason why any money should be sent to him by [his son]. You can tell [the student] for me, that his mother was an industrious hard working woman and that I hope that his conduct and efforts in school are such as to be an honor to her (Correspondence, Eastern Cherokee Agency File, Federal Archives and Records Center, May 7, 1920).

91

One may well ask why the superintendent waited several days to inform a Cherokee student boarding out of state about a death in the family. The out-of-state boarding school system created long separations, sometimes lasting for years, for Cherokee families. Even during major family crises or during summer vacations, students were seldom allowed to return home. Kinsmen were also hindered in their efforts to assist each other in the manner of the traditional Cherokee extended family.

Students tried repeatedly to return home, at least for summer vacations. In one case the director at Haskell recommended that a certain student, described as "very reasonable about [his] education and affairs generally," be allowed to return to the Cherokee reservation during the summer, only to have the request denied by the superintendent at Cherokee. The director at Haskell wrote:

> It seems rather an unnecessary expense for him to go home and back when it will take him but one year more to finish. However, he has not been at home but two weeks in seven years ... he cannot be blamed for wanting to see his people.

The superintendent's reply was, however, negative:

> I know just how [this student] feels about coming to the mountains to spend the summer, but if his health is good and he can find employment under your outing system during the vacation period I would not advise that he return to Cherokee until he has finished at Haskell. It is true that there is plenty of work at Cherokee but it has been my observation that nearly all, if not all, of the young men spend their money about as fast as it is earned and when the summer is over they have nothing to show for what they have done (Annual Report of the Commissioner of Indian Affairs, May 25 and May 29, 1920).

What the superintendent implied is that even "reasonable" students, like the one mentioned above, squandered their money if unsupervised. So despite ample employment at home, the student was denied permission to return to the reservation. And perhaps the superintendent was correct that few students had anything to show in the way of savings by the end of a summer at home. Perhaps, however, this was not due to squandering money but to participation in a traditional system of sharing money with family and friends in need. Such a system does deplete money which could be saved to purchase material goods, but the resulting lack of money does not mean unwise spending. Not only did the director at Haskell describe Cherokee students as "reasonable" about trips home, but the director at Chilocco did, too, saying they were "among the finest students we have and I find they do well on leaving school." Yet, Cherokee students were consistently denied permission to return home.

Even before the Quakers established their school among the Cherokees, the federal government had been developing a policy concerning boarding schools and the Eastern Cherokees. In his letter of August 16, 1880 describing the Eastern Cherokees, the Secretary of the Interior wrote:

> All [the Cherokees] appear anxious to educate their children, but prefer to have schools established at home, so all the children may attend instead of sending a few away. I have recommended that schools be established among them, but in my opinion better results will be reached by sending a number of children away from home to schools each year, to prepare for teachers, etc. The habits formed at such schools will be of very great advantage to them as well as to other members of the band (Quaker Collection 1882:45-46).

In other words, officials realized quite early that the students would acculturate more quickly in the boarding school situation.

Letters written from Cherokee students in out-of-state boarding schools to the superintendent at the Qualla Boundary frequently expressed dissatisfaction. They often requested advances on their annual money allotment, asked to be allowed to return to the reservation, and described unpleasant happenings at school. The only occupation the

93

educational system seemed to offer most Indian
girls was as maids to white families. Many whites
regularly wrote to the superintendent asking for
"Indian girls."

The superintendent's advice to Indian students to
learn a trade in order to earn "a good living" was
not always easy to accomplish as this letter written
by a boy in 1919 to the superintendent indicated:

> Well, I am very well and getting along very
> well with my schoolwork, I have also picked
> "Blacksmithing" as my trade and I am doing
> my very best to learn all I can about the
> trade ... I was to forty days for outing in
> which I should have been out working for
> money ... when the time came for me to start
> on my outing I went to the outing agent and
> told him I was ready to go to work, but in-
> stead of sending me out to work he told me
> to wait a few days ... he always said he
> had no place for me to work until I had
> only nine days to work before school started
> again (Correspondence, Eastern Cherokee
> Agency File, Federal Archives and Records
> Center, October 19, 1923).

Students were almost always encouraged to spend
their summers at the out-of-state boarding schools
they were attending to work at the trades they were
being taught. As the above letter indicates, such
employment was not always available. Even when
jobs were available, the pay was often unsatisfac-
tory, as revealed in this letter:

> You know I want to get an Education and I
> am working hard to get it. I guess you
> will let me go home next summer won't you?
> I beleave if I go home the folks would keep
> me because I had a hard time in getting
> them to let me come.... I stayed at
> Chilocco all during Summer and I worked
> Hard. I was a Carpenter all through. I
> am always spoiling my letter by asking
> you for help. A suit of clothes cost me
> a [whole] Summer's work. I made $32.00
> all the time I worked from the 9th day
> of July till Sept. 1st. Mr. Blair says
> that's the best he could do so I never

94

said anything. And that's the highest they
ever paid too. I did not want to cause any
trouble when they told me to stay I stayed
(Correspondence, Eastern Cherokee Agency
File, Federal Archives and Records Center,
October 19, 1923).

So students often stayed at the boarding schools
during the summer either unemployed or underpaid,
during the same era when employment was readily
available at Cherokee, if they had only been allowed
to return home.


EDUCATION AS SUPPRESSION OF CHEROKEE LIFE

Not all student letters were so discouraging. In
1918 a Cherokee boy wrote proudly from Hampton:

On Indian Day, February the eight, I am to
represent the South Eastern Indians in a
play which will show the loyalty of Indians
in different sections of the country. This
play will be given by the Indians, and I
wonder if you know the number of Cherokees
in the army and navy (Correspondence, Eastern
Cherokee Agency File, Federal Archives and
Records Center, January 19, 1918).

The superintendent's supposedly encouraging reply
was an elaborate distortion of Cherokee history.
After saying that Cherokee history was "one that
any Cherokee boy may be proud of," he listed the
great accomplishments of the Cherokees as: having
helped to destroy the Iroquois Confederacy, having
"espoused the side of the whites" during the American Revolution (one wonders whether the British or
the American colonists were the non-whites), the
Cherokee warrior Junaluska's having saved Andrew
Jackson's life during the Creek War, and the Cherokees' having been loyal to the Confederacy, which
must have seemed important to the superintendent,
who was himself a native southerner. The superintendent described the Battle of Horseshoe Bend,
during the Creek War, and lauded the "savage" custom of taking scalps when it was directed against
another group of Indians, instead of whites:

It is said that the Cherokees came out of

95

> the battle with hands full of [Creek] scalps
> and their teeth full of hair they having
> held the hair in their mouths while they
> cut off the scalps (Correspondence, Eastern
> Cherokee Agency File, Federal Archives and
> Records Center, January 30, 1918).

What the superintendent did not mention was that
during the Revolution the Cherokees in fact aided
the British, for which they suffered four devastat-
ing attacks in 1776 by American forces; that when
Jackson ordered the removal west of the Cherokees,
Junaluska regretted having saved Jackson's life;
and that significant numbers of Cherokees aided the
Union as well as the Confederacy during the Civil
War. It is interesting the superintendent went to
such length to convince the Cherokee boy to feel
proud of episodes in which Cherokees were enemies
of other Indian tribes, such as Iroquois and Creeks.
It distorted Cherokee history in order to praise
things white and condemn things Indian.

Few voices opposed such distortion, but Eastern
Cherokee writer Henry M. Owl made two significant
criticisms of Cherokee education during the era.
First, state educational requirements were not
taken into consideration by government schools,
and this step hindered Cherokee students in transferring to local public schools. Second, Cherokee
schools had few Cherokee teachers. Owl (1929:156)
notes:

> The schools have existed for more than
> forty years and in that period only about
> two Indian teachers have been appointed
> to work by the Government, and it would
> take an adding machine to accurately count
> the number of teachers that have held the
> positions during that time.

Letters from Haskell solicited Cherokee students
to be trained as teachers, but few Indians became
teachers to their own people. One Cherokee girl,
a product of boarding school experience via Haskell,
finally did teach Eastern Cherokee children for one
school year between 1930 to 1931. It is impossible
to flesh together the entire story of this girl
from the available records, but even a partial
account tells much about the Bureau of Indian

Affairs system of education during this era. In 1923, while still a student herself, the Cherokee girl wrote to the Eastern Cherokee Agency superintendent:

> It really doesn't seem possible that I have been away four years, but time does fly by ... I feel I would enjoy teaching [academic subjects]--much more than teaching sewing or cooking.... Mr. Peairs told me, he would promise me, that he would have me a position [teaching in Kansas] when I graduate. But Mr. Henderson, I have always felt when I get through here, I want to come back to Cherokee and begin with the little Cherokees of Carolina. I never dreamed of so many tribes of Indians [out in Kansas]. I guess every tribe feels their tribe is the best. I know I do (Correspondence, Eastern Cherokee Agency File, Federal Archives and Records Center, June 24, 1923).

Apparently, the Cherokee girl eventually realized her dream to teach the Indian people, but not immediately Eastern Cherokees. She first taught in at least two other Indian schools, one in South Dakota and one in Minnesota. When she finally taught on the Cherokee reservation, after years away as both a student and a teacher, she stayed only one year. Her brief career ended despite the superintendent's description of her as an "exceptionally good teacher" in his comments to the commissioner.

One can only speculate about why this Cherokee woman resigned after finally reaching her goal. Perhaps it was due to an illness or a desire to marry, or any number of reasons not relating directly to the educational system. Perhaps, however, her years of separation from the Cherokee people combined with the effects of the educational system worked to isolate her from her own people. The Bureau of Indian Affairs apparently discouraged her from teaching her own people, as they did many Indian teachers.

Several incidents in the era of B.I.A. education illustrate Cherokee distrust of the officials who worked with them as well as administrative aloofness from the Cherokee. In 1920 and 1921, for example,

Superintendent James Henderson of the Eastern Cherokee Agency corresponded extensively with Rev. A. E.
Brown of the Home Mission Board of the Southern
Baptist Convention, Department of Mountain Missions
and Schools, West Asheville, North Carolina. Brown
wanted to build a religious complex consisting of
a church, community house, and school, all adjoining
the boarding school. Henderson approved the idea
and urged the B.I.A. offices in Washington, D.C. to
approve the plan because, "the site is of no special
value to the school and these people are putting
forth efforts to christianize the Cherokees." Actually, at this time the Cherokees were already largely
Christian and mostly Baptist. They were running
their own churches, often conducting services in
the Cherokee language, and training ministers without white help. By the late nineteenth century almost all preachers on the reservation were Cherokee.

The Bureau of Indian Affairs objected to Henderson's
proposal informing him the proposed mission had to
be at least a mile's distance from the school, and
the Cherokees, themselves, would have to petition
for the mission. Henderson then obtained 250 Cherokee signatures on a petition requesting the mission be built. For reasons the available records
do not make clear, the plans for the mission never
materialized.

Yet, in an earlier letter from Henderson to Brown,
when hopes were high that Brown's Department of
Mountain Missions and Schools might become involved
with the Cherokees, the superintendent wrote about
plans for future educational work:

> If these plans [for new facilities] mature
> the Cherokee Boarding School will be able
> to carry the pupils to the point where they
> should enter high school and have the advan-
> tage of associating with white young men and
> women which we have found to be so necessary
> in the education of Indians.... [your money]
> might be expended with better results by
> taking the most promising young men and
> women away from reservation influences and
> putting them in some of your excellent
> missions schools where they would be com-
> pelled to measure up to the standard set
> for alert white students.... [also your Board]

might aid us very materially by establishing
community houses and a sufficient force of
workers to organize both old and young in
each community where they can be kept under
closer supervision.... Nor do I see any
reason why such a plan should fail, especially on this reservation where our Indians,
with few exceptions, have "one Lord, one
faith, and one baptism" (Correspondence,
Eastern Cherokee Agency File, Federal
Archives and Records Center, March 26, 1920).

These words reiterate the era's faith in off-reservation boarding schools. Henderson's hopes that
the entire reservation "can be kept under closer
supervision" also illustrates another distinctive
feature of the era: distrust of the Cherokees. It
contrasts sharply with the Quaker superintendent
Thomas C. Brown's words in 1882 that the good superintendent was "one in whom the Indians had confidence,
one who would visit them in their cabins...." Perhaps a diminished respect for the Cherokees, colored
by racism, is what characterizes the attitude change
from the era of the "Quaker Policy" to the era of
initial B.I.A. control: soliciting the advice of
the Cherokees by visiting with them in their homes
versus organizing them for "closer supervision."

Elderly Eastern Cherokees today remember having
their mouths washed out with soap or being beaten
when they dared speak Cherokee. One older man re-
members receiving such punishments and recalls the
ridicule he underwent on his first day of school
because he arrived wearing moccasins. The schools
almost wiped out the Cherokee language by such
tactics. But ironically, today this same man
teaches the Cherokee language in the schools to a
generation of Eastern Cherokees.

The harsh treatment of students and efforts to destroy the Cherokee language are confirmed by a most
intriguing eyewitness report from the 1920s. The
account is also interesting because the eyewitness
was John Collier, destined to become Commissioner
of Indian Affairs in the next decade, under Roosevelt. Scholars have been arguing about why Collier
became inspired to work with Indians as he did in
the 1930s. Some often have suggested the influence
of Taos Pueblo in New Mexico, but Charles J. Weeks

99

(1976) suggests the Eastern Cherokees were the
source of interest.  Collier was a native of Atlanta,
Georgia and made numerous camping trips near the
Cherokees.

The following  eyewitness account supports Weeks'
contention.  Collier (1941:3) wrote of how his
firsthand view of the boarding school on the Eastern
Cherokee reservation occurred:

> ... after three wintry weeks with very
> insufficient equipment on the highest of
> the Smokies ...  Lean and famined we ended
> a twenty-mile walk at Yellow Hill, the
> Cherokee Indian (government) school....
> The little boy inmates could not or would
> not talk English to each other, and they
> dared not talk Cherokee....  At length he
> [the superintendent] agreed we could eat
> and stay for the night.  This was an Oliver
> Twist place but with every light and shade
> of imagination disbarred....  Horror itself
> gave up the fight, in this place.  I had
> encountered Federal Indian policy of the
> self-righteous middle years.  Here was a
> place of pride of official Indian service
> ... where Indian boarding school children
> were to be fed on six cents a day, and not
> die....

Collier's eyewitness account is interesting not only
because of who made the observation but the context
in which it was made.  Collier, like few anthropologists or other social scientists of this era, had an
opportunity to view the school first-hand without it
being tidied up for an official visitor because
nothing special was done to impress the bedraggled,
unannounced camper.  He saw the school routine for
a day and a night, eating and sleeping there.  What
he saw horrified him.  Collier experienced the depression of boarding school life in general and
particularly the horror of a language being suppressed.  Later, when he became Commissioner of
Indian Affairs, he particularly singled out two
characteristics of Indian education which he wanted
to change:  the boarding school system and the efforts to suppress Indian languages.  If any good
came out of the early era of Bureau of Indian
Affairs control of Eastern Cherokee schools, it

surely must have been the effect it had on John
Collier. As an aside, it is unfortunate that
Collier's efforts to have the Cherokee language
taught in Cherokee schools under the New Deal failed.
It failed in part because of vigorous opposition by
more acculturated Cherokee adults who, by that time,
saw a return to the Cherokee language as a return
to "savagery." The forty years of forced acculturation had reaped harsh results.


CONCLUSIONS

The focus during this early era of Bureau of Indian
Affairs control of the schools was thus the suppression of Cherokee traditional culture and language,
an emphasis on out-of-state boarding schools, and
menial occupations for Cherokee students reinforced
by an emphasis on a vocational course of study.
Forced acculturation was accomplished through cor-
poral punishment, efforts to distort Cherokee history, and conspiracies with other agents of acculturation.

Certainly, better educational opportunities must
have been possible. One young Winston-Salem, North
Carolina woman, a music teacher, wrote idealistically
to the superintendent in 1918 about her goal of possibly teaching Indian students. The superintendent's
discouraging reply reflects his disdain for Indians
generally.

> I am quite sure that you are thoroughly
> competent to pass the required examination
> to teach. I feel, however, that your edu-
> cation has fitted you for higher work....
> While work in the Indian Service is honest
> and it offers great opportunity to do good,
> I feel that there are better things in
> life for you and I would suggest that you
> do not consider burying yourself and your
> talents in the Indian Service, as you in-
> evitably would have to do if you were to
> enter the Service (Correspondence, Eastern
> Cherokee Agency File, Federal Archives and
> Records Center, April 2, 1918).

Surely the superintendent meant teaching white
children when he wrote of "higher work" and "better

things in life." The young woman apparently made
no further efforts to get a position in a Cherokee
school and a potentially dedicated teacher was lost.

Despite such occurrences, a few sympathetic teachers
did obtain positions. Revealingly, the best paying
teaching positions were in Cherokee schools with
greater percentages of more acculturated "white
Indians." Teachers with seniority usually were
appointed. In 1915, for example, a teacher at Bird-
town Day School, described as "a good [school]" and
"in easy access of a good school population," received $720 a year in salary. At the day school in
Yellow Hill, central to the reservation, a teacher
could get up to $810 a year or more at the boarding
school. However, in the outlying districts, described as "secluded localities," teachers working
with more culturally traditional children at either
Big Cove, Snowbird Gap, or Little Snowbird Day Schools
received only $270 a year.

In 1930 and 1931 numerous letters between a sympathetic teacher at the boarding school and the principal reveal the principal often chiding the teacher
for lax discipline. After one incident when the
principal accused the teacher of allowing students
to stay out after an 8:30 PM bed check, the teacher
wrote angrily to deny the charges:

> I defy any one to make a report to the
> contrary.... It is my belief that your
> administration will be a success if you
> can show that you have one quality which
> you will need very much ... to possess
> in dealing with the Indians--and that is
> patience... (Correspondence, Eastern
> Cherokee Agency File, Federal Archives
> and Records Center, December 4, 1930).

Such a strong statement could not have endeared the
teacher to his principal. Four months later, after
other disagreements, the principal asked the superintendent to fire the teacher because he: "does
not have the initiative, forcefulness, industry and
cultural background so necessary for the best effi-
ciency."

The new superintendent declined to fire the teacher.
Perhaps the teacher was more sympathetic to Indians

and their educational needs because his wife was an
Indian, educated at Haskell, and trained for a "career" as a seamstress. Such teachers were, however,
rare during this era.

The discipline students experienced at the boarding
school was rigid. In the early 1930s reveille was
at 6:00 AM six days a week, and a bed check occurred
every evening at 8:30 PM, allowing an excessive nine
and a half to ten hours of sleep. Generally, it was
run like a military academy. The emphasis was on
vocational training, with the school's physical needs
being supplied by its students.

This era's most outstanding accomplishments were in
the improvement and construction of school facilities. The progressive emphasis during the following
"Indian New Deal" shifted from the physical improvement of the schools to their instructional improvement. Out-of-state boarding schools were de-empha-
sized while Indian traditional cultures were encouraged. Among the Eastern Cherokees, efforts to teach
the Cherokee language in the schools were instituted
under John Collier. But the previous forty years
of forced acculturation had made headway. Soon,
efforts to teach the language were abandoned because
"so few of the children were interested in learning
the language." Some Cherokees, probably the more
acculturated "white Indians," even termed such efforts "communistic."

One major feature of Cherokee education, the vocational emphasis, hardly changed at all from the era
of Quaker Policy, through the years of Bureau of
Indian Affairs control, and into the Indian New
Deal. This fact denotes even the less harsh, more
sympathetic eras were nonetheless acculturationist
and exploitive. Whites thought this type of training would best integrate Indians into the mainstream
of American life, at least American economic life.
Its goal can be summed up in this advice to a Haskell student, to "study hard and learn all you can,
so that when you are a grown man you will be useful
and happy" (Correspondence, Eastern Cherokee Agency
File, Federal Archives and Records Center, December
20, 1918).

A vocational education was supposed to create "useful," and thus "happy," people. Throughout all

these eras this goal was often left unfulfilled by
students well trained vocationally, but unemployed,
underpaid or trained again to do things they already
learned before entering school. The following description of Indian education under the New Deal
could well have described earlier eras:

> In addition to the usual academic courses,
> the Indian children are given practical
> training in vocational subjects, including
> dairying, farming, mechanics, woodwork,
> home demonstration and other practical
> studies (Collier 1941:8).

Despite some persistence of practice, 1934 marked
the end of the harsh period in Cherokee education
beginning in 1892. Ironically, the Cherokees had
already acculturated comparatively rapidly prior
to 1892. Before any schools were established among
them, the Cherokees were already predominantly
Christian, had adopted white material culture, and
were beginning to intermarry with whites. Scholars
often describe the Cherokees as one of the most
acculturated of all North American Indian groups.
Yet even a group already so much acculturated was
subjected to the harsh methods of forced acculturation of children. One can only wonder how much
harsher the system must have been on the Plains or
other, more traditional areas. The system created,
or furthered the creation of, a dependent people.
It was a system which labeled everything Indian as
bad, seriously distorted Cherokee history, and
nearly destroyed the language, to accomplish this
goal. The Cherokees became dependent on a Euroamerican system of education which gave them a new
history, a new and foreign language, and a new culture. Basic acculturating elements such as these
permeate the best as well as the worst of Cherokee
eras.

Today, many of the adult Eastern Cherokees are individuals educated during the initial era of Bureau
of Indian Affairs control. They feel lost when
they consider the traditionalists of their parents'
or grandparents' generation or the proponents of
revitalization among the younger generation. The
schools under B.I.A. control were a major force in
Eastern Cherokee acculturation, creating a dependency still permeating their lives. One might ask,

afterall, what else could be the result of an era when "horror itself gave up the fight."

FOOTNOTE

1. An earlier version of this chapter was presented at the 1976 annual meeting of the American Society for Ethnohistory. The basic research for this chapter comes from my 1971 M.A. thesis, <u>The Role of Formal Education Among the Eastern Cherokee Indians, 1880-1971</u>, University of North Carolina. I wish to thank my thesis committee: John J. Honigmann, chairman; John Gulick; and Dorothea C. Leighton; I also thank the Eastern Band of Cherokee Indians, John A. Crowe, Principal Chief, for all their help.

Primary source material on the early era of Bureau of Indian Affairs control comes mainly from records in the Eastern Cherokee Agency Files of the B.I.A. deposited at the Federal Archives and Records Center, East Point, Georgia. I would like to thank past director, Edward Weldor, present director, Gayle Peters, and the rest of their staff, especially political scientist, Charles Reeves.

REFERENCES CITED

Collier, John
    1941    Editorial. Indians at Work. September
           1-8.

Eastern Cherokee Agency File
    1892-    Eastern Cherokee Agency Correspondence.
    1958    Federal Archives and Records Center.
           East Point, Georgia.

Neely, Sharlotte
    1975    The Quaker Era of Cherokee Indian
           Education, 1880-1892. Appalachian
           Journal 2:314-322.

Owl, Henry M.
    1929    The Eastern Band of Cherokee Indians
           Before and After the Removal. Master's
           Thesis. University of North Carolina.

Quaker Collection
    1877-    Minutes of North Carolina Yearly
    1892    Meeting. Guilford College.

    1880-    Minutes of Western Yearly Meeting.
    1891    Guilford College.

Weeks, Charles J.
    1976    The Eastern Cherokee and the New Deal.
           North Carolina Historical Review 53:
           303-319.

Young, Virginia
    1894    A Sketch of the Cherokee People on the
           Indian Reservation of North Carolina.
           Woman's Progress 171-172.

CHAPTER 4

The Indian New Deal as Mirror of the Future

D'Arcy McNickle, Center for the History of the
American Indian, The Newberry Library, Chicago

We are moving far enough away from the 1930s and the
reform movement commonly termed "the Indian New Deal"
to view it dispassionately, without a sense of involvement. Strong lines were drawn up in those
partisan days, each side charging its opposite with
unworthy motives, each side dressing up its own purposes in seemly rhetoric. Now that the dust of combat has settled, one can begin to see what the true
issues were, what the gains and what the losses.

First, a brief description of the social, economic,
and political conditions which give rise to programs
of reform. One general set of circumstances prevailed
during the period. It was a time of deep, seemingly
inescapable depression--a time of long soup lines in
the cities, of rioting farmers in the countryside,
of bank closings, of unemployed businessmen selling
apples at street corners. One does not always see
behind the headlines and news broadcasts the reality
of economic disaster. I walked to work in midtown
Manhattan one morning just after a victim of the
times had leaped from a tall apartment building and
was spread all over the sidewalk. Even nature con-
trived to add to human misery, for that was a period
of the dreadful duststorms, when the topsoil of the
wheat-growing prairie states ascended into the jet
streams and swirled out over the Atlantic. I saw
that, too, standing in shock in a New York street.
It was a time when men began to talk about ecological balance, and a documentary film, "The Plow That
Broke the Plains," was viewed by hushed audiences.
Men came face to face with themselves in those days
and questioned the very society they had created,
and which had created them.

A time of doom, but it was also a time of opportunity. Under the lash of the desperate emergency,
social reform made giant strides. Banking methods
were overhauled; the marketing of securities was
regulated; vast holding company cartels were broken
up; systems of social insurance and unemployment

compensation were created. The management of national forests, grazing lands, wild life, water, and minerals was made responsive to the public interest. Vast public works projects were undertaken to repair some of the damage wrought through generations of heedless resource exploitation and abuse. Some of this concern for the environment, and some of the appropriated funds, managed to trickle down to the Indian community.

It is important to understand the conditions that prevailed in the Indian community. The older Indians of that period still lived with the defeats which many tribes experienced in the closing years of the 19th century. The tragedy of the first Wounded Knee affair was less than fifty years in the rear, a brief lifetime.

When Collier assumed the commissionership in 1933, the General Allotment Law had been operating for better than forty-five years, and in that interval some 90 million acres of land had passed out of Indian ownership; an estate of 138 million acres, all owned in common in 1887, had been reduced to 48 million acres. For the most part, the alienated lands were the best lands: the river bottoms, rich grass lands, prime forests. But land losses tell only part of the story. The allotment process, the individualizing of community-owned assets, created forces which had never before operated in Indian society. Families and individuals competed for choice lands, for water or other advantages. Outsiders intruded as homesteaders on so-called surplus lands, and inevitably meddled in the internal affairs of the tribe. Social structure was disoriented in many ways, as non-Indians married into a group, and kin groups were scattered throughout the reservation area. In each allotted reservation a class of landless, homeless individuals came into existence and, having no resources of their own, doubled up with relatives and intensified the poverty of all.

That, too, tells only part of the story. Tribes had been moved about like livestock until, in some cases, the original homeland was no more than a legend in the minds of old men and women. Children had been forcefully removed from the family and kept in close custody until they lost their mother language and all knowledge of who they were, while the schooling to which they were subjected was conducted as an exercise in animal training. Tribal religious practices, when they were not proscribed outright, were treated as obscenities. The bureaucratic apparatus had penetrated the entire fabric of Indian life, usurping tribal decision-making, obtruding into the family, and demeaning local leadership. It was totally oblivious of its inadequacies and its inhumanity.

Part of John Collier's initial problem, as the incoming commissioner, was to remove some of the tar with which he himself had plastered the Bureau. He had been an outspoken and caustic critic of the Bureau, and suddenly he was in the position of asking Indians to have confidence in the institution. While he occupied the office for twelve years, he never entirely extricated himself from the awkward situation.

One of his first acts, intended to moderate the harsh image of the Bureau, was the issuance of an order (Office of Indian Affairs 1934) declaring: "No interference with Indian religious life will be hereafter tolerated. The cultural history of Indians is in all respects to be considered equal to that of any non-Indian group. And it is desirable that Indians be bilingual—fluent and literate in English, and fluent in their vital, beautiful, and efficient native languages."

In a further early effort to undo the past, he secured the repeal of twelve obsolete laws, some dating from as early as 1790, which collectively placed inordinate power over civil liberties in the hands of Bureau officials. The repeal of these laws, needless to say, was not enough to change the authoritarian nature of the Bureau.

Collier, of course, is associated with the Indian Reorganization Act, which in the context of the Roosevelt administration was known popularly as the Indian New Deal. The legislation had been adopted by a reluctant Congress in 1934, reluctant because the Act by open declaration was a denunciation of the policies followed by Congress and national administrations through the previous half-century. The reluctance moreover went deeper than

bruised feelings. Most legislation as it emerges
from the Congressional mill bears small resemblance
to the bright promise that was fed into the hopper.
The Indian Reorganization Act was no exception.
Congress wanted the "Indian business" cleaned up,
but it was not ready or willing to transfer real
power to the Indian tribes. This unwillingness was
emphasized by the rejection of four critical features: (1) An orderly procedure for transferring
services and functions from the Bureau to an organized Indian community; (2) The creation of tribal
corporations for the management of reservation resources, with power "to compel" the removal of any
federal employee on grounds of inefficiency or
"other causes"; (3) A training program to prepare
Indians to take over and administer community services, including courses of study in Indian history
and culture; and (4) The establishment of a tribal
court system, with right of appeal to the federal
appelate court and to the Supreme Court

It was the first piece of major legislation dealing
with Indian affairs ever taken into the Indian country and discussed in open meetings. And here the
long history of bureaucratic misrule loomed as a
major challenge to Collier's reform program. At
every one of the regional meetings called to consider the pending bill, the motives and the purposes
of the Bureau were questioned, heatedly at times.
The distrust and suspicion voiced at these meetings,
and in subsequent meetings in Washington, were reflected in the tribal elections that followed. By
its terms, the act was not to apply on any reservation where a majority rejected it. Out of 258 tribes,
bands, and rancherias voting in these elections, 77
voted against application. The Navajo was one of the
tribes voting in the negative.

The bill as introduced in Congress was a document
of some fifty typewritten pages, but what emerged
was a scant six pages of print. The reduction in
bulk was not critical, but what was stricken in the
course of debate practically guaranteed that the
nature of the bureaucracy would not be altered. By
eliminating the provision giving the Indians a deciding role in the selection and retention of reservation employees, colonial rule was left intact.
By deleting the articles creating a federal Indian
court system, the control over law and order was

left in the hands of the Secretary of the Interior, and it encouraged the states, in later years, to seek to extend state law, and state taxation, to reservation lands.  One other deletion deserves passing mention.  If the article providing for courses of study in Indian history and culture and in administrative management had been retained, Indian studies programs might have been operating forty years ago.

The Indian Reorganization Act did retain two features central to Collier's reform program.  The first of these was the prohibition against any future allotment of tribal lands; the other was a watered-down provision dealing with tribal government and property management.  While the range of discretionary tribal action was greatly reduced from the original proposal, what remained was tacit recognition of the tribe as a surviving political entity with definable inherent powers.  The Act referred specifically to "All powers vested in an Indian tribe or tribal council by existing law"; and that, of course, included treaty stipulations and court decisions, as well as statute law.  In addition it recognized the right of a tribe to embody in a written constitution the power to "prevent the sale, disposition, lease or encumbrance of tribal lands."  Within this legal framework it became possible for an Indian tribe to function as a municipal body and to exert the common law rights of a property owner.

The legislation was not the emancipating instrument that had been hoped for, and within less than a decade of its enactment the nation was at war with the moneys authorized for salvaging the Indian community going elsewhere.  But the Act did mark the way into the future--if there was to be an Indian future.  In Collier's day that was not at all a certainty; indeed twenty years after the adoption of the Indian Reorganization Act, the Eisenhower administration almost closed out that possibility forever.

To go back a moment.  The misgivings and outright opposition expressed by many Indians during the hearings on the Indian Reorganization Act were symptomatic of more basic trouble.  Since the United States in 1871 renounced the policy of negotiating treaties with the tribes, a practice that had endured from colonial times, the Indians had not been

consulted in any major decisions affecting their
property, their family life, or the training of
their children. All such matters came within the
reach of a bureaucratic structure, which developed
attitudes and formalities impervious to Indian participation. And as the bureaucracy hardened, the
Indian community withdrew deeper into itself and
set up its own barriers to communication.

But Collier's problem did not come entirely from
the fact that for those sixty-odd years since the
renunciation of treaty-making the government had
barred Indians from assuming responsibility for
their own lives. The unseen and, indeed, the larger
problem had to do with the ethnic of social intervention which, in the 1930s, still functioned as a
tradition out of the 19th century--a heritage of
colonial administration.

In a major crisis that developed early in his administration the reluctance or the inability of the
bureaucracy to respond to human conditions had disastrous consequences. The occasion was the decision
to reduce Navajo sheep herds, the principal subsistence base of the tribe, in order to bring the
animal population into balance with deteriorating
range lands. Studies carried out by professional
agronomists demonstrated that top soil was blowing
away, perennial grasses were being replaced by annual
weeds of low nutrient value, summer rains were erod-
ing deep gullies and carrying mountains of soil into
newly constructed power and flood control reservoirs,
threatening to fill them with silt.

In designing a control program, Collier directed
that reduction would be on a "sliding scale," with
the largest reduction on the larger herds and a
lesser reduction on smaller herds, while herds of
a minimum size would be left intact. The directive
was later made specific in providing that herds of
up to 100 head of sheep would not be reduced. Herds
of that size were considered subsistence herds required to provide family support (Bureau of Indian
Affairs 1935:17923).

A report prepared soon after the reduction program
was initiated in 1933, states that: "The larger
owners flatly refused to make all the reduction
from their herds. After an all-night session (at

Tuba City, in November 1933) it was agreed ... that every Navajo should sell 10 percent of his sheep.... This same agreement became widespread over the entire reservation, since the large owners consistently refused to make the total reduction from their flocks" (Bureau of Indian Affairs 1935:17987). In practice, the owners of small herds found themselves under greater economic pressure than the owners of large herds; they sold out their entire holdings and found themselves completely dependent on the emergency work programs financed by the government. When these programs ran out of funds, real hardship followed.

Other complications quickly arose. The government had offered to buy sheep at prices ranging from $1.00 for ewes to $2.25 - $3.00 for wethers. Chee Dodge, the respected leader of the tribe, argued that the government should concentrate on the purchase of good breeding ewes, at better prices; otherwise, the Navajo livestock owners would offer only old ewes and other non-productive stock and reduction would not be achieved. These prices, however, had been established in Washington by the emergency relief administration, the source of the funds, and they could not be altered in the field. The disappointing results confirmed what Chee Dodge had predicted.

Perhaps the most serious oversight was the failure to recognize the fact that women were in many instances the principal owners of the family herds. Women were not members of the tribal council, however, and they were not consulted as negotiations went forward between the government and the tribal leaders. When the leaders returned to their families and found the women opposed to plans for reduction, any agreements with the government became meaningless.

What Collier did not discover until it was too late to intervene was that field employees sometimes resorted to coercive action. This interference occurred specifically in the eastern Navajo area, where it was expected that legislation, then pending in Congress, would be enacted and would result in extending the eastern boundary of the reservation to include an additional two million acres. In anticipation of the increased acreage, the Navajos of the area were induced to sell their goats, with the idea of eventually replacing them with sheep. By the fall of 1935 formidable opposition had developed against the legislation, making it unlikely that it would be adopted. Nevertheless the goat reduction program went forward. As Collier reported to the Senate subcommittee in the summer of 1936: "In my judgement, we should not have carried out the goat purchase program within the eastern area ... because we were no longer assured of the enactment of the boundary bill.... Why we did proceed with the goat purchases in this area, frankly, I don't know.... At the time we did not, at Washington, have any information, or evidence that duress was being, or was to be, employed anywhere. It was not directed to be employed, but on the contrary, all the sales were to be voluntary. However, before the close of the goat purchase operation, I began to receive... information that overpersuasion, and even duress, had in fact been employed in this area."

Elsewhere in his statement to the subcommittee, he commented: "the purchase was an error and I cannot, and do not desire, to evade responsibility for that error.... I am the Commissioner" (Bureau of Indian Affairs 1935:17801-02).

Such episodes were possible because the bureaucracy was the instrument of an older view of the relationship with the Indian people. In that older view Indians were incompetent to make decisions, especially when questions of a technical nature were involved--and livestock management was considered to be of that nature, even though Navajos had been successful herdsmen for several centuries. Indeed, their very success in increasing their herds was in part responsible for their predicament. In a chain of command situation, such as characterizes bureaucratic structure, responsibility is diffused; one is never accountable for some one else's mistakes.

Collier's hope of restoring to the Indian community some measure of self-government was diminished by the same impersonal, insensate play of bureaucratic forces. Anyone who has worked in government knows that project financing is based on performance. If funds allocated to a field project are not expended within a time limit, usually the fiscal year, it is assumed by those who approve budget requests that the money was not needed. The amount approved for a subsequent operating period will likely be reduced.

This leads to various strategems to keep ahead of
the finance wizards, the commonest of which is to
pile on expenditures before the end of the fiscal
period, thus demonstrating the accuracy of the original estimate and the soundness of the project.

The Indian Reorganization Act authorized federal
funds to assist tribes in formulating and voting on
written constitutions and charters of incorporation.
Collier intended that the organization documents
should reflect a tribe's traditional ways of arriv-
ing at decisions and selecting leaders.  To carry
out this purpose he recruited a staff of cultural
anthropologists, who were to work with the field
employees engaged in the program.  This move would
appear to be one of the first attempts, if not the
first, to use anthropologists as technical assistants
by a government agency.

The planning came to grief on two counts.  When it
was discovered in Congress that the Commissioner
was spending money on something called anthropology,
the appropriation was promptly disallowed and the
unit was abandoned although some anthropologists
continued working for the Bureau under other titles.
A more serious difficulty grew out of the fiscal
year syndrome.  To satisfy the budget watchers and
the wardens of the Treasury, it was necessary to
show progress in bringing the tribes under written
constitutions.  This involved sitting down in meeting after meeting and conducting a tribal drafting
committee through a maze of Whereas clauses and
Therefore, be it enacted resolutions.  Leaders, who
often were non-English speaking or who had only a
primary grade education, were exposed to the full
battery of Anglo-Saxon parliamentary syntax, and
they had to act before the end of the fiscal year.
The result was the hurried adoption of tribal constitutions prepared in Washington and based on conventional political instruments with no provision
for action by consensus or for the role of ritual
leaders.  The tribes were given tools, such as
majority rule, for which they had no accustomed
usage, and these became devices for community dis-
ruption and for petty demagoguery.

One should not conclude from this analysis of the
Navajo that no positive gains were registered during
the Collier administration.  The long record of

diminishing land and other resource holdings was halted. The total land base was actually enlarged by some four million acres, the first time in history that Indians gained instead of losing land. Credit financing was begun on a modest scale and made possible resource development and utilization, where previously Indians had leased out tribal and individual lands for lack of capital. A start was made, again modestly, in providing low cost housing. Day schools were built at a number of reservations as an alternative to the off-reservation boarding schools, and they were designed and operated as community centers, anticipating the movement of recent years to provide centers for recreation, adult education, and cultural activities.

These gains, modest as they were, were cut short by the crisis of war. When the shooting was over and Indian GIs and war industry workers came home, they found their reservations in ruins. Employment opportunities were gone, social services were severely curtailed (schools, hospitals, houses in disrepair or shut down entirely), and credit facilities denied. And presently, a hostile administration came to power committed to the ultimate extinguishment of tribal life.

What has come to the surface in tribal communities in recent years, notably at Wounded Knee and on the Pine Ridge reservation generally, is the anger that remained unuttered, but unappeased, for generations. It was an overwhelming anger growing out of the kinds of experiences suggested here; my account of these experiences has been mild and polite. Older Indians, still conscious of the defeats inflicted on their people in the closing years of last century, withdrew from open challenge and tried passively to live with the white man's inscrutable ways. That former period seems to have come to a crashing end.

The generation of Indian leaders now emerging lacks that consciousness of defeat which inhibited their elders. More than that, as a consequence of international wars, the collapse of colonial empires, rioting and burning in urban ghettos, an economy that destroys the environment, the white man seems not as invincible as he once seemed.

It was possible at Wounded Knee in 1890 for an army
unit--Custer's own 7th Cavalry, indeed--to slaughter
a Sioux camp of men, women, and children.  At that
same site in the winter of 1973, armored vehicles
and troop detachments surrounded another Indian camp,
but no slaughter occurred.  Two reasons suggest themselves.  The surrounded Indians had access to the
world beyond their lines, and they were able to ver-
balize their grievances to listeners who were sympathetic even though they might not understand what
was going on.  This access to public opinion was
enough to discourage hasty action by gun-carrying
troops.  An even more compelling restraint was the
changed circumstance behind that surrounding army.
Men in power no longer had a mandate to kill Indians
trying to protect their right to be themselves.
Perhaps that is a measurable gain.

Where, then, have we come?  One point certainly seems
clear.  Because Indians are discovering the uses of
power in modern society, it is no longer possible
to exclude them from the decision-making process in
matters affecting their property, their families,
the training of their children, or the nature of
the accommodation they choose to make within the
dominant society.  John Collier helped to make these
issues evident, but as a man of good will standing
outside the Indian community, he was limited in what
he could do.  He could not substitute his will and
vision for Indian will and vision.  Nor can any man
stand in the place of another.

That, too, is a discovery Indians have made in these
very recent years.  The simple demonstration of this
discovery is the astonishing growth of news media
operated by Indian groups reporting on conditions,
and the equally remarkable growth of political and
cultural organizations devoted to advancing Indian
interests.  The non-Indian "Friend of the Indian,"
that 19th century image of altruistic involvement,
is being told politely but firmly to stand aside.

Collier has been charged with turning the clock
back on Indian advancement.  The basis of the charge,
of course, was his insistence on extending religious
and cultural freedom to Indian groups and his commitment to the cause of revitalizing Indian society.
A modern critic (Kelly 1972) asserts that Collier
mistakenly assumed, from his knowledge of Indians

117

of the Southwest, "that Indians everywhere would
wish to return to tribal, communal life, if given
the opportunity."

What this writer fails to recognize, even in this
late day, is that Indians "everywhere" have always
been, and remain, more tribal, communal if you will,
or conscious of ethnic boundaries, than observers
from the outside generally realize. Already in
Collier's day the studies of A. Irving Hallowell
and others were offering evidence that culturally-
wrought personality persists even in circumstances
where the outward forms of behavior have accommodated to the dominant society.

Other critics of Collier's effort to build upon the
tribal past were people whose ideas had been formed
largely in the 19th century, who saw Native society
as incapable of development into modern forms. In
this view, the Native American existed in a world
devoid of logic, or sentiment, or dynamics. Indian
life came from nowhere and went nowhere.

Collier challenged this view in many published
statements and in his public career. He saw Indian
society as "not fossilized, unadaptive, not sealed
in the past, but plastic, adaptive, assimilative,
while yet faithful to ... ancient values." And
again he (1947:27-28) wrote: "Societies are living
things, sources of the power and values of their
members; to be and to function in a consciously
living, aspiring, striving society is to be a personality fulfilled."

Whether or not they are aware of John Collier's
insight in this matter, Indians today are discovering the truth that lies in this vision. This discovery accounts, in part, for the Indian studies
centers that have come into existence at major institutions across the country. The Navajo Community
College springs from this vision. In a harsher
mode, it accounts for the incidents at Wounded
Knee.

Indians were not held back by Collier's efforts to
build upon the tribal past. Instead, they have
plunged affirmatively into the twentieth century,
asserting their identity, and acquiring the skills
that will enable them to survive as Indians and
members of an Indian community.

REFERENCES CITED

Bureau of Indian Affairs
    1935    Circular dated May 1, 1935. Reprinted
            in Survey of Conditions of the Indians
            of the United States, Part 34, U. S.
            Senate.

Collier, John
    1947    The Indians of the Americas. New York:
            W. W. Norton.

Kelly, Lawrence C.
    1972    John Collier and the Indian New Deal:
            An Assessment. Paper delivered at the
            National Archives Conference in Research
            in the History of Indian-White Relations.
            Washington, D.C.

Office of Indian Affairs
    1934    Circular Number 2970. January. Mimeo.

CHAPTER 5

The Symbolic Value of the Little Big Horn
in the Northern Plains

Margot Liberty, University of Pittsburgh

June 24th and 25th, 1976, were difficult days for
National Park Service personnel at Custer Battlefield
National Monument in Montana. The Park Service had
been making a sustained effort to commemorate the
Bicentennial with appropriate ceremonies throughout
the country, but it faced special problems at Custer
Battlefield on the one hundredth anniversary of the
defeat by Sioux and Cheyenne Indians of the most
flamboyant military leader in American history.
This sensational event occurred one century ago in
the midst of the first Centennial celebration of our
nation's birth. "Generals ... rollicking at the
Centennial in Philadelphia while Custer falls in the
wilderness" were furiously castigated in 1876 by
Congress and others (Dippie 1970:163) as soon as
news of the disaster reached the east coast. In a
sense the outcry has not died down to this day. What
really happened to Custer and his illfated command?
What has happened to his reputation since? What
difference if any did his defeat make, to subsequent
U.S. Indian policy; and what difference does Custer
symbolism make today, to modern Indian peoples?
Some of these questions will be approached here,
if not finally answered, because with regard to the
Custer legacy it would appear that nothing is ever
finally answered (cf. Luther 1973).


THE SUMMER OF 1976

Events in the summer of 1976 need to be seen in
terms of the rise of militant leadership in the
American Indian Movement in the sixties and seven-
ties (Cohen 1976 and Bonney 1976). Two outbreaks
of newsworthy violence had occurred at the Bureau
of Indian Affairs in Washington in 1972, and at
Wounded Knee, South Dakota, the following spring:
both are of relevance here. Park Service personnel
and many others believed that a third such happening
was planned for Custer Battlefield during the Battle's

121

Centennial (the U.S. Bicentennial) summer, particularly on the actual anniversary of the battle itself.
Preparations were made to forestall such a development, or to minimize its impact, should it occur.
Memorabilia and archives were removed from the Battlefield Visitor Center. Twenty extra Park Service
rangers were called up from distant stations. Police from throughout Eastern Montana were on hand,
aided by posses of citizens with CB radios. The
Federal government withdrew from the town of Hardin,
thirteen miles from the site of expected trouble,
all VISTA workers until safer times should prevail.
In Billings, sixty miles away, provision was also
made for the safety of movie star Robert Redford,
in town for an environmental fund-raiser. It was
feared American Indian Movement sympathizers might
kidnap him from the Northern Hotel.

On the 24th and 25th, Battlefield gates were shut
tight against the regular flow of tourist traffic,
usually numbering several thousand visitors per
day at this time of year. Negotiations with members
of the surrounding Crow tribe for parking safely
beyond National Monument borders broke down completely. Sally's Last Stand, a tourist trap at the
bottom of the hill, enjoyed the most profitable day
of its life. Meanwhile, the Sioux caravan was on
the way--twenty-two carloads of participants in the
Lakota Treaty Council en route from South Dakota.
They expected to be joined by hundreds of Native
Americans from other states. Local authorities
estimated that as many as a thousand Indians might
demonstrate. The expected demonstrators had been
invited to camp on the adjoining Northern Cheyenne
Reservation at Austin Twomoons' place, where a com-
memorative Victory Dance was planned to last for
several nights, after whatever was to happen had
taken place.

Actually, "NOTHING HAPPENED," or virtually nothing,
as bannered by the Hardin Herald in its next issue.
"Perhaps the most dreaded week in our seventy year
history has passed totally without incident," reported the newspaper. "The town is still standing
... in fact congratulations are in order to the
Lakota Treaty Council and members of the American
Indian Movement who behaved much better than many
who (next) invaded town for the VFW Rodeo." There
was a tense moment at the Battlefield, nonetheless,

amidst Thursday's ceremonies as the Indian caravan
arrived with an upside-down U.S. flag which leaders
Russell Means and Oscar Running Bear carried onto
the speaker's platform. They were welcomed though
by "surprised officials" and encouraged to speak.
A sunrise ceremony went off smoothly Friday morning
(although considerably after sunrise) and even the
potential kidnapping or worse of George Armstrong
Custer III, on hand to lay a wreath, did not mater-
ialize. He was in fact hidden away in the Visitor
Center basement until the ceremonies were over. The
Park Service felt it had won the day although sharp
controversy on this point continues in some quarters
(Little Big Horn Associates Newsletter, August-
October, 1976).


THE ORIGINAL BATTLE AND ITS CONSEQUENCES

Moving now to consider the original battle and its
effect upon subsequent Indian policy, one can note
the effect it had upon members of the general American public at the time. They were celebrating the
Centennial in Philadelphia--open since May 10--with
great enthusiasm. Exhibits in a multitude of special
buildings stressed American world importance and
blossoming industrial might: "The exhibition was
at once a festival and an assertion of national pride
and purpose" (Weymouth 1976:15). (The Smithsonian
Institution recreated much of the Centennial's at-
mosphere in 1976. Many of its original exhibits were
shown in Washington at the old Arts and Industries
building for the Bicentennial.) It was the sixth
of the great World's Fairs, but the first to be held
in this country. It included, in the Government
Building, exhibits on the American Indian and his
culture; real Indians barely missed being on hand
as living specimens (Post 1976:77). There was instead "an immense array of curiosities: everything
from tepees to pottery, pipes, war masks and beaded
mocassins, crammed into every nook and cranny and
even suspended from the roof beams." Plains buck-
skin dresses were there, also a feathered dancing
stick and a pair of Sioux garters (Smithsonian 1976:
14). One wonders at the reaction among viewers of
this display when the first news came through from
the Little Big Horn.

For it was indeed a shocking defeat. The flower of

the U.S. Army, in many eyes at least, had been annihilated to the last man by savages one-half of whom
did not even carry guns (Dustin 1939; Graham 1953,
1962; Stewart 1955). Reaction was swift; within a
year the tribes of the Northern Plains were all on
reservations, their effective resistance broken
forever.

To understand this situation it is necessary to review some major events of U.S. Indian policy in order
to place the Custer Battle in perspective. In addition to signalling the end of Indian resistance in
the Northern Plains, it appears to have effectively
ended Grant's so-called Peace Policy begun in the
1860s (Dippie 1970:163, 174-175; Fritz 1963; Utley
1973:398) and to have added to the stimulus for land
allotment and assimilation. Eventually, it was
also to become a major symbol in movements demanding Indian independence, developing during the past
twenty years. All of these things are true despite
the comment, likewise correct, that in a military
sense the battle was unimportant:

> Ever since Sir Edward Creasy wrote his
> Fifteen Decisive Battles of the World in
> 1851, military experts have suggested
> additions to the list. Certainly ranking
> far down at the bottom of ... any such
> list would be the Battle of the Little
> Big Horn. It decided nothing. The vast
> horde that had done Custer in was never
> seen again. The subsequent campaign only
> hit and rounded up a few of its scattered
> bands, such as Custer expected to find in
> the first place. A recent assessment is
> that the Little Big Horn "sealed White
> minds against the American Indian." If
> it had, there would not be these thousands
> of items about that unfortunate fight.
> Not Waterloo or Gettysburg, nor any of the
> decisive fifteen, has had more ink splattered
> over it than the Little Big Horn (Don
> Russell, quoted in Luther 1973:2).[1]

Following the American Revolution, Indian policy had
gone through several major phases or periods. These
began with an early time of friendly relations and
trade, while Indian allies against British and Spanish forces in North America were still needed. This

era was followed by mounting desire for Indian land,
and the isolation of Indians themselves, after the
War of 1812. By the late 1840s, under the well
known Removal Policy spearheaded by President Andrew
Jackson, the deportation of Indians from most of the
eastern half of the United States was largely carried out. New territory brought new Indian populations within national borders, and new policies for
dealing with them. The Removal Policy was abandoned
for the Reservation Policy under Commissioner of
Indian Affairs George Manypenny after 1849. Manypenny supported allotment of land in severalty to
individual Indian owners, a policy which was later
adopted with a vengeance. Meanwhile, the Civil War
intervened; in the post-war period Congressional
investigation, made public in 1867, revealed deplor-
able conditions on the recently organized reservations. Grant's Peace Policy then set the direction
for developments on the Plains. It was an arrangement whereby Indians already on reservations were
placed under the control of missionaries, while most
off reservations were placed under the control of
the army. The army soon began campaigning to force
the off-reservation Indians onto them, a development
which led to many of the better known attractions of
the Plains Wars (cf. Utley 1953 and 1973). By the
1880s, with the fighting generally ended, attention
shifted back to land allotment and assimilation.
Later developments included the Indian Reorganization
Act of the 1930s, and the rise of urban Indians as
an important new political force after World War II
(Officer 1971:9-63).


MODERN SIGNIFICANCE OF THE LITTLE BIG HORN

Thus, the Custer fight served as an important bench-
mark, if nothing else, marking the end of Grant's
Peace Policy and ushering in almost fifty years aimed
at assimilating Indians into mainstream American life
while eradicating as quickly as possible every trace
of their own traditional culture. More importantly,
perhaps, it has attained new symbolism today. Custer as a figure of humor is familiar: nearly everyone knows at least one Custer joke, more often than
not unfit to print. Indian humorists are involved
as well as white. Bumper stickers stating that
Custer Had It Coming, and Custer Died For Your Sins,
were evident in Indian country considerably before

Vine Deloria Jr.'s Playboy article and subsequent
bestseller of 1969. John Stands In Timber was
telling a very mild, and printable, joke among the
Cheyennes in the 1950s: Custer it seems scoffed
at his scouts' warnings, telling them when they
found the predicted big village he was going to
abduct the best-dressed Indian girl and take her
along with him; and that his pause above the village
before attacking was because he was looking for her
(Stands In Timber and Liberty 1967:199). There are
many others. For a new, less printable example concerning Custer's putative death beneath an angry
Indian woman see Edmunds' 1976 "Can the Red Man
Laugh?" (1976:149).

But something else is happening as well. The Custer
episode is being interpreted increasingly by Indians
as a serious indication of Indian superiority over
white policies and institutions. Admittedly, there
is no direct cause and effect between Custer's down-
fall in 1876 and modern coal mining controversies
in the Northern Plains; but a symbolic reference
point does exist, and it will probably grow more
important. Current events among the Northern Cheyennes of Montana illustrate its significance.

The Northern Cheyennes are presently being called
"the most important tribe in the country" (Toole
1976:50-68) because of their very strong stand
against strip mining. Since 1972 they have essentially reversed the Interior Department's whole
coal leasing policy with regard to Indian lands.
Among other things, they succeeded in 1974 in can-
celling all leases let by Interior on their own
reservation between 1966 and 1973. They have been
to the Supreme Court of the United States to win a
unanimous decision in May, 1976, upholding tribal,
as opposed to individual allottees', interests in
further leasing for coal development (Northern
Cheyenne Tribe vs. Hollowbreast 44 CAPLCAPW 4655:
see Northern Cheyenne Research Project 1976:3-13).
This decision means that individual tribal members
will have to wait for coal development money until
the tribe as a whole decides what it wants to do,
and it may decide to do nothing, for a very long
time. To understand this development, remarkable
in a situation where extreme poverty has existed
for a century, and where the lure of plentiful cash
from coal leasing is thus strong, one needs to know

126

more about the Northern Cheyennes and their special land situation.

Briefly, they are a people whose resistance to white conquest and subjugation has been phenomenal (cf. Sandoz 1953, Stands In Timber and Liberty 1967, Sooktis 1976, and Weist 1977). Their new mobilization behind the coal issue has taken on something of the aspect of a sacred cause (cf. Northern Cheyenne Research Project 1976 and 1977, and nearly every issue of Tsistsistas Press, 1976-1979). Unlike most Plains tribes, they did not come under the provisions of the Dawes Allotment Act of 1877 until the 1920s. Individuals were not judged "competent" and thus able to sell allotted tracts to outsiders until the 1950s; and such land sales to outsiders were halted soon thereafter. The result was a small but unusually solid block of land in Indian ownership: on the Tongue River Reservation of 447,000 acres, 98 percent is Indian-owned and operated (61 percent or 270,000 acres held in common by the Tribe and 37 percent or 164,000 acres allotted to individuals). Only two percent or 10,000 acres is thus white-owned and operated (Northern Cheyenne Research Project 1976:4-15). The contrast to the situation on the adjacent Crow reservation (cf. Voget, this volume) is sharp. There, upon a vastly larger land base of 2,283,000 acres, whites control 88 percent; they own 709,000 acres and lease much of the remaining land within reservation boundaries (of which 1,297,000 acres are individually allotted and 227,000 acres are held in common by the Tribe). Only twelve percent of the total is thus utilized by Indians. There is no better illustration of the disastrous effects of allotment than in the contrast between these two tribes. The Crows, allotted early, had ample time to receive individual fee patents and then to sell to outsiders; the Northern Cheyennes, allotted late, were spared the land losses which generally ensued from allotment elsewhere. They have also consolidated non-Indian use by stopping all leasing of Cheyenne lands to whites, a practice which ceased in 1974; today all cattle on the reservation are owned by Indians.

In August of 1976 Northern Cheyennes again were in the headlines for challenging the construction of two additional 700-million-watt coal-fired generating plants at Colstrip 15 miles from the reservation, where the pollution from two such plants already in operation is clearly evident. On August 23, the Great Falls Tribune reported that the Cheyennes might hold the trump card in this increasingly complicated fight, via their petition to the Environmental Protection Agency for redesignation of the air quality standard over the reservation from the existing Class II to Class I, an unheard of prerogative. "The petition means," said Tribal Chairman Allen Rowland, "that we're in a bad habit of breathing fresh air, and we want to continue to do so" (Billings Gazette, August 22, 1976). "My own personal feeling is that I don't think Congress should say, 'Your air should be like this -- this number two.' Everyone should be able to choose the kind of air they have to breathe" (High Country News, July 16, 1976). The Cheyenne petition is the first of its kind in the country. At this time it appears the petition will be approved despite strong opposition from the mining interests, and from the Crows who wish to see coal development proceed (Environment Reporter, April 29 and May 6, 1977) although effective enforcement of its provisions will entail a grim and continuing battle (cf. Conoway 1973; Gold 1974; Josephy 1973; Smith 1975; and Northern Cheyenne Research Project, 1976 and 1977).[2] Rowland has also, to the utter amazement of the Cheyennes' Montana neighbors, offered to purchase in the name of the tribe the nearby community of Decker (along with Martha's Vineyard, Massachusetts) which was in the spring of 1977 talking about secession from its own state government. "We would like to buy Decker and incorporate it into the Northern Cheyenne Reservation," he said, pointing out various benefits which might derive from such an action. "For instance, we could conceivably extend our proposed Class I Air Quality designation to your area." Decker need no longer be a "resource colony of the State of Montana." The tribe could reactivate time-tested procedures long utilized by the Bureau of Indian Affairs with Indians by issuing Certificates of Competency to all eligible Deckerites: "Those unable to meet this test will be under our utmost supervision in all financial matters, to insure their continual well-being." Full tribal membership for Decker residents would not be possible, but a schedule whereby some might attain limited voting rights could be considered. In closing, he extended the purchase offer to the secession-minded residents of Martha's Vineyard: "We believe our special status is flexible enough to offer the same protection to that beleagured island" (Billings Gazette, April 6, 1977).

With this kind of sophistication, not to mention wit,[3] the Cheyennes have attained significant leadership among other tribes faced with the bitter issues of mining development. Twenty-two tribes are now organized as the Native American Natural Resources Federation of the Northern Great Plains (High Country News, January 2, 1976; Badhorse 1976: 22-23). The mining threat is most critical on six reservations: Northern Cheyenne and Crow, plus Fort Berthold, Fort Peck, Standing Rock, and Cheyenne River (Northern Great Plains Resource Program 1974:V20-V25). But other resources are at stake, including water. The Cheyennes and Crows are, in fact, now suing for primary water rights to the entire Rosebud Creek and Tongue River drainage systems in southeastern Montana. If the move is upheld, it could destroy the livelihood of hundreds of non-Indian ranchers throughout the area. The suit will not be resolved for many years. Meanwhile, however, the Cheyennes have also requested reassignment back to them of a large area of the public domain to help support their booming population. This area includes, symbolically enough, 550,000 acres of Custer National Forest, which would more than double the present reservation (Billings Gazette, December 12, 1975).

At Custer Battlefield June 25, 1976, American Indian Movement leader Russell Means referred to an earlier mineral craze in the Great Plains region--specifically, gold, discovered by Custer's expedition to the Black Hills in 1874. "Custer came into our country and invaded us for gold," he said. "Today we have a more sophisticated invasion by corporate giants. The issue is the same--mineral wealth. This time it is coal" (Sheridan Press, June 26, 1976). It is here that the new Custer image is most important. Other events continue to make headlines, such as the splashing of an intertribal urine sample upon the Custer statue in New Rumley, Ohio, by a group calling itself NAME (Native Americans Mending Errors), also on the battle's 100th anniversary (Little Big Horn Associates Newsletter, July 1976). Yet the real impact of the Custer

legacy among today's Indians lies elsewhere.  As
the Cheyennes said in 1976 at a high-power environmental meeting, "Custer tried to pressure us"
(Northern Rockies Action Group 1976:6-8; 14-15).
The implication is becoming increasingly clear on
fast-moving political fronts of the Northern Plains:
Custer's legacy--as a harbinger of Indian independ-
ence--is functioning as a very important symbol,
indeed.  In the words of Rubie Sooktis, in testimony
at the Northern Cheyenne Air Quality Redesignation
Hearing January 17, 1977,

> You know we are being surrounded not by the
> Blue Coats or Custer now, but the coal com-
> panies, that are surrounding the reserva-
> tion.  ... I am here to speak from the
> cultural point, from the Cheyenne way of
> life, the life that I have known and the
> life that I enjoy.  ... I think that the
> white man's way of life is a life that has
> its own demands and has its own meanings
> and its own rules.  The white man's way of
> life next to his heart is money and guilt.
> ... how do you fight against the gigantic
> dream, the white man's dream?  He's going
> to get it anyway some people have told me,
> he is going to get this land, but what
> about our dreams?  The dreams of Dull Knife
> and Little Wolf, the struggles they had and
> the price they had to pay so that we can
> benefit from that decision that was made
> almost 100 years ago.  ... we are again
> trying to survive, and we got no place to
> go.  Our air is in danger and we are sitting
> on top of the coal that people want and you
> look all four directions and you see all
> these coal companies, all these coal activ-
> ities, Colstrip and all those possible other
> plants.  We are totally surrounded and I
> don't think the Cheyenne people are going
> to surrender that easy, but we are also
> talking about survival.  ... we can survive
> on a physical basis but are we going to
> survive as a Cheyenne people in holding
> onto what makes us Cheyennes?  ... I guess
> we just have to find a way to survive, not
> only as Cheyenne people but to maintain
> what we have, what makes us Cheyennes, what
> makes us different from every other tribe,

from every other country, even the world.
And I am not only proud to be a Cheyenne
but I am fortunate to belong to a tribe
that still has human rights and still has
human laws (Northern Cheyenne Research
Project 1977:66-68).

The tribal stationery bears a picture of Little Wolf
and Dull Knife with the caption, "Out of defeat and
exile they led us back to Montana and won our Cheyenne homeland that we will keep forever." On this
point tribal members are virtually unanimous. "Custer Had It Coming;" and the coal companies' "Black
Dream" of exploitation may yet be next in this particular corner of Montana (Rubie Sooktis and others,
personal communication, July 1977) because of the
Cheyenne stand.


## FOOTNOTES

1. The battle is of more popular interest than ever.
Tal Luther's 1973 review provides 195 hand-picked
annotated references as an introduction to the lit-
erature, and these represent just the beginning.
Today new treatment is being provided by scholars,
e.g., analysis of the changing fortunes of Custer
in the media (Dippie 1974 and Hutton 1976) as well
as growth of Custer mythology in general (Dippie
1976). An entire organization, the Little Big
Horn Associates, exists to commemorate it. Visitors
at the National Monument near Hardin, Montana now
number close to 300,000 per year.


2. As this goes to press (August 1979), the future
of Colstrip plants 3 and 4 is still uncertain as
litigation continues. The Northern Cheyennes were
granted Class I air quality designation from the
Environmental Protection Agency in 1977--the only
such designation thus far in the entire United States.


3. Another example may be found in the testimony of
George Harris at the Northern Cheyenne Air Quality
Redesignation Hearing January 17, 1977. After a
tour by Cheyenne observers around coal plants at
Four Corners on the Navajo reservation, in which

the group visited a supposedly purified pond on which
floated numerous dead fish and ducks, the official
tour guide was questioned as to the cause. "Well,
they caught that guy unprepared, and he didn't know
just how he was going to answer it," Harris said,
"and the only thing he could think of was, 'Well,
they must have drownded'" (Northern Cheyenne Research
Council 1977:64). On the same occasion, Bertha
Medicine Bull, who was acting as interpreter, translated, instead of the routine spiel of the guide,
the pungent and critical comments of a Navajo woman
resident of the community seated beside her. Every
Cheyenne on the trip was convinced of the necessity
to ban strip mining on the Montana reservation.

## REFERENCES CITED

Abbey, Edward
    1977     The Second Rape of the West. Pp. 158-
            188 in Edward Abbey, The Journey Home:
            Some Words in Defense of the American
            West. New York: E. P. Dutton.

Badhorse, Beverly
    1976     Tzvyotanon: A Legend of Retribution
            Haunts Warlike Tribe's Efforts to Pre-
            serve its Culture and Exploit its Wealth.
            Billings Gazette, June 23, 1976.

Bonney, Rachel A.
    1976     The Role of AIM Leaders in Indian Na-
            tionalism. Paper presented at the 1976
            Meeting of the American Ethnological So-
            ciety, Atlanta, Georgia. Mimeographed.

Billings Gazette
            Billings, Montana.

Cohen, Fay G.
    1976     The American Indian Movement and the
            Anthropologist: Issues and Implications
            of Consent. Pp. 81-94 in Michael A. Ryn-
            kiewich and James P. Spradley, editors,
            Ethics and Anthropology: Dilemmas of
            Fieldwork. New York: John Wiley and
            Sons.

Conoway, James
    1973    The Last of the West:  Hell, Strip It.
            Atlantic 232:91-103.  September.

Deloria, Vine, Jr.
    1969    Custer Died for Your Sins.  New York:
            Avon Publishers.

Dippie, Brian W.
    1970    What will Congress Do About It?  The
            Congressional Reaction to the Little
            Big Horn Disaster.  North Dakota
            History 3:161-190.

    1974    Popcorn and Indians; Custer on the
            Screen.  Cultures 1:139-168.

    1976    Custer's Last Stand:  The Anatomy of
            an American Myth.  Missoula, Montana:
            University of Montana.

Dustin, Fred
    1939    The Custer Tragedy.  Ann Arbor, Michi-
            gan:  Privately printed.

Edmunds, R. David
    1976    Indian Humor:  Can the Red Man Laugh?
            Pp. 141-153 in Daniel Tylor, ed, Red
            Man and Hat Wearers:  Viewpoints in
            Indian History.  Boulder, Colorado:
            Pruett Publishing Co.

Environment Reporter
            Washington, D.C.:  The Bureau of
            National Affairs.

Fritz, Henry E.
    1963    The Movement for Indian Assimilation,
            1860-1890.  Philadelphia:  University
            of Pennsylvania Press.

Gold, Raymond W.
    1974    A Comparative Case Study of the Impact
            of Coal Development on the Way of Life
            in the Coal Areas of Eastern Montana
            and Northeastern Wyoming.  Missoula:
            University of Montana.

Graham, W. A.
    1953    The Custer Myth:  A Source Book of
            Custeriana.  Harrisburg:  The Stackpole
            Co.

    1962    The Story of the Little Big Horn.  Har-
            risburg:  Military Service Publishing Co.

Great Falls Tribune
            Great Falls, Montana.

Hardin Herald
            Hardin, Montana.

High Country News
            Lander, Wyoming.

Hutton, Paul
    1976    From Little Big Horn to Little Big Man:
            The Changing Image of a Western Hero in
            Popular Culture.  Western Historical
            Quarterly 7:19-45.

Josephy, Alvin M., Jr.
    1973    Agony of the Northern Great Plains.  Pp.
            71-100 in Audubon:  Magazine of the
            National Audobon Society.  July.

Liberty, Margot
    1975    The Cheyenne Indians.  For Plains volume,
            Handbook of North American Indians
            (forthcoming), Smithsonian Institution,
            Washington, D.C.

Little Big Horn Associates Newsletter
            Little Big Horn Associates, Box 27046,
            El Paso, Texas.

Luther, Tal
    1973    Custer High Spots.  Fort Collins,
            Colorado:  The Old Army Press.

North Central Power Study
    1971    North Central Power Study:  Report of
            Phase I, Volume I.  Study of Mine-Mouth
            Thermal Powerplants with Extra-High
            Voltage Transmission for Delivery of
            Power to Load Centers.  Prepared under
            the Direction of Coordinating Committee,
            North Central Power Study. Mimeographed.

Northern Cheyenne Research Project
    1976    The Northern Cheyenne Air Quality Re-
            designation Report and Request. Lame
            Deer, Montana: The Northern Cheyenne
            Tribe.

    1977    The Northern Cheyenne Air Quality Re-
            designation Report and Request in Three
            Volumes. Lame Deer, Montana: The
            Northern Cheyenne Tribe.

Northern Great Plains Resource Program Staff
    1974    Northern Great Plains Resource Program
            Draft Report. Denver, Colorado.

Northern Rockies Action Group
    1976    Proceedings of the Native American,
            Environmentalist and Agricultural Work-
            shop, December 10-12, 1975, Billings,
            Montana. Helena, Montana: Northern
            Rockies Action Group.

Officer, James
    1971    The American Indian and Federal Policy.
            Pp. 6-85 in Jack Waddell and Michael O.
            Watson, eds., The American Indian in
            Urban Society. Boston: Little, Brown
            and Co.

The Plains Truth
            Billings, Montana

Post, Robert C.
    1976    1876: A Centennial Exhibition. Wash-
            ington: Smithsonian Institution.

Rosenberg, Bruce A.
    1974    Custer and the Epic of Defeat. Univer-
            sity Park, Pennsylvania: Pennsylvania
            State University Press.

Sandoz, Mari
    1953    Cheyenne Autumn. New York: McGraw Hill.

Sooktis, Rubie
    1976    The Cheyenne Journey. Ashland, Montana:
            Religion Research Center. Mimeographed.

Smith, Helena Huntington
 1975    The Wringing of the West.  The Washington
         Post (Outlook Section), Washington, D.C.
         February 16.

Smithsonian Institution
 1976    A Supplement to 1876:  A Centennial Ex-
         hibition.  List of Objects Exhibited.
         Washington, D.C.: Smithsonian Institution.

Stands In Timber, John and Margot Liberty
 1967    Cheyenne Memories.  New Haven:  Yale
         University Press.

Stewart, Edgar I.
 1955    Custer's Luck.  Norman, Oklahoma:
         University of Oklahoma Press.

Toole, K. Ross
 1976    The Rape of the Great Plains:  Northwest
         America, Cattle, and Coal.  Boston:
         Little, Brown and Co.

Tsistsistas Press
         Lame Deer, Montana (Northern Cheyenne
         Newspaper).

Utley, Robert M.
 1953    The Celebrated Peace Policy of General
         Grant.  North Dakota History 20:121-142.

 1973    Frontier Regulars.  The United States
         Army and the Indian, 1866-1891.  New
         York:  Macmillan Co.

Weist, Tom
 1977    A History of the Cheyenne People.
         Billings, Montana:  Montana Council
         for Indian Education.

Weymouth, Lally and Milton Glazer
 1976    America in 1876:  The Way We Were.
         New York:  Random House.

# INTRODUCTION TO PART II

The previous chapters have shown the growth of
Indian political organization in face of extensive
contact with Euroamericans. The Cherokee and Navajo
reactions to forced acculturation indicate a basic
vitality in resistance to change while the Wabanaki and
Northern Cheyenne reveal a capacity for doing more
than resisting. The Cheyenne illustrate a pattern
for achieving a new way of life that will incorporate much of their old values and customs. In short,
Native Americans are adapting new political forms
and tactics that allow them to retain a distinct
life style, and the choices they make about adapting
the new or retaining the old will be their choices.

In Part II the authors describe this process among
the Seminole of Florida, the Crow of Montana, the
Inuit and Cree of Quebec, the Dene in the Northwest
Territories, and the Inuit of the Canadian Arctic.
In some cases a new political organization is barely
emerging; elsewhere pan-native organizations are
combining the strengths of numerous groups. Whatever the degree, it is clear that Native Americans
are not content with the domination of the larger
society. They are acting and speaking out against
a form of colonialism that has been and is exploiting them and their resources. The following chapters document current developments in Native political organization while recording the drama of Indians speaking for themselves.

Chapter 6 vividly portrays the effects of the trust
relationship on the Seminole. The almost total
management of their affairs by the Bureau of Indian
Affairs has left the vast majority of them apathetic
about any form of government. Despite large-scale
federal aid for a cattle raising program, the Seminole remain in poverty, and the federal program has
not encouraged either leadership or entrepreneurship.
Garbarino provides not only the historical background
leading to their situation but also describes its
present consequences. She sees little chance for
economic development without a corresponding development in local self-government. Nevertheless, some
Seminole manage to exert leadership accommodating
to highly different expectations from whites in the
BIA and fellow Seminole on the reservations.

Garbarino portrays the difficulty of such a role
and analyzes its effects on personality. Her further description of other Seminole personality
types is invaluable for an understanding of how
federal domination affects reservation Indians.

While white contact invariably brings some disrup-
tion as shown by Garbarino, Native cultures have
also shown a remarkable persistence, even in extreme
circumstances such as the Cherokee. Voget explores
how Indians manage this persistence. In his study
of the Crow and Iroquois Voget brings many years
experience to analyzing the process of acculturation
and searching for the factors that explain why some
groups, such as the Wabanaki, retain a high degree
of integration. In Adaptation and Cultural Persistence among the Crow Indians of Montana he notes the
importance of land, language, ideology, ceremony,
and a type of economy as basic for the persistence
of distinct life styles. Although his analysis is
for Crow, its applicability to the Penobscot and
Passamaquoddy, as well as the other communities
described here, is obvious. What is not so obvious
is the importance of ideology and ceremony and their
relation to a total way of life, including economics
and politics. Voget's description of current Crow
life vividly portrays this relationship and demonstrates why Indian political organization cannot be
expected simply to duplicate the forms and content
of neighboring white communities. The chapter exemplifies the point that the goal of self-determination
for Indians cannot mean they will be just like other
Americans. Rather they must be seen as having the
right to determine how they will form self-governing
communities of Indians.

This problem is explored further by Barger in his
description of Inuit and Cree Adaptation to Northern
Colonialism. The Canadian administration has insisted that there is but one law for everyone; as a
result the Cree and Inuit councils are constrained
in their decision-making. Their reactions parallel
those described by Garbarino among the Seminole.
However, the Inuit and Cree have lost much of their
apathy given the new emphasis on development of resources. Traditional leadership styles remain, but
leaders are now expected to assert the values and
ideology of their people. Also, Cree and Inuit

differences are being minimized while their similarities as minorities are emphasized. Although separate Inuit and Cree organizations have formed to pursue their own interests, alliances between them are being forged similar to those among the Wabanaki. In this process the Inuit and Cree explicitly recognize the value of land and language in preservation of their heritage, and Barger captures the drama of the Cree and Inuit recognizing their ideology must be retained through their own efforts. The chapter has Native peoples clearly speaking in their own words about the factors analyzed by Voget for the Crow. Beyond doubt, the Cree and Inuit will maintain their distinct identity while making adaptations to new economic developments.

This theme is presented even more vividly by the Dene, Metis, and Inuit who appeared before Justice Thomas Berger. In Helm's chapter about Indian Dependency and Indian Self-Determination, Native peoples speak cogently of their needs to protect their heritage while at the same time adapting to the economic development schemes of the larger society. Helm ably summarizes the historical setting which led to dependency. She then uses excerpts from Berger's extensive hearings to show how well the Natives recognize the paradox of accommodating to development while attempting to preserve their former values. The process is especially well illustrated by the Dene whose newly emerging national entity is contrary to the organizational principles of the former bands. Support and leadership for this new authority must come from novel adaptations. The experiment surely will produce frustration and dissatisfaction, as illustrated by the comments concluding Helm's chapter, but the price of self-determination must be matched against the costs of outside domination.

McElroy presents a similar picture in her analysis of the politics of Inuit Alliance Movements in the Canadian Arctic. This movement coincided with the Bicentennial, and the Inuit face problems similar to the American colonies as well as the Dene. How much will a federal union affect life on the local level? Can the values and ideology of local life persist in the face of an over-arching political alliance? While the Inuit struggle for answers, they are actively pursuing an organization capable of meeting the demands thrust upon them by development from the south. Their former mode of interacting on a personal basis is giving way to the informality of one political organization negotiating with another. In the process, pan-Inuit associations are rapidly gaining strength. While most individuals still operate in these associations as Inuit, following traditional norms for appropriate behavior, they are recognizing a need for change in order for Eurocanadians to understand the assertion of their rights. The change is illustrated in the Tapirisat organization where young Eskimo are exerting influence and building alliances with other Native peoples. Yet older Inuit, too, recognize the problem. McElroy reports the words of one of them who could be speaking for most North American Natives: "We do not need the pity, the welfare, the paternalism and the colonialism which has been heaped upon us." Instead, "The presence of our ancestors within ourselves is very strong. The will to survive is there." Drawing upon such resources, Natives can be expected to determine much of their own future.

The determination will not be easy. Most members of the larger societies fail even to understand the issues. The authors of this book hope their work will contribute to a better understanding, but they realize that comprehension of the problem is only a first step. Final self-determination and choices about the future must remain in the hands of Native Americans themselves.

CHAPTER 6


Independence and Dependency Among the Seminole
of Florida

Merwyn S. Garbarino, University of Illinois
Chicago Circle


This paper sketches the events and circumstances
that have created a politically dependent society
out of an amalgamation of traditionally independent
groups of southeastern Indians.  The first part summarizes the history of the Seminole Indians (cf.
Swanton 1922, 1946), leading to a discussion of the
tribal framework within a dominant society.  The
thesis is that the history of conquest and subsequent political control by the federal government
could not but result in dependency for the Indian
society as a whole, a dependency which even now only
a very few individuals are beginning to sever.


SEMINOLE ORIGINS

Independence marked the very formation of the entity
that came to be known as Seminole.  That tribe was
a late development, nonexistent as a group before
the middle of the eighteenth century.  Independence
is implied by the meaning of the Muskhogean word,
seminole.  It has been given various translations:
wild, undomesticated, runaway, renegade, separatist,
all of which may be glossed to mean a group of Indians who fled into Florida--then Spanish territory--
to avoid control by British settlers who were taking
the lands of the southeastern Indians.

There were no Seminole to greet Ponce de Leon and
his men, the first Europeans to set foot on the
Florida peninsula.  In 1513, the aboriginal inhabitants were primarily the Timucua in the northern
region and the Calusa in the southern.  Along the
east coast other smaller tribes were probably allied
with or paying tribute to the larger groups.  The
names of these smaller societies are largely unknown
to most people today.  Tekesta, Jeaga, Ais, for example.  Native populations who met Spanish explorers

of the west coast, the Apalachee among others, have
long since become extinct.

The Spanish in Florida in the sixteenth and seventeenth centuries were not settlers. Instead, they
established forts and depots along the coast to
protect and succor their galleons carrying bullion
from Mexico to Spain. They did not compete with
Indian populations for farmland. At the worst, the
Spanish used some natives for labor. Missionary
priests made many conversions, and in general, European and Indian relations were peaceable, the Indians
benefitting from the passage of European goods,
domesticated animals, and crops. However, cultural
contact was accompanied by European microbes against
which the aboriginal populations had no immunity.
The mortality was high, and whole communities were
wiped out by the eighteenth century.

By 1700, other Europeans had entered Florida. The
French tried to establish a Huguenot community on
the east coast only to be driven out by the Spanish
while the British raided Spanish forts. These Europeans left descriptions and pictures of the Florida
natives, pictures in the style peculiar to European
art of the day, showing classically proportioned
males and females--noble savages in their daily pursuits, hunting, eating, cultivating. Perhaps descendants of those so depicted contributed to the
heterogeneous population that became known as Seminole by the middle of the eighteenth century.

England, France, and Spain, struggling for control
of the eastern regions of the North American continent, came into conflict with one another as well as
with the Indian tribes allied with each. Warfare
became endemic in the late seventeenth century, and
mortality from fighting and disease depopulated the
native towns. By the decades when Britain controlled
Florida, 1763-1783, the disrupted aboriginal tribes
of the peninsula had been infiltrated by small splin-
ter groups of southeastern Indians like Creek, Yamas-
see, and Yuchi. A Creek majority formed the nucleus
of what became the Seminole, but the others also
contributed to the new group which doubtless absorbed
remnants of the original Florida groups as well as
some escaped slaves of African descent. Though all
were referred to as Seminole by the time of British
possession, two languages were spoken, both of Musk-

hogean stock: Muskogee and Mikasuki. These two languages, mutually unintelligible, are still spoken by the Florida Seminole of today. All the Indian people who moved into Florida speaking other languages, for example the Siouan Yuchi, gradually abandoned their own and began to use one or the other Muskhogean tongue (Swanton 1925).

In 1783, when Spain regained control from Britain, Florida had become a refuge for runaway slaves and white outlaws from Georgia and the Carolinas. Florida Indians sometimes joined these renegades in their harrassment of the settlers across the border, and irate United States citizens called upon the state militia and federal troops for support. Spain was too weak either to control the Florida natives or come to their aid during the border violence. It was merely a matter of time until the United States pressed hostilities into valuable Indian lands in Spanish Florida.

A chief of an Alachuan band called for a union of all Florida Indians to mount an uprising against the encroaching whites, and the Shawnee chief, Tecumseh, traveled to Florida and other parts of the South in an attempt to unite all Indians in intertribal harmony. Tecumseh had long dreamed of a mighty Indian alliance that would halt the invasion by the Europeans, but none of these attempts at unified defense ever materialized.

Following the War of 1812 many Indians of the Southeast who sided with England, including a thousand additional Creek, fled to join the Seminole. In this way the Creek element was strengthened, and their language became dominant. The flight into Spanish territory of Indians who had supported Britain angered and worried the United States. General Andrew Jackson, on orders of the Secretary of War, readied his troops for action along the border. He did not stop at the border, but entered the northern area of the peninsula not only to punish Indian warriors who had taken refuge there but also to recapture slaves of African descent who had fled into Spanish territory.

Some Seminole owned black slaves, but the Indian institution of slavery differed from that in white society. Slaves of Indians often intermarried with the Seminole or with free Negroes, and the children of such unions were free. Free Blacks lived in villages, much like the Seminole villages, cultivating their lands, and often carrying arms for defense. Such a condition held great appeal to the slaves in the southern United States who persisted in their flights to freedom in Spanish Florida. The weakness of Spain tempted the United States military to pursue the fugitives. The Florida border became a battleground. Jackson expressed the view that the United States should take possession of Florida and believed he had authority to march down the peninsula.

Jackson drove the Spanish and the Seminole southward, outnumbered and outgunned. By 1819, the United States held virtual control of Spanish Florida and signed a treaty to purchase Florida. The hostilities of 1817-1818 that led to this treaty mark the First Seminole War. The territory passed formally to the United States in a ceremony in 1821 and with it passed control over the Seminole. But the problems that led to Jackson's entry into Florida did not cease with the treaty. Conditions remained much the same: slaves still ran away to take refuge with the Indians who protected them, and the Seminole raided United States military establishments and settlers' homes and farms. In 1824, the Seminole were removed to a reservation area in the central peninsula, carefully set back some miles from each coast. The United States government considered the coastal regions particularly vulnerable to attack from unfriendly European powers and intended to keep the area free of unfriendly domestic groups.

The Indians were dissatisfied with the lands assigned them. Too little of it was good farm and pastureland; too much was sand or marsh. In a short time the Seminole were raiding again. When severe drought ruined an entire year's crops, violence became widespread. Hostilities were often exacerbated by adventurers and gunrunners for their own aggrandisement. Agitation grew among settlers in Florida to have the Indians there removed to Indian Territory.

144

ATTEMPTS AT SEMINOLE REMOVAL

The policy of Indian removal from all of the southeast to Indian Territory was gaining wide popularity
among the white citizens and their representatives
in Washington (cf. McReynolds 1957).  In exchange
for their traditional tribal lands in the East,
Indians willing to move west were promised new lands
and money payments.  Many of them moved because they
could see little future in the Southeast.  A few
Indians, however, were adamant in remaining.  To
convince the Native people to move west, the government offered to take some leaders to the new territory to make their own appraisal.  A few Seminole
went to view the land, and although many agreed that
it was good farm and pastureland, they neither wanted
to move personally nor had the authority to agree to
tribal removal.  In addition, the government planned
for the Seminole to live with the Creek, and no Seminole thought well of that idea.  Nevertheless, the
government claimed the delegation had given consent
to the removal--they had done nothing of the sort--
and began arrangements for the transfer.  Antagonism
climaxed and the Second Seminole War (1835-1842)
began.  That war cost the government twenty million
dollars and the lives of nearly 1,500 soldiers.
During that conflict the Seminole best known to his-
tory--Osceola--became the major leader.  He rigor-
ously opposed the surrender of Indian rights and
became the figure around whom the Seminole rallied.

After a long, bloody stand in determination to stay
in Florida, the Seminole were defeated, and the
majority moved to the West.  However, a few refused
to be dispossessed and fled farther south down the
peninsula into the cypress swamp and sawgrass regions.  Until the Civil War, the government tried
various tactics of persuasion to convince those
remaining to go west, even bringing delegations
from Indian Territory to coax the refugees.  However,
the new dwellers of the everglades staunchly refused
to leave.

After a brief and futile military excursion to flush
the Seminole from the southern Florida territory,
the government turned its energies toward the greater
conflict of the Civil War.  From that time the Florida Seminole were left largely on their own, isolated

and undisturbed. The sawgrass and cypress swamp regions were undesired by white settlers, and the Indians had several decades in which to recover from past aggressions and adjust to a new environment. During the Civil War period, the number of Seminole in South Florida was certainly less than 1,000, probably less than 500.


SEMINOLE IN THE POST CIVIL WAR PERIOD

The first real investigation of the Indians who remained in Florida occurred in 1880 when Clay MacCauley (1884) made an ethnographic study on behalf of the newly organized Bureau of Ethnology. MacCauley, using interpreters, seems never to have discovered that there were two languages spoken, for he refers throughout his report to "the" Seminole language, and the phonetic recording he made of some words is apparently only in Muskogee. He gave the population of all Seminole in Florida as 208, probably an inaccurate figure, considering the difficulties of making a census at that time.

He found Indian settlements scattered from one about 65 miles north of Lake Okeechobee to one on the Little Miami River, about ten miles west of Biscayne Bay. In other words, by the last quarter of the nineteenth century, the Florida Seminole were living in an otherwise uninhabited region far south of the lands they had occupied during the eighteenth century. However, it was a territory with abundant animal and plant foods. In fact, it was the territory of the extinct Calusa, who had been hunters and gatherers, not agriculturalists, so plentiful were the wild foods. The agreeable climate made few demands for clothing and shelter, and the Seminole people maintained their scattered settlements with very little white contact. MacCauley says that a white halfbreed child and its mother would be put to death, that the only mixed blood Seminole were children of Indians and Blacks.

Contacts with outsiders, infrequent though they were, supplied the Seminole with calico, gingham, and flannel. Other ready-made articles from white traders were steel knives, guns and ammunition, shawls, scarves, blankets, beads, trinkets, and rarely, shoes. In general, MacCauley found the Seminole

antagonistic to white people and their ways though
eager to obtain many items of material culture.

Seminole settlements at the time of MacCauley's
visit were largely self-sufficient camp units composed of extended or nuclear families. Work varied
by age and sex but not rigidly. In fact, each adult
was capable of handling all kinds of work. Each
camp could, should the occasion arise, become totally
self-sufficient provided the desire for European
goods did not become an emotional necessity instead
of a luxury. But the trend toward dependency upon
trade goods was clearly present. For example, the
art of making pottery had been replaced by widespread
use of iron kettles and pots.

Two of the settlements were organizationally independent of the other three, while the latter were
loosely bound in what MacCauley called "a simple
form of government," having a council composed of
representatives from each of the three groups. The
council met annually under the direction of two
medicine men who were considered leaders. However,
MacCauley was unable to learn the object of the
council's deliberations or the extent of its decision-making powers.

By the last quarter of the nineteenth century, the
Seminole were using United States currency as a
medium of exchange and standard of value. MacCauley
reports that the unit they adopted was not the dollar
but the quarter. The Indians obtained money in exchange with traders for buckskins or received credit
in written form for future purchases. Records were
kept in the form of marks on paper, one for each
quarter or four to a dollar. MacCauley was informed
that the annual value of Indian trade at Miami was
about $2,000, a larger sum than would have been true
of trade with other bands since the Miami group did
business with whites more regularly than the others.
However, all bands had to trade with outsiders to
obtain the desired European goods.

MacCauley worried about the enervating effects of
the lush environment and the possibilities that the
Seminole, whose bravery and pride had been demonstrated by their nearly two centuries of warfare,
would be destroyed by the fact that they had no
further retreat. Describing them as strong, fear-

less, haughty, and independent, MacCauley anticipated a decadence of their moral strength as they
were forced to submit to the dominant American society. MacCauley foresaw a great and rapid change
resulting from the immigration of white settlers
into Florida and attempts to drain the swampland
and everglades. He hoped that Indian and white
would become friends, but he recognized ancient
barriers would probably fall slowly and painfully.


## THE EVE OF THE INDIAN REORGANIZATION ACT

Fifty years after MacCauley made his survey, the
Commissioner of Indian Affairs ordered another.
Roy Nash, who did the study in 1930, calculated
that the area over which the Seminole hunted and
roamed was about 40 by 140 miles, or approximately
the size of Connecticut. Recognizing the difficulty
of an exact census, Nash (1931) estimated the population between 500 and 600. Though his report
pointed out changes that had occurred during the
time elapsed since the MacCauley report, he also
indicated many cultural retentions like dugout canoes and traditional clothing for women. Women had
begun to sew their traditional, colorful garments
on Singer sewing machines cranked by hand or by foot
pedal. In marked contrast to MacCauley's findings
of 1880, Nash reported that white-Indian offspring
had become a matter of course.

Since MacCauley's visit, popular winter resorts like
Miami, Ft. Lauderdale, and Palm Beach had developed.
In 1880, no railroad ran south of Orlando; by 1930,
one had been built along the eastern shore of Lake
Okeechobee to Key West. Others crossed from east
to west or ran down the west coast to Naples, but
these rail lines had little impact on the Seminole.
More important to them were a few hard-surface roads
connecting cities on the coasts to those in the interior. However, trails from any of these roads to
the Indian settlements still required oxen or dug-
outs in the wet season.

In 1930, although wild foods, particularly meats,
were still staples, some items like coffee, grits,
salt and sugar were regularly bought from grocery
stores. Common to most camps were chickens and a
few hogs. Some families owned one or two oxen and

a wagon, and a few had victrolas operated by a hand-crank.  The Seminole grew no tobacco though they cultivated corn, beans, tomatoes, and other vegetables.  The Indians obtained a small cash income from the sale of furs and hides of racoons, alligators, otters, and deer.  Some employment was available for the men as guides to white hunters during the open hunting season, and some women sold Seminole dolls.  Nash (1931) observed that the small income from these sources was frequently used for payments to bootleggers for liquor.

During the two decades of British rule, a young naturalist, William Bartram, had traveled in 1774 among the Seminole living in the northern area. Bartram (1958) wrote that the Indians not only had free range of the whole peninsula but regularly crossed to Cuba and the Bahamas in large dugout canoes.  By the time of MacCauley's visit, the Seminole range had been greatly reduced, and the camps were confined to five main groups in the southern region.  MacCauley wrote there was no further retreat for the Indians.  Nash found that MacCauley had misjudged.  In four of the five settlements that existed during MacCauley's time, the Seminole had been crowded out by cattlemen, hunters, and the expanding urban areas.  Left to the Indians were the swamps and everglades alone.

By 1930, some Seminole groups had begun living at tourist centers during the winter.  The owners of those centers encouraged the Seminole to exhibit themselves to the curious tourists, and the Indians apparently enjoyed it, or at least found the pay ($6.00 per week per family) enough to smother any objections.  In the past half century, Nash concluded, the Seminole had been driven into the most inhospitable swamps in Florida; robbed of all security; forced to abandon their cattle; and forced into increasingly insecure economic positions.  They progressively had lost tribal organization and had become drunkards and beggars.

THE PRESENT RESERVATIONS

In 1911, federal legislation created two reservations for the Seminole still in Florida.  On the east coast near the city of Hollywood, Dania Reservation--now called Hollywood Reservation--was established on slightly more than 480 acres. Today the federal headquarters, the Seminole Indian Village (a tourist attraction), and the Arts and Crafts store are located on this reservation convenient to the public on U. S. highway 441. Big Cypress Reservation was also established by the 1911 legislation. Located approximately 30 miles south of Clewiston and 140 miles northwest of Miami, the federal reservation of nearly 43,000 acres abuts on the territory of a state reservation of an additional 108,000 acres.

In 1935, Brighton Reservation on the northwest shore of Lake Okeechobee was established, almost 36,000 acres of higher and better drained land than at Big Cypress. The inhabitants of these three reservations form the Seminole Tribe of Florida. The Miccosukee Tribe, organized in January, 1962, is a separate political entity, although most members are related to members of the Seminole Tribe of Florida. The Miccosukee people live on federal trust land along the Tamiami Trail; they too have hunting and fishing rights in the state reservation. The inhabitants at Brighton speak Muskogee which they call Cow Creek, while Mikasuki is the language of the Trail Indians and those at Big Cypress. Both Muskogee and Mikasuki speakers live at Hollywood (Garbarino 1972).

The Seminole did not take advantage of the Indian Reorganization Act until 1957 when they organized under a constitution which created the Seminole Tribe of Florida. The constitution of the new organization provided for a Tribal Council and a Board of Directors, an innovative division of powers with the former body primarily concerned with political matters and the latter formed to direct business activities such as development and management of tribal resources. Both council and board consist of five members elected by members of the tribe. (The Miccosukee Tribe has its own, separate organization.) The powers of both council and board are subject to the approval of the Secretary of the Interior or his authorized representative. This limitation on tribal decision-making obviously can constrict independence in many areas where other United States citizens have decision-making rights limited only by the laws of the land.

Today the Florida Seminole live in dwellings that

range from the traditional open-sized, palmetto-
thatched structure called a chickee, to modern
ranch houses comparable to general Florida housing.
Houses of all types are wired for electricity, and
many homes have telephone service.  As in every
community a range of education and income indicates
a range in possessions.  Almost everyone who lives
in the ranch houses has a diversity of major appli-
ances like refrigerators, washers, and television
sets.  Most families have a car and some have more
than one, but perhaps the universal appliance is a
portable, battery operated radio.  Every household
has at least one.

Most employment comes from agricultural labor and
the Indian Service or the Tribe.  Some people have
college or post-high school degrees, while others
are on welfare.  However, the average income and
average educational level are below the average in
the general population, and many of the people in
the post-forty age group speak little or no English.
Some people own herds of cattle pastured either at
Big Cypress or at Brighton though owners do not have
to live on either reservation.  Competent and dili-
gent craftworkers can add more than $1,000 a year
to the family income by sale of traditional clothing,
dolls, and other items that are marketed through the
Arts and Crafts store.

In short, the Seminole isolation from the dominant
society has not precluded their loss of independence
since they have become ever more enmeshed in an economic system in which they are far from equal participants.  Having learned new desires, they had to
find ways of attaining them.  The result was economic
dependence upon the dominant society.  Even more
entangling and frustrating than the economic dependence is the constriction of their political situation.  Even after organizing into a corporate body,
the Seminole Tribe of Florida, the group remained
unable to make important community-binding decisions
because of the controls exerted upon them by the
Bureau of Indian Affairs (Garbarino 1967).


SEMINOLE POLITICAL DEPENDENCY

John Collier, Commissioner of Indian Affairs between
1933 and 1945, hailed the Wheeler-Howard (or Indian

Reorganization) Act of 1934 as legislation that
would enable Indians to organize themselves into
self-determining communities. Among other things,
the Act encouraged the creation of local tribal
governments and corporations that would presumably
allow elected Indian officials to make community-
binding decisions. It also created a revolving
loan fund so incorporated tribes could borrow money
for various tribal enterprises. It seemed to Collier
and others, both Indian and white, that the Bureau
had become an agency of control and exploitation
rather than one for protection and advisement. Collier saw the Act as a way of ending the Bureau's
monopoly of Indian affairs, leaving it a service
and "within limitations" a regulatory agency.

In 1957, the Seminole Tribe of Florida was organized
under the provisions of the Indian Reorganization
Act. The question to be explored is the degree to
which that organization has resulted in true self-
government and decision-making. Has the tribe gained
independence similar or equal to communities in the
general American society? This goal has been prevented by restrictions written into the tribal constitution, which itself had to be approved by the
Secretary of the Interior. The restrictions keep
the Seminole community from true political independence commensurate with that in outside society. In
fact, one may argue the Indians have very little
control over programs largely designed for them by
outsiders and channeled through the local representatives of the Bureau of Indian Affairs.

If decisions in finance, housing, education, public
works, and other sectors are made for a community
by outsiders; if significant jobs are controlled by
those making such decisions; and if the people of
the community consider it futile to contest those
decisions, then that community cannot be considered
independent. True, all communities are subject to
laws of the various levels of government, but many
spheres of decision-making exist in which they have
a wide range of choice. For the Seminole of Florida,
the situation differs from that of the general American community, for the federal agency exercises
control over such resources as money and credit,
employment, information and knowledge, and legality
to a degree not experienced in the wider society.

Examination of the decision-making operation within the structure of the Seminole Tribe will give insight to Seminole dependency on the federal agency. Though the tribal constitution clearly provides for a decision-making structure through the election of tribal officers, no major sector exists where decision-making is completely free from veto by the agency. The greatest power wielded by the federal representatives comes from agency control over tribal finances. The tribal Board of Directors must have approval from and supervision by the Bureau of Indian Affairs to borrow money from the Indian Credit Fund on behalf of the tribe. The Board Charter specifically states that the Bureau will have this control. Even the choice of attorneys to represent the tribe, as well as their fees, must be approved by the Bureau.

Individually, any Indian seeking economic assistance from the United States government is under supervision to a degree not found among borrowers in the general population. By the tribal constitution, the Branch of Credit of the agency must approve loans for business, housing, and cattle purchases, and it also has the power to take repayment out of cattle sales before a seller gets a check for the proceeds. Officials in the credit branch believe they must maintain this financial control until the Indians have more education and experience. They have a point, of course. The cattle program is heavily subsidized by the government, and it would likely fail if the government abandoned it. But how can individuals learn the financial side of cattle raising if they are never allowed the experience of being responsible for debts? In fact, the government persuaded some Seminole to purchase cattle when they had little interest in becoming cattlemen, people who had ridiculously unrealistic expectations of wealth and no appreciation of the work and problems involved with livestock management. Indians who may become competitive stockowners in the general market have been seriously hampered by the inefficient and incompetent owners the government has allowed to join the program, and it has cost more to maintain participation of some owners than can possibly be recovered in sales. The government is caught in the dilemma of whether the cattle program should be self-sufficient and competitive with others, or whether it should be open

to all Seminole regardless of aptitude. The solution
has been to continue heavy subsidies and controls
over expenditures and sales and to hope that the un-
economical owners will drop out of their own accord.
But this decision has all been governmental. In the
meantime, those Seminole who could learn to handle
the financing are not allowed to do so and are kept
dependent upon the agency.

In addition to controls specified in the corporate
charter and the tribal constitution, the agency staff
and various expert consultants exert control in many
ways through their command of greater information and
knowledge, and through their ability to direct employment. Lack of familiarity with day-to-day business
affairs limits choices by most Seminole. Few have
information about loans or understand interest and
principal. When they apply to the agency to borrow
money, even for as simple a project as digging a
well, they rarely understand what is involved in repayment. The agency staff is too harried--or perhaps
too unaware--to find time for thorough explanation.
It is very difficult for most Seminole to borrow in
the general money market, so they feel dependent on
the agency and resentful of that dependency.

A form of control through knowledge is especially
visible at meetings where agency representatives
are able to use rules of procedure, writing of min-
utes, resolutions, and motions to direct the course
of events. Government personnel always have the
right to attend meetings because the tribe operates
with government funds. Since the Seminole cannot
quote regulations the way the agency representatives
can, knowledge of rules of order produces very effective control by the government whose employees continue to feel supervision is necessary to prevent
disastrous decisions. They are afraid to let the
Indian make decisions.

The few Seminole who have occupational skills and
experience have been coopted by the Bureau of Indian
Affairs. The best paying jobs available to the
Seminole come from employment within the Bureau.
These are various positions within the agencies and
work with the schools, on land development, and as
heavy equipment operators on the road program. People fortunate enough to hold these positions are
among the most highly paid Seminole, but they must

conform to work standards of the federal government
to obtain and keep these jobs.  Since the employment
is very desirable, the workers tend to avoid rocking
the boat through disagreement with the agency.  Even
jobs with the tribe fall under control by the agency
both through its control of tribal expenditures and
because the tribal officials must turn to the agency
for direction.  Since the Seminole themselves are
not capable, or at least feel themselves incapable,
of supervising tribal work, the agency has become
the employer, in effect, although the tribe finances
the salaries.  The agency sees to it that the men
and women they want are those to be hired.

The next question to be raised concerns independence
in internal decision-making.  Within the community
certain persons may be considered cultural brokers--
negotiators with the outside.  They are the elected
officials who have been elected precisely because of
their willingness to play an arbitration or negotiation role.  The recruitment of this leadership has
been largely self-selection in that those so selected
are willing to play this role and proclaim their
willingness.  They are also people acceptable to the
bureaucracy personnel who are aware of the position
of these cultural brokers as intermediaries in the
communication system between the agency and the Indians.  The fact that lines of communication in both
directions--agency to Indians, Indians to agency--
run through the leaders reinforces their position.
They become buffers between the agency and the people, a position permitting some leeway and independence.

Nevertheless, this independence is far from unre-
stricted.  It is hedged about on the one hand by the
controls written into the tribal constitution and
on the other hand by the political traditions of
the Indian society.  Decision-making by unanimity
has long been a custom of the Seminole people, and
the elected leaders try to achieve unanimity for
the simple reason that there is always a chance
that decisions will not be implemented unless based
on the consensus.  The community holds the potent
weapon of passive resistance and hostility.  Leaders
can reduce the probability of such reaction by de-
laying decisions until the community backs them.
Consequently, the leaders often do not make decisions
though they have the legally bestowed right to do
so.  The resulting postponement may be particularly

galling to agency officials who must operate under schedules not observed by the tribal members. Programs voted by Congress usually have a terminal date for implementation, and community passive resistance can put pressures on the agency and in effect modify agency control over the people.

Modification of agency control through passive resistance is minor, however, when compared to the dependency of leaders and people alike in financial and technological matters. Agency personnel are very powerful in these spheres, and Indian leaders are in no position to disagree on the basis of the intrinsic merits of government proposals because the leaders lack information about alternatives. They can only disagree on the basis of what the people will or will not accept.

It is rare that Indian leaders "lead" in the sense of initiating action. This style of leadership appears autocratic and undesirable to Indians who would resent such behavior. Instead, Indian leaders make sure they have the support of their people by persuasion or cajolery no matter how much time may be consumed in getting it. However, the Indian officials, knowing that their constituents will oppose a measure the leaders and the agency deem necessary, may approve it anyhow and blame the decision on the agency, explaining that the Bureau of Indian Affairs forced them to make the decision. Such an explanation is usually accepted. While the Indian leaders do not have to make any particular decision, they may do so if they are in general accord with the agency officials, but they need some kind of alibi for their constituents. The people seldom doubt the agency can force decisions on Indian leaders.

In general, the tribal members consider the agency to be authoritarian. Though they may like individuals within it, they are reluctant to deal directly with the people at the agency, preferring to operate through elected Indian officials. The only real power these officials have lies in their mediator roles. If the leaders refused the service, the people might have to make contact with agency representatives themselves. By and large, they do not wish to do that. The reverse is also true. Bureau employees achieve contact with reservation inhabitants largely through the Indian leaders, reinforcing

the power of the latter as mediators or cultural
brokers. The small degree of independence the Indian
leaders do have is the result of this interaction
channeled through them. Their job is to fuse agency
policy with social choice. It is not an easy one.

The structural situation of decision-making is only
one dimension of Seminole dependency. Significant
psychological components also exist. Seminole differ
from one another temperamentally, and these differences appear in individual perception of the need
for social action. Certain characteristics set apart
those who seek leadership from those who remain followers. Not only do the would-be leaders have a notion of practical politics, they also hold a more or
less explicit political ideology which involves, among
other things, plans for expanding their own position.
These emphases vary from the traditional image of
leader in some ways; for example, the people do not
expect their leaders to assert themselves in internal
matters. However, while desiring leaders who are
sensitive to group consensus, the people want them
to be firm toward the outside--primarily the Bureau
of Indian Affairs. Obviously, leaders require a
flexible personality. Successful leaders among the
Seminole show just this ability to adjust to situations. At the same time, the leaders must be examples
to the rest of the community in their industriousness
as defined by the dominant society. They must also
be temperate people displaying self-control and patience. All these characteristics describe personality types that are effective under slow bureaucratic
mechanisms while being able to operate within the cultural tradition. The requirements of acculturation
appear to demand these characteristics of steady day-
to-day application. In other words, current socio-
political conditions favor certain personalities.

Careful examination of individual responses to authority shows that some Seminole are attempting to
break free of government control. I will use the
term, "independent," to designate people who either
are or aim to be decision-makers, or those who are
not afraid to take a position opposed to those in
authority. "Dependent" people are those who try to
do what they perceive as desired by others in authority. The dependents are compliant and susceptible
to suggestions and examples.

Independent Seminole are self-confident and speak
of long-range goals. They are concerned for the
community, for its problems, and for its improvement.
They demonstrate a high degree of control over impulsive actions and a marked ability to delay gratification and to plan for the future. They are able to
assess situations, make choices, and accept responsibility for their actions. Generally, they hold themselves in high esteem; they are the people who vote
regularly and who assume leadership. This group is
not large, probably little more than ten percent.

Dependent Seminole are much concerned about what
others think of them. They seek approval and are
uncomfortable with the idea of being different.
Generally, they lack initiative and seldom develop
their own opinions. They vote irregularly and usually only because they feel external pressure to do
so. Most Seminole fall into this category.

The relationship of independent to dependent is
necessarily complementary--two sides to the same
coin. Thus, the leaders must understand the problems of the followers and to an important degree
resolve or conquer these problems within themselves.
The resolution often is not understood by the followers who perceive it as a sell-out to the Bureau of
Indian Affairs or to the dominant society. Followers
expect leaders to assert themselves in external matters but to adhere to traditional behavior patterns
internally. Such behavior often appears hypocritical
to outsiders, and the more acculturated leaders themselves tend to find it two-faced. Dependence upon
the leaders in external affairs can consequently
create conflict. It certainly results in ambivalence
toward the leaders who may be resented if they are
successful and scorned if they are not. These reactions are not usually overt but expressed in gossip
and innuendo. Although it is probably less unpleasant than open ill feeling, this suppressed resentment is hard to accept. It tends to build up into
an explosive situation that can be destructive.
Again, flexibility to fllow whatever courses the
various situations require is an essential quality
in leaders. They must be able to bear in-group
aggression as well as assert themselves on behalf
of the group before the dominant society, and they
must recognize that what seems to the Seminole like
loyalty to traditions is often viewed by outsiders

as backwardness or intransigence. Recognition of
all this requires some very sophisticated reasoning
as well as steadfast character. It is hardly surprising that few individuals actively seek leadership.

Another type of individual may be described as "contradependent." People of this type take a consistent
position in defiance of authority. They are fatalis-
tic, believing they have no control over their own
destinies. They are impulsive, undisciplined, and
seek instant gratification. They are often angry but
even more often apathetic. Much of their defiance
comes in the form of passive-aggressive behavior,
doing nothing when action is called for and ruining
others' plans. They do not think about the consequences of their behavior, instead blaming fate,
other people, or the Bureau of Indian Affairs for
their condition and dissatisfactions. Most people
in this category are males; they comprise about ten
percent of the population. Their common complaint is
"What's the use?" Unfortunately, this group tends to
affect the dependents' thinking about many community
matters. The contradependent philosophy of futility
reinforces an already present sense of political
alienation among the dependents. It is all too easy
to blame everything on the agency.

The contradependents may be people who would have
been successful leaders under other conditions: for
example, conditions that require a burst of energy,
a flamboyant style of thrust and parry. They might
well have fit in with the traditional war chief model
of authoritarian leadership for a specific goal and
a limited time. But this is speculation. What is
fact is that they are unable to adapt themselves to
either leadership or followership under present conditions of acculturation. Their political values
and personalities are not appropriate to the current
situation.

CONCLUSION

Group action requires sensitivity to others, organization, and cooperation. It also requires the freedom to make choices. A case can be made that cur-
tailment of this freedom by the agency has brought
about an increase in individual dependency to the

point of indifference or contradependence. Examination of political participation, as measured by frequency of voting in tribal elections, shows a decrease in voters over the years. Reluctance to participate is expressed by "What's the use?" The blame for such a large degree of dependency and alienation must be laid on the restrictions created by the Bureau following policy determined by Congress.

For several generations the bureaucracy has treated Indians like children. And like children, the Indians have often responded with petulant resistance, consistent disagreement with authority, and passive-aggressive behavior. They feel dependent upon the government, and they feel resentful. This condition repeats itself as each generation provides a model of behavior for the next and as the young Seminole experience the same situations and the same treatment by the bureaucracy that afflicted their parents. They are caught up in a philosophy of fatalism. Such a paternalistic relationship does not allow Seminole communities to mature. Dependency is not a question of unemployment, though that contributes to it; nor is it a question of formal education, though the lack of that contributes to it. The dependency of the Seminole as a community is directly attributable to government restraint on their decision-making autonomy. To learn to think in terms of a future time horizon, Seminole must be allowed the responsibility for the future and learn to face the fact of their own accountability. Dependency breeds present-orientation and present-oriented individuals tend to be dependent. It is a positive feedback spiral, and people in this position rarely learn to make plans and implement them.

Data indicate that outsiders make decisions for the Seminole in areas of finance, housing, public works; that outsiders control significant employment; and that the Seminole people have largely given up the struggle for self-determination as a community because they have been denied opportunity to learn from experience. People with personalities suitable to tasks of leadership exist within the Seminole population. Roles and relationships exist to allow cross-cultural communication through the leaders as cultural brokers, but decision-making mechanisms and rights are denied by a bureaucracy that fears expensive mistakes--and doubtless fears the blame for those mistakes.

The honest desire of Bureau officials to protect the Indian people is seen by many as an insult to adult Indians. Compounded of guilt for past behavior and largely inaccurate romantic notions about contemporary Indians as museum pieces who for unstated reasons cannot compete with other human beings in the modern world, government policies continue under the delusion that Indians cannot make do for themselves. Those policies have become, in fact, self-fulfilling prophecies. Many Indians have come to believe in their own dependence--or at least they have learned to act as though they do.

REFERENCES CITED

Bartram, William
    1958    The Travels of William Bartram.
            Naturalist's Edition.  New Haven,
            Connecticut:  Yale University Press.

Garbarino, Merwyn S.
    1967    "Decision-Making Process and the Study
            of Culture Change," Ethnology 6(4):
            465-470.

    1972    Big Cypress:  A Changing Seminole
            Community.  New York:  Holt, Rinehart
            and Winston.

MacCauley, Clay
    1884    The Seminole Indians of Florida.
            Annual Report, Bureau of American
            Ethnology, No. 5.  Washington, D.C.:
            Smithsonian Institution.

McReynolds, E. C.
    1957    The Seminoles.  Norman:  University
            of Oklahoma Press.

Nash, Roy
    1931    Survey of the Seminole Indians of Florida.
              71st Congress, 3rd Session, Senate Docu-
              ment 314. Washington, D.C.: Government
              Printing Office.

Seminole Tribe of Florida
    1957a   Amended Constitution and By-Laws. Holly-
              wood, Florida.

    1957b   Amended Corporate Charter and By-Laws.
              Hollywood, Florida.

    1965    Cattle and Pasture Regulations.
              Hollywood, Florida.

Swanton, John
    1922    Early History of the Creek Indians and
              Their Neighbors. Bulletin, Bureau of
              American Ethnology, No. 73. Washington,
              D.C.: Smithsonian Institution.

    1925    Social Organization and Social Usages
              of the Indians of the Creek Confederacy.
              Annual Report, Bureau of American Eth-
              nology, No. 42. Washington, D.C.:
              Smithsonian Institution.

    1946    The Indians of the Southeastern United
              States. Bulletin, Bureau of American
              Ethnology, No. 137. Washington, D.C.:
              Smithsonian Institution.

    1952    The Indian Tribes of North America.
              Bulletin, Bureau of American Ethnology,
              No. 145. Washington, D.C.: Smithsonian
              Institution.

CHAPTER 7

Adaptation and Cultural Persistence
Among the Crow Indians of Montana

Fred W. Voget, Southern Illinois University
Edwardsville

INTRODUCTION

Any survey of culture contact situations creates an
impression of great variability both with regard to
the processes and effects of acculturation. Throughout this arc of acculturation societies range from
ones which have successfully maintained a high degree
of cultural viability to those which present little
more than tattered shreds of the past. However complex the factors accounting for cultural variability
and persistence, five conditions appear to favor the
successful adaptation of traditional institutions to
altered circumstances. Without attention to priority,
these conditions are: (1) a homeland with which an
ethnic population can identify and where they can
cluster; (2) a localized economy, or a functional
complementarity with the work world of the dominant
society, which supports basic social reciprocities
and traditional statuses; (3) a social and ceremonial
institution which permits identification with a cultural tradition; (4) an ideology which rationalizes
the use of traditional forms and procedures as well
as causal-functional contrasts between one's own lifeways and those of the alien culture; and, (5) a living
language which not only demarcates the group from
outsiders but also shapes the meaning of what people
desire and anticipate in their social relations.

These conditions may be forcefully present in the
persistence of single institutions as illustrated
by the high steel workers of Caughnawaga. In their
case, the integrity of a traditional small group
organization was accommodated to employment in the
wider society without correlating it with other
native-based institutions (Mitchell 1960; Freilich
1958). Persistence of the informal hunting, work
and war party organization was facilitated by a continuity in the functional compatibility of the work
the Caughnawaga Iroquois participated in as their
circumstances altered. In all these work ventures--

163

fur trapping, lumbering, log rafting, river trans-
port--as well as in the four-man riveting gang of
high steel, the Caughnawagans preserved not only the
virtues of their small group organization but also
the shallow liaison which generally characterized
their relations with the European (Voget, Caughnawaga field notes). Within their own work group they
were sequestered from direct individual competition
and supervision by whites, and at the same time,
they followed a life style emphasizing the aggressive demeanor, high risk, high pay, comradeship,
voluntaristic independence, and prestige of the old
time warrior.

In the Caughnawaga case, all of the cited factors
are present, from the reservation homeland to use
of a traditional language. It is, of course, to
be expected in the light of Malinowski's (1960:53)
analysis of the nature of institutions and their
functional integrity.

The five factors are equally visible in instances
where a large measure of cultural continuity and
integration has been maintained, as in the case of
the Hopi and Navaho Indians. The success of efforts
to renovate and to reintegrate cultures threatened
by dissolution also underscores the importance of
these conditions. The rebirth of the Seneca nation
under the reorientation brought by Handsome Lake's
prophetic teachings in 1800 was possible because
they possessed a homeland and could support themselves economically (Wallace 1970). Consequently,
the Seneca sustained traditional relationships of
the social and political order. In language and
ceremony they continued to express and experience
their cultural identification.

The Crow Indians of Montana again illustrate how
traditional institutions can be combined to achieve
a sense of historic identity, direction, and cultural continuity. Despite heavy pressure for
changes, conservatives have welded traditional kin
reciprocities to the circulation of wealth, thereby
strengthening social ties and converting the generous fulfillment of kin obligations into prestige.
The socioeconomic organization is reinforced by
modified traditional religious ceremonials and world
view which evoke social reciprocities, permitting
individuals to achieve personal successes with traditional means while affirming their Crow identity.

HISTORIC LOCATION, POPULATION, AND TRADE CONTACTS

In pre-reservation times the Crow population is estimated between 4,000 and 5,000. While accommodating
to their seasonal and trading needs, they divided
during the 1820s into two major bands, the Mountain
and the River Crow.

Like their Dakota, Blackfeet, Cheyenne, and Arapaho
enemies, the Crow were bison hunters. They maneu-
vered between the Rocky Mountains on the west, the
Big Horn and Absaroka ranges to the south and west,
the Black Hills and Powder River on the east, and
the Missouri River to the north. The Yellowstone
River, and its main tributary, the Big Horn River,
constituted the heart of their historic homeland.
According to tradition, the Crow once were affiliated
with the village-dwelling Hidatsa of the Upper Missouri (Curtis 1970:4:38-39; Lowie 1935:3-4). In
legend, a quarrel over distribution of the succulent
manyplies of a dead bison started the Crow westward.
In all probability this migration occurred early in
the eighteenth century. In their Yellowstone drainage homeland, where they probably displaced Shoshoni,
the Crow found themselves in a favorable trade situation. From the Shoshoni, Flathead, and Nez Perce
they obtained horses and augmented craft production
for trade with villagers to the east, obtaining European hardware and corn from them.

William Clark traversed Crow country in 1805, the
very year that the trader, Larocque, introduced the
tribe once again to direct trade contact. Between
1805 and 1880 the Crow accommodated to the fur trade
without modifying their seasonal round. During the
1840s they annually marketed about 5,000 bison robes.
In 1875, according to the Report of the Indian Commissioner, the Mountain and River Crow brought in a
total of 9,400 bison robes and 95,000 pounds of
other furs for a combined value of $71,125.

Their situation in the Yellowstone area favored them
as middlemen in trade exchanges between the western
tribes and villagers on the Upper Missouri. They
maintained this position into the middle of the
nineteenth century, but with increasing difficulty.
They constantly had to defend their northern boundary
against the Blackfeet, and with the southwestward
drift of the Cheyenne, Arapaho, and Dakota toward

mid-century, Crow were hard put to defend their homeland.

Friendly relations with the "Yellow Eyes," as they called the invading whites, was an integral part of Crow pragmatic diplomacy. They signed a treaty of friendship in 1825, renewed their permission to the government to build roads and forts in 1851 at Fort Laramie, and in a treaty at the same location in 1868 surrendered over 30,000,000 acres. The treaty of 1868 in effect established a reservation for the Crow, but they, as other Plains tribes, did not become locked into this system until around 1882-1883 when the great bison herds were decimated.

BASIC INSTITUTIONS OF TRADITIONAL CROW CULTURE

The seasonal migration, clustering, and dispersal of bison dictated the movements, clustering and dispersal of the Crow. As bison concentrated in the summer, so the Crow came together for the kill and moved as a tribe under the direction of a Camp Chief. Summer was the preeminent time for gathering with relatives and for holding religious ceremonials like the Sun Dance.

A family, commonly uniting a number of brothers in a cooperative unit, cared for basic needs. Husbands hunted while wives processed animal and plant products, provided the skin-covered tipi, and fashioned clothing. The family was integrated into a wider clan organization which regulated marriage and determined the basic rights, obligations, and civil protections of individuals. Crow clans were matrilineal and exogamous, and headed by a chief. Lowie (1935) recorded thirteen clans, five forming linked pairs, and one with a group of three. The cooperative and social ties between linked clans were so strong that membership in one clan was tantamount to membership in the other. The solidarity of these clan-phratries was so strong that intermarriage was discouraged.

Crow society was an "open society," stressing individual mobility through the acquisition of wealth and of reputation earned through war honors and raiding for horses (Lowie 1912:9:228-240; Voget 1964). Retired warriors with powerful spirit guardians

constituted an elite which shaped the careers of
young men by offering counsel and the protective influence of supernatural power--for a fee. A warrior-
medicine-man often dreamed of locating the enemy and
perceived foes bested in combat, the necessary pre-
condition for success. This information and blessing
were conveyed to a protegé, usually a near relative,
son-in-law, or friend of his own son. Such dreams
often were quite specific with regard to details.
Speaking of the dreams with which Sees-The-Living-
Bull blessed him, Two Leggings (Nabakov 1967:166)
reported:

> .... The events he foretold always came
> true. He had given me his medicine and now
> he gave me his dreams and visions which
> brought me many victories as the summers
> and winters passed.

The reputations of great men thus were sprinkled pro-
fusely with "miracles"--the timely prophesy of the
enemy's fate at the hands of an avenging Crow warrior,
the drawing of buffalo to the camp, or the raising or
driving away of rain clouds. Such men drew others
about them, as Iron Bull, whose sister's sons ate at
his table daily and rode his fine horses in exchange
for their care. Iron Bull also generously fed a number of old men in his lodge daily, supplying the meat
through his own skill as a hunter (Curtis 1970:4:51).

Warrior-medicine-men of reputation acted as "chiefs"
who ran the society with one of them recognized as
head chief over the whole tribe. Their advice in
band and tribal councils was acknowledged as most
worthy. Hence, their recommendations usually prevailed, but on critical issues they were sensitive
to the "yeas" and "neas" of younger men, as well as
the counsel of leaders of military societies. A
chief's career generally began with achievement of
four conventional war honors: striking first coup
on the enemy, wresting a weapon from the hands of an
enemy, cutting a horse picketed in front of a tipi
in the enemy camp, and leading a war party which
brought back horses or scalps without loss of life
(Lowie 1912:9:238-240; Curtis 1970:4:12-13). From
that moment the warrior became a war captain, entitled
to carry a medicine pipe. Further horse raids, coups,
and scalps enhanced reputation until retirement from
war around the age of forty. At this time a man

continued his successes vicariously through the careers of younger men upon whom he conferred dream blessings.

In their world view the Crow developed a power-controlling support system inspiring confidence to conquer the unpredictable dangers threatening life and success. The world and the heavens were alive with power conferred by the Creator on insects, birds, animals, stones, streams, sun, moon, and stars. A concentration of extraordinary power brought extraordinary things to pass. The path to control and to safety was simple--people must seek out these powers and concentrate them for their use. By eating a grizzly bear's heart one became like a grizzly--fearsome, but cool and ever ready to take advantage of an opponent. The road to power, however, was not easy. The search involved a torment of the flesh by fasting and wailing in wakeful prayer at secluded mountain vistas where spirit helpers were known to come. Aroused by the determination and pitiable condition of the powerless human being, a spirit helper adopted and conveyed power to the supplicant. Secure in this spirit-father--child relationship, a Crow confidently mobilized power at those "moments of truth" when confronting danger. Indeed, in their most profound public ceremony, the Sun Dance, the Crow drew upon all their war captains and those with special medicines to mobilize and to concentrate spiritual power to revenge themselves upon the enemy.

Crow pursuit of war honors, wealth, reputation, ceremonial distinction, and social and political influence drew economy, social organization, knowledge system, religion, and political organization into a functioning alignment of institutions. Reciprocal exchanges between a man and his matrilineal kin and his father's matrikin constituted the core of social relationships. A father's matrikin provided him with life-protective dreams and guided his career with wise counsel and prophetic blessings. Such "clan uncles" also honored their "children" whenever they achieved some distinction, whether in killing a first deer or returning as a coup counter. At such time a grandfather (father's clan) might hold a feast and distribute goods in his grandchild's honor. In turn his matrikin feasted his father's clansmen and distributed horses, shirts, leggings, and other valuables to them at "give-aways."

168

The kin exchange, in conjunction with a "purchase"
of power and rights to perform prestigeful functions
in public ceremonials, served as major instruments
to circulate surplus wealth.  The exchange system
opened the door to some concentration of wealth and
privilege in the hands of ambitious warrior-medicine-
men and their kin.  To obtain the hand of a chief's
daughter required more horses and other goods than
daughters of less-renowned families.  Moreover, the
extraordinary supernatural power commanded by a war-
rior-medicine-man invited "purchase" of some of it
by young men eager to move up in the world.  Membership in military and ceremonial fraternities, as well
as rights to perform special ceremonial functions,
circulated wealth through a kind of purchase in that
four things of value were donated by the applicant.
The goods offered for fraternity membership usually
were distributed to members at large, but payments
for ceremonial rights were made to the owner.  The
kin of a Sun Dance sponsor were obligated to assemble
many goods to give to the medicine bundle owner directing the ceremony.  The Eagle Medicine-Man, who
dedicated the eagle's nest of the Sun Dance lodge,
also was entitled to take four things from the goods
collected.

While the principle of reciprocity was the keystone
of Crow social relationships and cooperation, the
exercise of public rights must be validated by either
reputation or "purchase."  Commonly those of reputation were invited to carry out important ceremonial
functions, and these tasks required some gift in
payment for the service.  The linkage between a successful career and social reciprocities between in-
laws was especially vital to the social order.  The
most direct route to public reputation and influence
was through warfare.  Success in war not only confirmed supernatural patronage but also provided horses,
the prime measure of wealth and the prized gift in
social repayments.  A distribution of wealth in public "give-aways" reinforced and extended reputation
since the  individual fulfilled his social obligations and proclaimed that prized virtue, generosity.


TECHNOLOGICAL CHANGE AND SOCIO-ECONOMIC ADJUSTMENT

Almost one hundred years have passed since the Crow
arrived at their present reservation with Crow Agency

as the administrative center.  During this century
they have been exposed to, sometimes forcibly, the
religious, economic, educational, and political institutions of the dominant culture.  This contact
has produced individuals with varied acculturational
experiences and orientations.  An increasing number
are being trained as teachers, nurses, secretaries,
alcoholic counselors, road machine operators, carpet
machine operators, auto mechanics, and welders.  Tribal
politics and negotiations with government and coal
developers have familiarized present-day Crow with
the nature of administrative machinery and the politics of administration.

Of the approximately 6,000 Crow, some 40 percent have
found work in towns adjacent to the reservation or in
the industrial cities of the Pacific Northwest and
California.  The reservation possesses paved and
graded roads, elementary and high schools, a hospital,
and local clusterings of country stores, service stations, and short-order eating places.  Crow for the
most part dress in clothes purchased in Hardin, Sheridan, or Billings.  Men and boys follow the cowboy
tradition while women effect a modest modishness with
dresses, jeans, and at times shorts.  Nearly every
family owns an automobile or pickup.

The Crow are situated on land where they formerly
lived.  Approximately 1,297,000 acres of a 2,283,000-
acre reservation are in the hands of individual allottees while 277,000 acres are under Tribal ownership.  Non-Indians own 709,000 acres.  As of 1965 the
Crow used but 12 percent of their allotted and tribal
grazing, irrigated, and dry farm lands, while non-
Indians used 88 percent (MRBS-R187).  Of an estimated
760 Crow families, only 55 were engaged in a combined
stockraising and farming venture in 1964.  These 55
families accounted for approximately 72 percent of
land used by the Crow.  Cattle owned ranged from a
half-dozen head to 676.  For the 23 families possessing 100 head and over, wage labor, per capita payments, lease income, and land sales were important
but not vital income supplements.  For the area, it
is estimated that successful ranching requires close
to 200 breeding cows.  If the 23 families owning over
100 head are taken as successful ranchers, then but
3 percent of the Crow are engaged in an efficient
stockraising venture.  This figure also includes 20
whites married to Crow women.  According to the

Missouri River Basin Report (1968, Report No. 187)
families headed by "non-Crow spouses" and "low-bloods"
averaged 145 and 129 cows respectively, while "high-
bloods" and "full-bloods" averaged 81 and 44.  Those
making the report felt that the high- and full-blood
groups lacked the incentives for efficient dollar
return on investment.  They also indicated that the
high- and full-blood operators were less willing to
add income through wage labor, since they earned but
one-fifth of the wage labor income reported by the
50 operators surveyed.  High- and full-bloods constituted 40 percent of the stockraisers.

Availability of lease income has been a central factor in the economic adjustment of the Crow.  Some 66
percent derive their income from a combination of
land rents, welfare payments, land sales, and per
capita payments.  It would appear, however, as if
lease income has provided a sufficient base, when
augmented by wage labor and per capita payments and
assistance from kin, for mobilizing funds for "give-
aways" and sponsorship of Peyote and Sun Dance ceremonies.  The Crow thus have been able to marshall
adequate surpluses locally, and to apply these to
their own social and ceremonial ends with minimum
involvement in the work world.

The Crow also have adapted the seasonal rhythm of
their former life to a round of social and ceremonial
activities which at times brings one or two districts
together, and which culminates in a grand tribal encampment in August at Crow Agency.  The social round
begins in September, with everyone planning for the
next annual encampment.  September and October are
relatively quiet except for a Tobacco Society adoption and Peyote meetings.  In November districts
celebrate Veterans' Day with wardances, and Crow set
out for Oklahoma to compete in intertribal hand games.
At Thanksgiving, districts sponsor special dances as
warmups for Christmas and New Year's celebrations.
At Christmas and New Year's, districts extend invi-
tations to each other.  Guests belonging to the same
clans as district officers responsible for the dance
are honored by being called on to head a dance procession or to act as drummers.  Between January and
March the Crow hold a dance on Washington's Birthday
at Crow Agency, practice the hand game, and attend
basketball tournaments.  Sun Dance prayer meetings
may begin in March or April after the first thunder,

and in April the Crow hold Oklahoma and Northern
Cheyenne hand game teams in a Junior and Senior competition. In May the districts compete to determine
the best junior arrow throwing team, to be followed
by a senior tournament in June. June is also a major
occasion for Catholics, who celebrate Corpus Christi
with a parade dance, feast, and "give-aways." Sun
Dances may be performed in June, July, or August,
though July is favored. By mid-August the Crow
again converge upon Crow Agency for their tribal
encampment, to enjoy socializing, good eating,
dancing, horse racing, and status enrichment.

At all social gatherings individual Crow exploit social relationships to increase public recognition
and lay a foundation for public and ceremonial office.
As one Crow put it, the Crow have a "bad habit," trying to outdo one another in a generous distribution
of goods. There is a sensitivity about public reputations and a constant vieing with one another. Cur-
iously, in 1805 Larocque (1910) described the Crow
as showing a more competitive spirit amongst themselves than other tribes he had visited.

Two principles apparently govern Crow thinking about
holding public office and performing public functions.
First, a public action requires an actor to possess
a valid title for his performance. Second, continuous performance of public functions requires reciprocities in which an individual repays social or ceremonial services with gifts. One also must periodically
honor kin by distributing wealth in their behalf.
The basic axis of social and economic exchange links
a person and his or her matrikin with a father's
matrikin. The relationship between brothers-in-law
constitutes a secondary axis of exchange.

A valid title for public acts is conveyed in four
ways: by right of a personal-public reputation
based on prestigious achievements; public conveyance
of a right by an authorized holder; by inheritance
in conjunction with gift purchase; by purchase with
gift and service. A distribution of goods at a public gathering usually was essential before exercise
of a right.

The emphasis the Crow presently place on the passage
of wealth to convey a valid right to a public function means that no one can achieve prestige without
entering into the "give-away" and secondary exchange

172

relationships. The route of the "give-away" is especially important for election to tribal offices, such as chairman or secretary. Use of a ceremonial name on public occasions requires the recipient to repay the donor validating the right with a "give-away." In one case a prominent Crow politician prevented criticism of his candidate by bestowing his ceremonial name publicly on a known critic. Immediately, clan relatives of the erstwhile critic dug into their pockets for money to repay the donor on the spot. The recipient has not made public use of the name because he has not validated his title with a "give-away."

In the inheritance of "medicine bundles," normally conveyed from father to son, the usual procedure is for a son to purchase the bundle with four gifts of value. The same holds for purchase of a right to take the lead in a ceremonial procession, or to sing a special song. Veterans alone enjoy a kind of instant status since they share with warriors of old the mantle of success, namely, the testing of one's power over the mystical power of the enemy. Crow youths generally carried medicine feathers or peyote talismans to protect themselves during military service. At the time of his departure for the army, a youth is honored with a feast and a small "give-away." On his return, a veteran's father, in cooperation with the son's clan relatives, will hold a large "give-away" to increase the son's status. A safe return from combat evokes the idea of power, and veterans are invited to bless ceremonial functions and to wish for success in team competitions.

Husband and wife share the heavier burden in accumulating goods to honor a son with a "give-away," with the wife's maternal relatives secondarily obligated for substantial amounts. A modest "give-away" will cost around $800 and the more prestigeful several thousands of dollars. Adoption into the Tobacco Society (Beaver Dance) takes between $4,000 and $5,000. In a $2,000 give-away, a father would be expected to contribute about $200. The more prestigeful and costly the items distributed, the more reputation increases. Decorated boots, saddles, and serapes obtained from Old Mexico are more esteemed than locally purchased items. Inflation has pressured expenditures upward. For example, when Crow give a handcrafted and beaded buckskin dress, they are honoring the person with a gift of about $700. At the same time status

competition has driven up expectations. Thus, to
reciprocate the honoring of one's sister with a give-
away by her husband's kin, a brother will strive for
a "give-away" in which he can give his brother-in-
law a race horse with registered papers (Voget, Crow
Field Notes).

"Give-aways" and repayments for medical or other
services take planning and saving, perhaps for several years. As one perceptive informant put it, the
Crow "know how to save for a 'give-away,' but they
don't know how to save for tomorrow. They want to
outdo each other. That's the economy of this tribe."
However, once a reputation has been established,
wealth follows as a "clan uncle" is invited to pray
for his "children" and to carry out ceremonial or
curing functions. In any "give-away," goods are
distributed in priority to outstanding "clan uncles."
Persons with little reputation receive less or are
ignored. During the full moon prayer meetings of
the Sun Dance, the medicine man invites outstanding
Sun Dancers to take places around the altar. These
assist with prayer smokes and with their own medicine
powers for which they are repaid by the sponsor, and
by those for whom they prayed, with a blanket or
money.

In their social competition the Crow intermingle
contemporary achievement situations with traditional
ones. Above all others, Peyotists use their meetings
to stress education. As children complete a grade,
or the elementary sequence, they are honored with a
peyote meeting where modest wealth is transferred to
the medicine man and to clan uncles invited to be
present and to pray. Usually at this time the sponsor, whether father or a maternal uncle, will vow to
give another meeting if "child" or "nephew" successfully completes further education. The achievements
of children in making teams, winning honors, and in
going away to school give them a central place in
"give-away," competitions. The focus on children
is quite in the spirit of the "give-away," for one
distributes goods not on one's own behalf but in
honor of another. The desires of children for new
dance outfits, horses, automobiles, trips and the
like--often querulously voiced in invidious comparison with the families of peers--are carefully considered by competing parents.

The Crow Fair and Rodeo is the prime setting for a

"give-away" because of the large number of people
present.  Special honorary positions have been created for those willing to stage a grand "give-away."
In 1976 an eleven-year old, Burton Pretty On Top Jr.,
was made honorary President of the Fair Board in
knowledge that his parents and clansmen would vali-
date his title with a "give-away."  Moreover, the
annual Crow Fair and Rodeo would be incomplete without "give-aways" by important tribal officers, who
thereby solidify their public images and testify to
their continuing support of Crow traditions.  Inter-
district and intertribal competitions also provide
excellent staging for "give-aways" honoring team
players.  At the "arrow throwing," when district
teams reach ten points, and at each subsequent ten
points, veterans are honored with the invitation to
recite their war deeds as a blessing for the success
of their respective teams.  Adoption into the Tobacco
Society as well as selection as a princess of American Indian Days are equally worthy for honoring a
child with a "give-away."

Some 30 percent to 40 percent of the Crow appear to
be involved in the "give-away" system.  Of these,
perhaps one-fifth constitute the elite, or approximately 8 percent.  The elite includes elders who are
frequent recipients of donations at "give-aways" and
who have established their reputations through "give-
aways."  These elders exercise considerable political
influence not only because their words are heard with
respect but also because they actively groom their
"children" for public office.  Contemporary elders
resemble the chiefs of old since they are rivalrous
and serve as nuclei for political factionalism.  They
sustain their positions with an aura of mystic power
conveyed by dreams assuring the good health and success of their protegés.  These elders uniformly follow traditionalized religious expressions, such as
the Sacred Sweat, Peyote, Sun Dance, and Tobacco
Society.

Membership in a Christian church is no bar to participation in the "give-away" system.  Baptist, Catholic, Mormon, and Four-Square Gospel members sponsor
"give-aways."  Only the Pentecostals abstain, and
they naturally are described as greedy and stingy
since they do not live up to the cardinal virtue of
generous giving symbolized by wealth distribution.

175

However, at the last election, evangelically-oriented Crow, aroused for the first time to enter politics seriously, succeeded in capturing the tribal chairmanship.

## TRADITIONAL RELIGIOUS PROCEDURES AND MODERN WORLD VIEW

Social reciprocities channeled through the clan and marriage relationships are not the sole axes for the contemporary circulation of services and of wealth. As of old, religious ceremony stimulates a flow of demands and reciprocal exchanges between kinsmen. Back of religious practice lies a traditional philosophical vitalism that grants power to all creatures, objects and growing things--with the possible exception of man. By its very size and relation to the cycling of summer warmth and winter cold, the sun occupies a special place in the power system. The bison, so important in the past for meat, shelter, sewing materials, containers, and robes, remains a commanding source of power. Sun Dancers look to the time when the bison will run over them and give them some power. The eagle also is exceedingly powerful, conveying the quality of success, symbolized by the grasping of its prey. However, it is not the lesser or greater distribution of power among the world's creatures that is important. The important fact is the qualitative differences of power and power concentration. Respect for the powers of animals and plants may lead even a college-educated hunter to offer the foreleg of a slain deer to the "water spirit."

In the vitalistic world of the Crow, the key to success lies in tapping power and in concentrating it in tangible symbols--body paintings, songs, and feathers seen and heard in dream or vision. In the private quest, to which individuals may be led by dreams, the supplicant receives power as a gift from the spirit-helper. At other times the power and its tangible symbols are obtained from a medicine man or clan uncle. The down feather from the eagle's breast, or the peyote button, properly blessed by the owner, becomes a talisman warning recipients of dangers and protecting them with right choices. A feather or peyote talisman is useful in all competitive situations--the arrow throw, hand game, horse racing, or basketball. A "little medicine" bag also

is a good thing to have along when undergoing surgery.
During World War II medicine feathers blessed by John
Truhujo, the Shoshone medicine man who introduced the
Sun Dance to the Crow in 1941 at the invitation of
William Big Day, were in great demand for those going
overseas (Voget 1948b).  Regarding use of Peyote in
World War II, a veteran reported to Kiste (ms. p. 79):

> I carried two peyotes in a little deerskin
> bag.  When I was in a tight spot ... I'd
> take that bag out and lay it down in front
> of me.  I'd pray and I'd see the right way
> to do things.  To get out of a jam.

Whether prayer is directed to a spirit or simply to
power associated with a talisman is a matter of opinion among individual Crow.  It appears that the prag-
matics of cause and effect are more important than
the metaphysics of the power source.  In this regard
contemporary differences in interpretation echo those
found by Lowie (1935) when searching for metaphysical
distinctions from elderly informants.  Understandably,
the introduction of peyote as a new source of power
leads some to think the old medicines have lost their
effectiveness.  After all, the conditions of life
which made the obtaining of power and the attachment
of spirit-helpers possible evaporated with the passing
of the old days.  The sheep and cattle of whites now
spread over the land and intrude into all but the
most inaccessible of spirit domains.  Yet the introduction of the Sun Dance from the Shoshone has stimulated a search for power in the traditional way,
with some going to Cloud's Peak in Wyoming, a favorite
place of old, as well as to Castle Rock near Pryor.
Fasting and sweating are still important elements for
changing one's luck, to get rid of illness, to resolve
difficult decisions, and to determine whether to seek
power.

Linkage of the traditional world view with Peyotism
and the Sun Dance has preserved the general integrity
of traditional religious ceremonialism among the Crow,
even though both ceremonies are imports.  Peyotism
spread to the Crow from the Northern Cheyenne sometime between 1910 and 1914 following participation
by Crow in Northern Cheyenne meetings (Kiste ms. pp.
3-4).  The Sun Dance was introduced in 1941 by William
Big Day of Pryor, with the assistance of John Truhujo,
a Shoshone medicine man (Voget 1948a, 1950).

Curing is integral to both Peyotism and the Sun
Dance. At the outbreak of World War II both were
used to extend protection to Crow youth in service.
However, the Sun Dance evokes a greater feeling of
tribal unity and effort than Peyotism because it
requires more community cooperation and resources
than a peyote meeting. The Sun Dance exerts a special appeal because the bison head, eagle, willows,
brush lodge, fasting, dancing, and use of "medicines"
clearly recall traditional forms and procedures. The
kin exchange system also is reinforced since relatives are expected to build the dancers' stalls,
bring sage and cattails to cool the body, and to loan
medicines and body paintings. The public nature of
the ceremony draws attention to the affirmation of
kin support when it is known that relatives do not
believe in the Sun Dance. A veteran chosen to tend
the fire may use the occasion to honor clan uncles
and nephews in the dance with a gift of blankets and
cigarettes. As the dance ends, participants ask
clan uncles to bless them, in return giving their
uncles blankets, coverlets, money, and horses. The
Sun Dance is now part of the annual calendar of public events, with July and early August performances
preceding the tribal encampment at Crow Agency.

THE INTEGRATIVE FUNCTIONS OF PAST AND PRESENT RELIGION

Two borrowed ceremonial complexes emphasizing native
forms, meanings, procedures, and functions are significant events in the acculturative history of the
Crow. Through a common emphasis on curing both Peyotism and the Sun Dance carry out functions which the
medical practice of clinic and hospital do not fulfill. Diseases are omnipresent, and medicine men
claim individual cures of chronic illnesses which
baffle medical doctors. Beyond this, native-based
ceremonials provide expressive testimonials of ethnocultural identity. In the Sun Dance the costume
is filled with symbols of the past--medicine feathers, eagle down "breath" feathers, eagle bone whis-
tle, body paintings, and wrap around kilt. More
important, in using old techniques based on a traditional world view, participants live out their
identity, self-moved and directly involved in their
own personal needs.

As a public ceremony, the Sun Dance provides a more

visible and challenging affirmation of faith than
Peyotism. Sun Dances draw more non-Indian visitors,
whose questions need answers, and who can be told
that the Indian worships the Creator just as whites.
The public doctoring of individuals focuses attention
on cures and facilitates rapid dissemination of "miracles." People hear good words spoken by elders in
behalf of the Sun Dance and the sponsor of the ceremony. Here too, they are told that the Sun Dance is
a powerful instrument helping the Crow to attend the
annual encampment at Crow Agency with full purses and
happy hearts. The Sun Dance forestalls sickness and
death; hence, because of the Sun Dance, people can
taste the full enjoyment of socializing together as
a tribe--dancing, feasting, racing horses, and having
a good time.

The church community, as the state, serves as a primary vehicle for identification of self, in-group,
and out-group. In the acculturative experience of
American Indians, religion provides a particularly
sharp challenge to ethnocultural identity because of
the persistent attacks on the world view and moral
basis for action which support the traditional life-
style. For this reason, as political and economic
independence falter, the religious institution serves
to reintegrate the community despite schisms (Aberle
1966; Berkhofer 1963; Barnett 1957; La Barre 1971;
Linton 1943; Slotkin 1956; Spicer 1954; Voget 1956;
Wallace 1956). Moreover, in traditional cultures
religion frequently performs an integrative function.
During bison hunting days when Crow suffered losses
to Blackfeet and Sioux, the Camp Chief asked young
men to fast for power to change the luck of the Crow.
Chief Plenty Coups (Linderman 1962:69) notes this
dedication to the public welfare when telling about
his medicine fast:

> ... Of course I had spoken to nobody of my
> dream, but when I came in sight of the vil-
> lage my uncles began again to sing the Praise
> Song, and many people came out to meet us.
> They were all very happy because they knew
> I now had Helpers and would use my power
> to aid my people.

The power quest thus was not just a private search
for personal wealth and reputation; the careers of
outstanding chiefs reveal the search was equally

for the common welfare. In former times dream experiences were important for both private and public policy. Plenty Coups' dream forecast the spread of the whites, and in the violent wind storm which destroyed three of four trees on the mountain, only the tree which housed the chickadee survived. The chickadee was Plenty Coups' Medicine Helper, and Yellow Bear (Linderman 1962:73-74), one of the Crow "Wise Ones," considered the communication most prophetic:

> .... He was told to think for himself, to listen, to learn to avoid disaster by the experiences of others. He was advised to develop his body but not to forget his mind. The meaning of the dream is plain to me. I see its warning. The tribes who have fought the white man have all been beaten. By listening as the Chickadee listens we may escape this and keep our lands.

> The Four Winds represent the white man and those who will help him in his wars. The forest of trees is the tribes of these wide plains. And the one tree that the Four Winds left standing after the fearful battle represents our own people, the Absarokees, the one tribe of the plains that has never made war against the white man.

Coyote Runs, an old warrior present when Plenty Coups told Linderman (1962:75) of his dream-fast, commented:

> We traveled by that dream. The men who sat in that lodge when Plenty-Coups told what he had seen and heard knew a heap better than he did that it was time the Crows turned their faces another way. They saw it was best to do something to prove their friendship to white men, and they began to watch for a chance, too. When they found it, the Crows pointed their guns with the white man's, and some of us died and we lost many horses.

Nothing today indicates powerful dreams shape public policy, although dreams still influence personal decisions. However, the ancient linkage between religion and public welfare is promoted through the careers of medicine men who use their power to cure

and to prophesy. During World War II dream prophecies forecast the August date of the end of the War
against Japan, and visions of ships were taken to
mean the imminent return of victorious soldiers.
Prayers at Sun Dances and Peyote meetings invariably
include blessings for the Crow people and the world
at large. Occasionally, a desired political goal is
introduced into prayers for the common good. The
political process, of course, evokes the image of an
institution closely connected with public needs.
However, the political process is so interlocked
with obligations to kin and supporters that it cannot adequately focus the idealism of the people.
Hence, the religious institution emerges as a special vehicle for advancing the common good and for
living out a Crow identification. One well-traveled
and sophisticated Crow considers his reservation to
be the "religious capital" of the Indian world.

Persistence of the Crow world view in modified religious ceremonial is not simply a matter of the mani-
fold ways in which a traditional institution can be
adapted to changed circumstances. Both Peyotism and
the Sun Dance embody in their procedures basic values
associated with the traditional religious expression.
The individual is self-moved, responding to the im-
mediacy of his own needs or those of relations. In
his quest the individual builds his own "hot-line"
to a power-helper who helps or warns him. An overwhelming desire or concern, usually confirmed in
dream clues, sparks this active engagement. Thus a
younger brother sacrifices himself in the Sun Dance
to forestall evil from the family of an older brother
active in politics. He hopes to prevent illness, or
death in the family, or injuries from an auto acci-
dent. The process is not concerned with doctrinal
matters, or with taking a stand in a church community.
Rather the spiritual relation is strictly between a
person and his God. Doctrine is set not so much by
belief as by forms and procedures, subject to varia-
tion according to rules governing one's own revealed
medicine. Individuation, if not individuality, is
a cultivated aspect of both traditional and present-
day Crow ceremonials. The pragmatic orientation of
the Crow again is revealed by their use of the vow.
Here the individual contracts to sacrifice himself
only upon getting what is desired.

In sponsoring a Peyote meeting, or in electing to

undergo the rigors of the Sun Dance, a person frequently sacrifices himself in the interest of kin.
Such personal sacrifice reinforces kin ties, especially those linking older brothers and sisters to
younger siblings.  During World War II fathers, older
brothers, and maternal uncles entered the Sun Dance
in order to bring a son or younger brother safely
home, while elderly clan uncles, mothers, aunts, and
sisters fasted in the lodge.  But Peyote meetings
and the Sun Dance may also be used to win scholar-
ships and to complete a high school or college education.  There is nothing desired, to which Peyotism
and the Sun Dance cannot be adapted, including elim-
ination of "bad habits."  However, without the value-
principles embodied in procedures accenting the Crow
approach to individuality, aboriginal ceremonials
would be deprived of a strong support for their persistence.


SUMMARY AND COMMENTARY

Anthropologists long ago showed the importance of the
nature and kinds of contact for the rate of cultural
exchange, including what is available for acceptance
or rejection, and the development of contra-accultur-
ative tendencies.  These theoretical orientations
received a more formal expression in the concept of
interactional fields which accompanied a focus on
structural-functional-interactional relationships
(Wilson and Wilson 1968; Lesser 1961; Voget 1963 and
1975:757-760).

The Crow demonstrate how a group subject to heavy
assimilative pressures over a hundred-year period
can forge a relatively bounded interactional field
insulating them from direct and intense contacts
with the wider society.  The limited nature and frequency of contacts facilitate maintenance of core
institutions supportive of traditional status goals,
procedures, and life style.  Five factors have favored
this cultural persistence:  (1) possession of a homeland with which the Crow identify themselves as a
people; (2) a local economy permitting both maintenance of social reciprocities among kin and attainment
of traditional statuses using Native procedures;
(3) Native religious ceremonies which reinforce the
social system and which activate a sense of identity
by use of traditional forms and procedures; (4) a

world view of cause-and-effect relations bringing
meaning to Native religious forms and procedures,
and expressing the self-moved individuality and
involvement traditional to the Crow outlook; and
(5) a living language.

The combination of social, economic, and ideological-
ceremonial institutions constitutes a traditionalized
system relatively insulated from frontal acculturative assault.  Economic viability is central to the
bounded quality of the contemporary social and cultural system.  A system of land-lease rentals and
per capita payments generates a surplus which permits
some one-third to two-fifths of the Crow population
to set their objectives according to traditional
views of social reciprocities and status achievement.
Of the estimated 75 to 100 families engaged in the
give-away distribution, some 15 constitute an elite.
Since the local lease economy establishes nothing
more than an indirect complementarity with the wider
society, the bounded quality of the localized interactional field is sustained.  Presently the Crow
utilize but 12 percent of land in use, and the sale
of land to non-Indians, unless checked within the
next few years, could mean that the Crow will own
less than half the reservation lands.  Of the approximately 6,000 persons on the reserve, whites comprise
about 44 percent.  On the other hand, exploitation
of coal reserves on the ceded and reservation lands
promises to extend the indirect complementarity governing socioeconomic relations with the wider society
by a substantial increase in available per capita
payments, thereby strengthening the insularity of
the traditional sociocultural system.

The adaptive persistence of Crow culture has been
achieved in large part by pouring new wine into old
bottles.  New status-achieving situations have been
created for "give-away" validation out of participation in sports, school graduations, scholastic honors, honorary positions associated with the Crow
Fair and Rodeo, and election to tribal office.  These
innovations supplement the traditional statuses of
war veterans and of medicine men practicing in Peyotism or the Sun Dance.

Owing to acculturative pressures Crow culture has
been subject to considerable erosion.  For example,
the mother-in-law--son-in-law avoidance is fading,

183

and clan exogamy is no longer an important consideration in marriage. The "sassing" of clan uncles is said to be on the increase, and young wives more often quarrel with a husband's relatives. Narrators of ancient myth and warrior exploits no longer are found at public gatherings, surrounded by an appreciative audience of young and old. Grandmothers and grandfathers do not strive to fill the imaginative minds of grandchildren with living memories of the bison hunting days.

Crow culture, indeed, is losing its traditional form-content and some of its social practices. However, the social, economic, and ideological-ceremonial framework here described promises to maintain the basic structure and value orientations until the present interactional system is breached by new relationships. In the perspective of change, the maintenance of traditional social relationships, ideology, and ceremonial have been vital to persistence. Here are to be found the forms, meanings, procedures, and objectives through which the individual can live out an identity as a Crow. At present there is no great stirring to seek an identity through political action as found in the American Indian Movement. This may come in the future, but the apparent viability of the contemporary sociocultural system suggests that such political action is far distant.

REFERENCES CITED

Aberle, David F.
      1966    The Peyote Religion Among the Navaho.
              Chicago:  Aldine.

Barnett, Homer
      1957    Indian Shakers:  A Messianic Cult of
              the Pacific Northwest.  Carbondale:
              Southern Illinois University Press.

Berkhofer, Robert F., Jr.
      1963    Protestants, Pagans, and Sequences
              Among the North American Indians,
              1760-1860.  Ethnohistory 10:201-216.

Curtis, Edward S.
      1970    The North American Indian.  The
              Apsaroke, or Crows 4:3-126, 175-180.
              New York:  Johnson Reprint Corporation.

Freilich, Morris
      1958    Cultural Persistence Among the Modern
              Iroquois.  Anthropos 53:473-483.

Kiste, Robert
      MS      Crow Peyotism.

La Barre, Weston
      1971    Materials for a History of Studies of
              Crisis Cults:  A Bibliographic Essay.
              Current Anthropology 12:3-44, including
              commentaries.

Larocque, Francois
      1910    Journal of Larocque from the Assini-
              boine to the Yellowstone.  Publication
              No. 3, Canadian Archives.  Ottawa.

Lesser, Alexander
      1961    Social Fields and the Evolution of
              Society.  Southwestern Journal of
              Anthropology 17:40-48.

Linderman, Frank B. (orig. 1930)
      1962    Plenty Coups, Chief of the Crows.
              Lincoln:  University of Nebraska.

Linton, Ralph
1943    Nativistic Movements. American
        Anthropologist 45:230-240.

Lowie, Robert H.
1912    Social Life of the Crow Indians.
        Anthropological Papers of the American
        Museum of Natural History 9:181-248.
        New York.

1935    The Crow Indians. New York:  Farrar
        and Rinehart.

MRBS-R 187
1968    Crow Cattle Ranching Operations.
        Missouri River Basin Investigation,
        Project Report 187.  Billings, Montana:
        Bureau of Indian Affairs.

Nabakov, Peter (ed.)
1967    Two Leggings:  The Making of a Crow
        Warrior (based on a manuscript by
        William Wildschut).  New York:
        Thomas Y. Crowell Company.

Malinowski, Bronislaw
1960    A Scientific Theory of Culture and
        Other Essays. New York:  Oxford
        University Press.

Mitchell, Joseph
1960    The Mohawks in High Steel (abridged and
        revised).  In:  Edmund Wilson, Apolo-
        gies to the Iroquois, 3-36.  New York:
        Farrar, Straus and Cudahy.

Slotkin, J. S.
1956    The Peyote Religion.  Glencoe:  Free
        Press.

Spicer, Edward
1954    Potam, a Yaqui Village in Sonora.
        American Anthropological Association,
        Memoir No. 77.

Voget, Fred W.
    1948a   Individual Motivation in the Diffusion
            of the Wind River Shoshone Sundance to
            the Crow Indians.  American Anthropolo-
            gist 50:634-646.

    1948b   The Diffusion of the Wind River Sho-
            shone Sun Dance to the Crow Indians
            of Montana.  Ph.D. thesis, Yale
            University.

    1950    A Shoshone Innovator.  American Anthro-
            pologist 52:53-63.

    1956    The American Indian in Transition:
            Reformation and Accommodation.
            American Anthropologist 58:249-263.

    1963    Cultural Change.  In:  B. J. Siegel,
            ed.  Biennial Review of Anthropology,
            228-275.  Stanford:  Stanford Univer-
            sity Press.

    1964    Warfare and the Integration of Crow
            Indian Culture.  In:  W. Goodenough,
            ed.  Explorations in Cultural Anthro-
            pology, 483-509.  New York:  McGraw-
            Hill.

    1975    A History of Ethnology.  New York:
            Holt, Rinehart and Winston.

    n.d.    Caughnawaga Field Notes.

    n.d.    Crow Field Notes.

Wallace, A. F. C.
    1956    Revitalization Movements.  American
            Anthropologist 58:264-281.

    1970    The Death and Rebirth of the Seneca.
            New York:  Knopf.

Wilson, G. and M. Wilson
    1968    The Analysis of Social Change Based
            on Observations in Central Africa.
            Cambridge:  Cambridge University Press.
            (orig., 1945)

CHAPTER 8

Inuit and Cree Adaptation to Northern Colonialism[1]

W. K. Barger, Indiana  -  Purdue University
at Indianapolis

Western culture has had a different impact on the
Indian and Inuit (Eskimo) peoples of the Far North
than among the Native inhabitants of the United
States and southern Canada.  Until the 1950s, the
presence of Euroamerican society was limited primarily to exploration, trade, missionary activities,
and pockets of mineral exploitation.  The few whites
in the North remained in isolated posts, adopted many
of the Native ways, and largely acted as middle men
in the exchange of furs for Western goods.  The fur
trade, and the mission activities which followed,
stimulated a number of changes in the economic and
social fiber of Native cultures, but the Indians and
Inuit still maintained a large degree of independence
and self-sufficiency.

Following World War II a new wave of Euroamerican influence swept the North.  Military radar bases were
established, and exploration of the area intensified
to discover natural resources.  In Canada and the
United States, an increased sense of social responsibility gave rise to bureaucratic agencies which administered developmental programs.  For the first
time, large numbers of Euroamericans appeared in
northern settlements; these whites came in a dominant social, political, and economic role.  Native
peoples were drawn into new towns and became involved
in a wage-labor and expanded market economy, Western
education, bureaucratic administration, and other
institutions of the national societies.  Recent developments have stimulated many changes in the traditional cultures of the northern Indians and Inuit.
New constraints and new opportunities have impinged
upon their independence and guided their alternatives
in the modern world.

Some researchers have seen the northern Natives as
doomed for extinction (Jeness 1928); others have
predicted they are becoming a subordinate caste in
the national societies (Graburn 1969:218-232, Ferguson 1971, and Vallee 1971).  In another view the

189

FIGURE 1: EASTERN CANADA

190

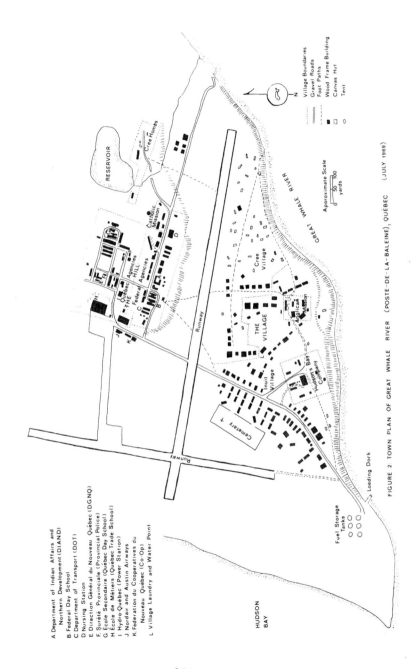

A Department of Indian Affairs and
   Northern Development (DIAND)
B Federal Day School
C Department of Transport (DOT)
D Nursing Station
E Direction Général du Nouveau Québec (DGNQ)
F Sureté Provinciale (Provincial Police)
G École Secondaire (Québec Day School)
H École de Métiers (Québec Trade School)
I Hydro Québec (Power Station)
J Nordair and Austin Airways
K Federation du Coopératives du
   Nouveau Québec (Co-Op)
L Village Laundry and Water Point

Village Boundaries
Gravel Roads
Foot Paths
Wood Frame Building
Canvas Hut
Tent

Approximate Scale

0   50   100
        yards

FIGURE 2 TOWN PLAN OF GREAT WHALE RIVER (POSTE-DE-LA-BALEINE), QUÉBEC    (JULY 1969)

191

Inuit and Indians of the North are adapting: while
at a disadvantage in relations with the dominant
whites, they maintain a positive ethnic identity and
develop a viable role in the national society (Barger
1976, 1977, and n.d., and J. Honigmann and I. Honigmann 1965 and 1970). This report will explore the
fate of the Native inhabitants in the Far North in
terms of two issues: the nature of internal colonialism which Euroamericans have imposed, and the
adaptations of the Native peoples to this new system.
These issues will be examined primarily among the
Inuit and the Cree Indians of Great Whale River,
Québec.

This colonialism involves domination of the Native
majority in the Far North by a foreign, immigrant
minority, the Euroamericans (Lieberson 1961, Brody
1975, and Cardinal 1969). This system differs from
classical colonialism by occurring within the national
boundaries of the dominant society. Otherwise, it
is much the same in social, political, and economic
structure. The whites enjoy the highest status in a
stratified social system. They also possess the power
and authority to impose their will in policies and
administration. As a result, the dominant society
receives the greatest economic benefits.

Many whites in the North demonstrate sincerity, dedication, and a sense of service in their relations
with the Native peoples. Some have actively contributed to the adaptation of the Indians and Inuit,
particularly teachers and missionaries who have been
more closely associated with the Inuit and Indians.
Other whites, including administrators and foremen,
are at times relaxed and flexible in dealings with
Natives, as when a worker wishes to be absent from
his job to go hunting. But these individuals, along
with those more overtly prejudiced, are often constrained by the colonial system, which directs affairs in the North in terms of goals of the dominant
society. This colonialism is evident in many set-
tings across the North and is well illustrated in
the case of Great Whale River.


COLONIALISM IN GREAT WHALE RIVER

Great Whale River is a small town in Nordic Québec
located on the southeastern shore of the Hudson Bay.

In 1971, some 550 Inuit, 350 Cree Indians, and 125
English and French Canadians resided in Great Whale.
The settlement lies on the border of the Arctic sea
and tundra environment and the inland Subarctic taiga
and riverine environment.  In aboriginal times, the
Inuit were oriented toward a subsistence in the Arctic setting while the Crees subsisted in the Subarctic zone.

Though Europeans sporadically appeared in Nordic
Québec since Hudson's voyage in 1610 (Cooke 1964),
the fur trade was not fully initiated in the region
until 1732 when the Hudson's Bay Company opened a
trading post at Richmond Gulf.  Posts were later
operated at Little Whale River and other sites.  In
1857, a permanent post was built at Great Whale River,
and the fur trade became firmly established in the
region.  Angelican missionaries soon followed, and
by 1900 most Crees and Inuit had been converted to
Christianity.[2]

In 1955, the construction of a radar control base
for the Mid-Canada Line introduced a new era of change
at Great Whale (Barger 1976, 1977; Barger and Earl
1971; and J. Honigmann 1972 and 1975).  Inuit and
Crees migrated to Great Whale to work on construction
and maintenance jobs.  The federal government established agencies to administer housing, educational,
health, and other programs to the Native peoples.  In
1964, the provincial government initiated administrative and service agencies in Great Whale.  Its presence has been increasing steadily in recent years.
When military operations ceased in 1968, Great Whale
became a federal and provincial administrative center for the western half of Nordic Québec.[3]

New influences were introduced to the Inuit and Crees
with the development of a modern Northern town.  These
changes included congregated settlement patterns,
permanent housing, subsistence based on wage labor
and expanded market exchange, community services such
as education and health care, and a national political
system.  There were several variations to a Western
model of modern community life, including geographic
isolation, limited communication with the larger national society and with other northern settlements,
the absence of a viable means of economic production
at the local level, and a nonrepresentative local administration.  Several special features also distinguished Great Whale:  two native ethnic groups were

present; and the Eurocanadians, a migrant minority, were socially, politically, and economically dominant over the Inuit and Crees.

In 1971, social domination was clearly evident in the social structure of Great Whale. The Eurocanadians formed an upper white class, and the Inuit and Crees a lower Native class. Substrata divided each class. Among the whites, the white collar, administrative workers enjoyed more prestige than the blue collar technicians. The English Canadians, mostly federal employees, and the French Canadians, mostly provincial employees, maintained more social ties within their own group. Within the Native strata the Inuit enjoyed greater socioeconomic status than the Crees. The three main ethnic groups each resided in segregated neighborhoods. The Eurocanadians were concentrated on "the Hill," the old base area, while the Inuit and Crees lived in separate sections of "the Village," the old post site by the river shown in the map.

Political domination is clearly evident in Great Whale. Administration of Native affairs is controlled by Eurocanadians. Policies concerning housing, job training, education, health, welfare, and political and legal affairs are made in the higher levels of Canadian bureaucracy and are implemented on the local level by Eurocanadians. Administrators are primarily responsive to higher officials who appointed them. Decisions are mostly made without the contribution of Native peoples. In fact, consultation with the Inuit and Crees generally takes place only after policies have been made, and the emphasis is on how decisions can best be implemented rather than formulated.

The Eurocanadian judicial system was also imposed on the Inuit and Crees. In trials of Native defendants in 1970, court officials often stated, "There is one law for all Canadians, whether they be white, Eskimo, or Indian." These laws, however, reflect Eurocanadian norms alien to the Native people; they do not acknowledge that Inuit and Crees have their own norms. The Inuit and Cree councils possess very little legal power, though they do command some moral authority within their communities.

The Eurocanadians in Great Whale also enjoy far greater economic benefits than the Native peoples.

The highest-paying, highest-prestige, and supervisory positions are all held by whites. In some cases whites were brought North to perform jobs local natives are qualified to do, such as operating heavy equipment. Those Inuit and Cree who were employed are in lower-skill and lower-paying positions, like carpentry and temporary construction. The Eurocanadians in Great Whale also enjoy a noticeably higher standard of living. They are provided with modern housing and furniture, electricity, plumbing and other conveniences. Government programs provide the Inuit and some Crees with housing which is far better than in traditional times, but living conditions are still inferior to the whites.

The colonial system in Great Whale is likewise evident in interethnic relations. Social activities are segregated along ethnic lines. The Great Whale Community Association limits its membership to Eurocanadians. This organization operates a bar and holds seasonal parties on a segregated basis, even though they are in government buildings. The Inuit and Crees hold movies and dances in the Village; few whites attend these events. Visiting and other interpersonal activities also occur mostly within ethnic groups. On a personal level the Eurocanadians in Great Whale largely see themselves as representatives of a more "advanced" way of life. With their own culture as the standard, they judge the Inuit and Crees as "progressive" or "backward." At the same time, they also hold a romanticized view of traditional Native life, as "simple" and free from the worries of modern civilization. The Inuit and Cree, for their part, show deference toward the whites, and they also display respect for the technological accomplishments and large-scale organization of the national society. Otherwise, both peoples exhibit ultimate faith in their own ways.

One important aspect of interethnic relations in Great Whale is that whites generally favor Inuit over Cree. This discrimination was influenced by several structural and behavioral factors. Historically, separate federal agencies administered the Inuit and Crees. The Department of Northern Affairs (D.N.A.) was responsible for the Inuit, and an agency was located in Great Whale. The Indian Affairs Bureau (I.A.B.) handled administration of the Crees, but the nearest agency was in Fort George, some 150 miles south.  Thus government programs in housing, job training, and other areas were readily available to the Great Whale Inuit while few benefits seemed to filter up to the Crees.  Even when D.N.A. and I.A.B. were reorganized into the Department of Indian Affairs and Northern Development (D.I.A.N.D.), separate administrative arrangements were maintained, a system which the Crees preferred.  In 1971, a new program promised to provide the Great Whale Crees with better housing conditions, but they generally received far fewer benefits than the Inuit.  It should be noted that the provincial Direction Général du Nouveau Québec (D.G.N.Q.) also favored the Inuit over the Crees, particularly in the area of employment and community services.

On a behavioral level, the Eurocanadians also discriminate more against the Crees.  While the whites see both Native groups as somewhat "primitive," they polarize the Inuit and Crees in terms of their own values and standards.  Some whites, for example, speak of the Inuit as more "progressive" and the Crees as more "backward."  As evidence, they point out differences in housing, job performance, continued education, and other signs reflecting middle-class Eurocanadian norms.  In many ways, however, these views are a self-fulfilling prophesy, related to Eurocanadian structural discrimination.  The Eurocanadians also interpret many aspects of Inuit and Cree behavior in terms of their own norms.  For example the ready smiles of the Inuit and their diligence in performing tasks are seen as "friendly" and "industrious," while Cree reticence and norms of economic equality are seen as "unfriendly" and "unambitious."  Two exceptions to these patterns of discrimination are worth noting:  the French Canadians display more romantic views of the Crees than the English; they are more prone to interpet Cree reticence, for example, as "stoic."  Also, sincere friendships are generally not observed between whites and Inuit, though relations as a whole between the two groups are more friendly and cordial.

In summary, the Great Whale case clearly illustrates the system of internal colonialism in the Canadian North.  The Eurocanadian minority dominates the Native majority socially, politically, and economically. The Inuit and Crees, however, respond to this colonialistic system with initiative and innovation by making functional changes in their social structures and world views.

INUIT AND CREE POLITICAL ADAPTATION

In traditional times, the hunting camp was the main Inuit social unit. Five or six related families were led by a headman. Leadership was informal and achieved (See Hoigmann 1960 and 1962; Balikei 1959 and 1964; Graburn 1969; and Wilmott 1960). The headman's influence was based on his proven hunting abilities, experience, wisdom, moral behavior, and kinship ties. Graburn (1969:56-61) notes that the Inuit have no word for "obey." They use a term meaning "follow," and their word for leader means "thinker." This small, flexible structure was well adapted to a hunting and/or trapping subsistence where survival required dispersal and mobility. It should be noted that the Inuit were relatively independent during the fur-trade period, largely managing their own affairs.

After the town emerged at Great Whale in the mid-1950s, significant changes occurred in the Inuit social structure. New events influenced Inuit social organization as early as 1957. Leadership was still invested in the headmen of the different camp groups that migrated to Great Whale, and no one person exercised wide influence. The role of Eurocanadians noticeably increased, however. The Northern Service Officer, who acted as employment agent and managed relief payments, attempted to create an Eskimo Community Advisory Council. The stated goal was eventual self-government, but Balikci (1959) notes that the real functions of the new council were to facilitate communication between the agent and the Inuit community. This arrangement largely benefitted whites because the agent retained full authority. The system was imposed by outside authorities; it denied the Inuit any real voice in administration. It also ignored important features of Inuit social structure. As a result, few real political developments were achieved.

By the early 1970s, however, considerable changes in Inuit social organization were occurring. The traditional kinship and camp affiliations were still present, but they had merged into a larger, cohesive community system. Developments were particularly

197

evident in social structure and political views. Changes in political organization occurred on both local and regional levels. In Great Whale, leadership remained based on achievement, but the criteria shifted from land-oriented skills to town-oriented abilities. Most members of the Eskimo Community Council, for instance, were men who held technically-skilled jobs and had a relatively secure standard of living. During elections in 1970, several Inuit stated they preferred men able to deal with government authorities and speaking English.

The Council, itself, had become a viable force in community affairs. It called public meetings to discuss social problems, such as drinking and a growing generation gap. It also passed several "rules" to manage such problems, including a curfew for younger people and speed limits for snowmobiles. It organized community events such as movies and holiday festivals, and it appointed a "policeman" to oversee these events. The Council had little official power, but it exercised moral authority in community affairs. The local Inuit generally abided by its decisions. The Council actively represented the local Inuit in external affairs. Leaders called meetings with government officials at all levels and assertively presented Inuit views and positions. In one meeting, for example, a leader asked for Inuit teachers in the school to ensure the children did not forget their language and traditional ways.

The Great Wale Inuit also engaged in regional Native affairs. Leaders regularly attended meetings of Inuit councilors from northern Québec settlements. In 1970, almost all adults joined the Québec Indians Association; several years after I left Great Whale, I was told they had switched to join the newly-formed Northern Québec Inuit Association. In 1971, leaders participated in the formation of the national Inuit Tapirisat or Eskimo Brotherhood.

Another new order of development involved political views. Traditional concepts were not concerned with a role in the national society, but by 1971 the Inuit had formed clear positions on aboriginal rights related to three main political issues: self-determination, claims to the land, and preservation of their ethnic heritage.

The Great Whale Inuit consistently expressed a desire to run their own affairs, and they resented their lack of voice in policies directly affecting them. In a meeting with high government officials Inuit leaders stated:

> We don't want to be told either by Québec or the Ottawa Government [what to do]. We have to say first what we think.... Our aim, living in our own territory, is to more and more control our own affairs, and to choose who we want to assist us to manage our own affairs.... If the government wants to change anything, they should consult us before making or proposing any changes. For a long time Eskimos have been on this land. Now they would like to be master of this land and govern it.

A key issue in self-determination is claims to land inhabited for generations. Inuit leaders made this clear:

> The first and main concern here is the land .... I'm merely saying that the Indian and Eskimo people in the North who live in this land should have deeds to their land.... Once we get the land, in time we will be able to manage it. Then we won't need an outside government. We ourselves, the people of this land, will run it the way we want.... Our land here is part of the country of Canada. Those groups [in Canada] who have title to their own land, they decide how it is to be run. Why shouldn't the Indians and Eskimos do the same in their own land?
>
> (Pointing to a map of Nordic Québec) The Eskimos and Indians are presently living there now. They would like to own this land, not by the White man, but free to run their own affairs.

A strong motivation in self-determination is concern for aboriginal hunting rights and preservation of culture and language.

> Church people and government people keep

reminding us we should not lose our customs,
and this we understand very well. We understand that the Eskimos can only keep their
culture if they are the ones who run the
land.... I visited Indians in the south....
They lost their own customs and language.
We don't want this to happen here. One of
the ways to prevent this is to make sure we
are bosses in our land.

In forming these views, the Inuit incorporate a number of ideas contributed by several concerned outsiders, including missionaries, teachers, government
workers, and regional Native leaders. Regardless of
the origin of these ideas, the Inuit see them as
relevant and incorporate the concepts as their own;
they are expressed as Inuit views.

In summary, the Inuit of Great Whale achieved significant developments in their social structure and
political views. These changes were a response to
the colonialistic system which had been imposed upon
them. The developments are remarkable given that
Inuit leaders were all raised in hunting camps. The
Great Whale Inuit desire to be full citizens of the
national society; but they seek to achieve this along
with the maintenance of their special status and
unique heritage, as Inuit.

Traditional social organization among the Crees focused on family and lineage units (Honigmann 1962,
1964). Leadership was based on age and sex. Lineage
elders, particularly older men, had the greatest
authority; others could gain influence through demonstrated abilities, moral behavior, wisdom, and generosity. The process of consensus governed group decisions. An issue was discussed informally until a
position was reached agreeable to everyone. When
individuals disagreed, they generally abstained in
order to preserve social harmony. Traditional Cree
social structure was well adapted for small, mobile
groups where subsistence was often marginal. Band
chiefs were primarily traditional leaders, functioning more as group spokesmen. In 1964, however, this
leadership structure began to alter under pressure
from the local Indian agent and the missionary (Robbins 1967). In this year, two elections of the band
council were held. In the first, the Crees sat in a
circle and discussed candidates; after several hours

a chief was agreed upon without a formal vote. This consensus process placed a traditional leader in the role of chief. However, dissatisfaction with this choice led the Indian agent to void the decision. In a second election, the Indian agent presided. People were seated in rows facing the front, and parliamentary procedures were followed including formal nominations and a secret ballot. This election produced another chief whose role was defined as an intermediary between the Crees and government authorities and as a higher moral figure within the Cree community. The little information available on this new type of chiefs indicates they functioned as traditional leaders but with conflicting demands. They were apparently expected to meet advisory, achieved standards within the Cree community and to be assertive in dealings with government agencies.

By the early 1970s, important changes in Cree social organization were emerging. Traditional kinship ties remained important, but as among the Inuit, new developments were evident in social structure and political views.

Changes in political organization were observed on local and regional levels. In Great Whale, a new dual structure of leadership solidified in 1970 with elections for the Cree Band Council. Within the Cree community, traditional patterns persisted; lineage elders and the consensus process still influenced group positions. A new type of leadership emerged, however, to represent the community in external affairs. Young men who had reputations for being assertive in dealings with whites were elected to the council. These new leaders were expected to demonstrate some traditional behavior such as generosity, but other criteria included knowledge of English and even aggressiveness with Eurocanadian officials. While the Cree community as a whole tended to insulate itself from the whites, the young leaders actively and assertively presented group goals to government authorities. This new dual structure was an innovative approach both to preserve traditional norms and to meet more effectively white domination.

The Great Whale Crees also were active in regional Native affairs. In 1970, almost all adults joined the Québec Indians Association, and leaders regularly attended meetings of this organization. They later joined the Grand Council of the Crees of Québec when the Québec Indians Association was reorganized. Another new order of development involved political views. As among the Inuit, large-scale political concepts were limited, but by 1971 the Crees expressed clear positions on self-determination, claims to the land, and preservation of their ethnic heritage. Additionally, they voiced concerns about socioeconomic development. They likewise pressed for a goal of determining their own fate, rejecting policies made without their consent. Cree leaders, for example, told high government officials:

> The Eskimos and Indians who were here before [the whites] should not be ordered around.
>
> I think the Indians and Eskimos should be their own government, and their chiefs and counselors should be responsible for considering what is important. We will decide what we want to do. If any proposals originate from the government, we do not have to submit to it.

Again, ownership of their traditional homeland was seen as a key in this self-determination:

> We want titles to our land.... Who is responsible that we can't get the right to build our houses where we please? We were here first.
>
> By existing legal agreements, the land belongs to the Indians and Eskimos. But the White man does what he wants on the land. If an Indian or Eskimo went down south and tried to pitch his tent or house on land belonging to the White man by legal title, he would have to get permission and pay for it. This should also happen in this land with Indian and Eskimo land.

A major motivation to achieve self-determination was preservation of aboriginal hunting rights and Native culture and language:

> We have been down south, and seen where [Indians] don't have rights.... The chief

of that reserve says all rights to hunt have
been taken away. We still have these rights,
but if they are taken away people would
starve.

We don't want to follow the example [of
Indians in southern Québec].... They got
assistance, but lost much, including hunting rights.... Those people in that reserve no longer speak their language. I
am afraid of that for here too.

Another issue was a demand for more government support in economic and social development. The Crees
resented the greater benefits received by the Inuit
and strongly expressed their desire for better housing, jobs, educational opportunities, and community
services.

Several concerned outsiders had actively contributed
to Cree views, including regional Indian leaders,
missionaries, teachers, and government workers. Regardless of the origin of these ideas, however, the
Crees synthesized the concepts with their own, and
the views expressed were truly Cree in nature.

In summary, the Great Whale Crees made significant
alterations in their social structure and political
views in response to the colonial system imposed upon
them. These achievements were largely made by leaders
raised in hunting camps. Though they desired many of
the benefits of the larger national society, they were
willing to participate in it only to the extent that
they could maintain their unique status and heritage
as Crees.


INUIT AND CREE POLITICAL COOPERATION

The Great Whale Inuit and Crees each responded to
the system of northern colonialism in somewhat different manners. This divergence can be traced to
variations in ethnic norms and to different socioeconomic conditions. Still, both groups shared a
common "Native" status in the town and were subject
to the same domination by Eurocanadian society.
Thus, the Inuit and Crees found that their separate
concerns overlapped. In these circumstances, they
frequently cooperated to achieve common goals.

Political cooperation most often occurred when both
peoples opposed particular government policies.  On
these occasions, both Inuit and Crees elected to
meet jointly with government officials.  Leaders
referred to both groups in stating their political
positions.  At these meetings, the Inuit and Crees
presented their individual goals, but they both emphasized that they stood together on common issues.
The Inuit and Crees worked to establish greater independence for Natives, a status they both shared.
A completely unified stance between the Inuit and
Crees is not likely to occur.  Each people has a
unique ethnic identity which they wish to preserve.
Each also has its own set of needs and goals.  But
the Inuit and Crees also have common positions on
some issues and have shown they can unite to achieve
them.


A CASE ISSUE:  THE ROAD TO NATIVE POLITICAL AUTONOMY

From 1964 to 1976, a series of events related to native autonomy occurred in northern Québec.  Three of
the events illustrate both internal colonialism and
Native political adaptation.  The first involved a
move to transfer administration of the Inuit and
Crees to provincial authorities.  Historically, the
federal government had administered Native affairs,
an arrangement which Québec preferred (Richardson
1972:58-59).  But in 1964, the federal and provincial
governments agreed to transfer this responsibility to
Québec.  The facilities and equipment of the old radar base at Great Whale were subsequently turned over
to D.G.N.Q., which began providing all town services.
In 1969, the federal D.I.A.N.D. issued a white paper
which outlined a termination policy for the Native
peoples of Canada who would become "normal" citizens
of the provinces like other Canadians.  Québec responded positively to this new policy, and the two
governments worked out a five-year transfer plan which
would become a model for termination.  In line with
these agreements, most federal personnel assigned to
Nordic Québec after 1969 were French Canadians.

The Inuit and Crees strongly objected to these moves.
In a series of meetings, they clarified their position
saying they preferred federal administration over
Québec.  They resented the unilateral manner in which
the policies were made and implementation begun.

Both the Inuit and Crees pointed out no provisions were made regarding their claims to the land.[4] They believed Québec was far more interested in the rich natural resources than in Native welfare. They feared cultural extinction, a fate they had observed among Indians in southern Québec, and they were concerned about the lack of guarantees should Québec secede from Canada. This issue stimulated many of the political developments among the Inuit and Crees. Both peoples formulated clear views of their political positions and began organizing on a regional level.

The federal and provincial governments did not directly respond to the Native positions. In a January 1970 letter to the Inuit councils of northern Québec, the ministers of D.I.A.N.D. and D.G.N.Q. stated: "We propose to make some changes.... We need your help in bringing about these changes, and we want to get your views on how they should be carried out." Consultation with the Native peoples focused only on how the policies could best be implemented, not what the policies should be. In a series of meetings, high government officials answered the issue of self-determination by saying: "If the Indians and Eskimos after getting the necessary knowledge can administer their own affairs, I feel that both Québec and Ottawa would be happy to allow them to do this." Eurocanadian authorities saw self-determination as something they reserved for themselves to determine when the Natives were "ready." Regarding land claims, in 1969 the Minister of D.I.A.N.D. told the Great Whale Inuit and Cree councils: "You talk about the land. All land in [northern] Québec is owned by the provincial government." Other officials stated a year later: "No matter how much you want [it]..., it is very difficult to get control of this land." And: "[We] cannot give you an answer about the land.... If [you] want to put together [your] proposal, that's fine. But [until you take official action] we can't settle that." Québec claimed the land with the federal government supporting the claim. They both indicated that Native positions were invalid because they had taken no official [legal] action to substantiate their claims.

Another event in the push for autonomy was a surprise move by Inuit councillors from northern Québec settlements in 1971. At a meeting on the transfer issue, they stated their intention to form a Native regional

government as part of the provincial structure; the
Crees could join this government if they wished.
The Inuit chairman later reported that this idea was
originally suggested by a trusted government worker
who had long experience in the North and who spoke
fluent Inuttitut (Eskimo). Following the meeting,
the Inuit leaders sent a letter to the Minister of
D.I.A.N.D. This letter was drafted in French by
government officials and stated: "The Eskimos of
Québec are studying the possibility of forming a
regional government structure, and believe it necessary that their point of view be taken into consideration."[5] In this letter, the meaning of "intend" in
Inuttitut was altered to "are considering;" the Inuit
did not read French, and it was not learned if they
realized or approved of this change in meaning.
Government authorities responded by saying they
would study the matter, but as far as is known no
concrete action was taken by either federal or provincial officials. The Inuit move, however, reflected considerable political initiative.

Another event influencing Native political autonomy
was the James Bay hydroelectric project (Richardson
1976, Québec 1976). In 1971, Québec announced the
formation of a provincial corporation to dam the
rivers of James Bay, including Great Whale River,
to provide hydroelectric power for southern Canada
and New York State. This massive project was clearly
designed to benefit the mainstream Eurocanadian society; little consideration was noted for the Native
peoples whose homeland would be partially flooded
and disrupted by an influx of whites. The policy
was conceived and implementation begun without
prior consultation with the Crees or Inuit.

This project solidified Native political developments
which had already begun. The Crees and Inuit rallied
behind this issue and formed regional Native associations, the Grand Council of the Crees of Québec and
the Northern Québec Inuit Association. They took
their case to the courts with the help of federal
grants. They specified preconditions; before they
would discuss the James Bay project, they wanted
their aboriginal rights and claims to the land clarified. In 1973, after five months deliberation, the
court issued an injunction to stop all development
activities and to cease interference with Native
rights. Provincial authorities appealed this decision.

A week later, the Québec Court of Appeals set aside the injunction after five hours' deliberation. In making this judgment, the justices stated Native rights were irrelevant to "the general and public interest of the people of Québec which is opposed to the interests of about 2,000 of its inhabitants" (Richardson 1976:301).

The Natives carried the issue to the Supreme Court of Canada, but three new events intervened at this time. First, Québec made an offer to settle the dispute, and second, the federal government threatened to withdraw its financial support which enabled the Natives to pursue their case. The third event was a further decision by the Québec Court of Appeals, ruling that James Bay was not Native land but a "frontier;" that is, Eurocanadians far outnumbered the Natives, and the Natives themselves were too much acculturated to be considered as aboriginal inhabitants. The court also ruled that the royal charter giving Rupert's Land to the Hudson's Bay Company never guaranteed aboriginal title to the land.

Under increasing pressure, the Crees and Inuit negotiated a settlement in 1975, and this agreement was ratified in 1976 (Québec 1976). They gave up all claims to the bulk of the territory in northern Québec. In return, they are to receive: $225,000,000 over a twenty-year period; exclusive rights of use and occupancy in limited areas around settlements and traditional campsites; and aboriginal rights of use but not occupancy in traditional hunting and trapping areas. Native hunters and trappers will be guaranteed a minimum income to enable them to pursue traditional activities. In addition, local and regional Native corporations will be established.[6] Elected councils will have the power to make ordinances, impose fines, levy taxes, and issue licenses. They will be responsible for community planning and services, education and justice, and they will review the environmental and social impact of development projects.

This agreement has not yet been fully implemented, and many questions remain about the autonomy of the Crees and Inuit of northern Québec. Yet two aspects of the settlement are clear. First, the Eurocanadians have gained many political and economic benefits for an apparently nominal cost. Second, the Inuit and

Crees have shown initiative and innovation in pursuing their goals. They have achieved significant results in establishing self-determination and political autonomy although it remains to be seen what viable role they will attain in the national society.

## THE POLITICAL FUTURE OF THE INUIT AND CREES

Three principles are evident in the political adaptation of the Great Whale Inuit and Crees. First, both peoples seek to maintain their group autonomy. They consistently act as if they are independent and self-directing. Even though they possess little official power, they assume the initiative and moral authority and then show innovation in confronting the dominant society. The second principle is that the Inuit and Crees expand their world views to include political goals relevant to their new circumstances. For example, issues are stated in terms forcing government officials to respond, and Native positions are taken up in the courts. The third principle is that both the Inuit and Crees organize politically on local, regional, and national levels. Their positions on the James Bay issue, for instance, were represented by Native associations, and this move had great impact on the Eurocanadian political institutions. Judging from the Great Whale case, political adaptation involves a process of syncretism; that is, traditional ways are synthesized with new views and structures to form a new system (Barnett 1953:54-56). But this new ethnic system is still unique. The Inuit are still Inuit and the Crees are still Cree in heritage.

The future of the Inuit and Crees as Canadian Natives remains open. They have achieved some of their political goals, though it remains to be seen how these will be implemented. It is certain they will face new issues in time. Yet they have shown the initiative and independence to work out their own viable role in the national society. With this sense of responsibility for their own fate their future holds much promise.

# FOOTNOTES

1. This report is largely based on field research in Great Whale River, Québec, from 1969 to 1971. I wish to thank John J. Honigmann for the opportunity to conduct research in Great Whale during the summers of 1969 and 1970, and for his personal support and encouragement. My appreciation is also extended to the Wenner-Gren Foundation for Anthropological Research and to the National Institute of Mental Health for their support of field work from 1970 to 1971. I particularly wish to express my gratitude to the Inuit, Cree, and Eurocanadian people of Great Whale who shared their lives with me and taught me much about life in the process.

2. For reports dealing with the Inuit and Crees of Great Whale and areas during the fur-trade period, see: Cooke 1964; Garigue 1957; I. Honigmann and J. Honigmann 1953; J. Honigmann 1951, 1952, 1960, 1962, and 1964; J. and I. Honigmann 1959; Lips 1947; March 1964; Rogers 1964a, 1964b, 1965, and 1969; and Speck 1931.

3. For reports dealing with Great Whale and adjacent areas during the town period, see: Arbess 1966; Balikci 1959, 1961, and 1964; Barger 1976, 1977; Barger and Earl 1971; Chance 1968; Chance and Trudeau 1963; Dryfoos 1970; Graburn 1969; Hall 1973; J. Honigmann 1972 and 1975; Johnson 1962; Vallee 1964 and 1967; and Willmott 1960 and 1961.

4. The land issue is complicated, but some argue the Inuit and Crees have a legal claim (Richardson 1972:49-84). These claims are based on a royal proclamation of 1763 and the Act of 1912 whereby the District of Ungava became part of Québec. The Act of 1912 stipulated Québec was to negotiate with the Native peoples of the area to settle land and aboriginal rights, but negotiation never occurred. (See Québec 1976:xiii-xiv).

5. My translation. The original reads: "Les Esquimaux du Québec étudient la possibilité de

mettre sur pied une structure regionale de government et croient nécessaire que leur point de vue
soit pris en considération."


6.  The Great Whale Inuit and Crees are to be
separately incorporated, though they will jointly
administer some lands.

REFERENCES CITED

Arbess, Saul E.
1966    Social Change and the Eskimo Co-Operative
        at George River, Québec. Ottawa: North-
        ern Co-ordination and Research Center.

Balikci, Asen
1959    Two Attempts at Community Organization
        among the Eastern Hudson Bay Eskimos.
        Anthropologica 1:122-135.

1961    Relations Inter-éthniques à la Grande
        Rivière de la Baleine, Baie d'Hudson,
        1957. National Museum of Canada Bulletin
        No. 194.

1964    The Eskimos of the Québec-Laborador
        Peninsula. In, Jean Malaurie and Jacques
        Rousseau (eds.), Le Nouveau-Québec.
        Paris: Mouton.

Barger, W. K.
1976    Adaptation to Town Life in the Canadian
        North: A Cross-Cultural Model. Paper
        presented at the Meeting of the American
        Anthropological Association, Washington,
        D.C.

1977    Culture Change and Psychosocial Adjust-
        ment. American Ethnologist 4:471-496.

n.d.    Great Whale River (Post-de-laBaleine):
        From Trading Post to Town. In, William
        C. Sturtevant (series editor) and June
        Helm (Volume editor), Handbook of North
        American Indians, Vol. VI: The Subarctic.
        Washington: Smithsonian Institution.
        In Press.

Barger, W. K., and Daphne Earl
1971    Differential Adaptation to Northern
        Town Life by the Eskimos and Indians of
        Great Whale River. Human Organization
        30:25-30.

Barnett, H. G.
1953    Innovation: The Basis of Cultural
        Change. New York: McGraw-Hill.

211

Brody, Hugh
    1975    The People's Land.  Markham, Ontario:
            Penquin Books.

Cardinal, Harold
    1969    The Unjust Society, Edmunton:  M. G.
            Hurtig.

Chance, Norman A.
    1968    Conflict in Culture.  Ottawa:  Canadian
            Research Centre for Anthropology.

Chance, Norman A., and John Trudeau
    1963    Social Organization, Acculturation, and
            Integration Among the Eskimo and Cree.
            Anthropologica 5:47-56.

Cooke, Alan
    1964    The Exploration of New Québec.  In, Jean
            Malaurie and Jacques Rousseau (eds.),
            Le Nouveau-Québec.  Paris:  Mouton.

Dryfoos, Robert J., Jr.
    1970    Two Tactics for Ethnic Survival -
            Eskimo and Indian.  Trans-Action 7:51-54.

Ferguson, Jack
    1971    Eskimos in a Satellite Society.  In,
            Jean Leonard Elliott (ed.), Minority
            Canadians, Vol. I:  Native Peoples.
            Scarborough, Ontario:  Prentice-Hall.

Graburn, Nelson H. H.
    1969    Eskimos Without Igloos.  Boston: Little
            Brown.

Hall, Lawrence W., Jr.
    1973    Great Whale River Eskimo Youth.
            Anthropologica 15:3-19.

Honigmann, John J.
    1951    An Episode in the Administration of the
            Great Whale River Eskimo.  Human Organi-
            zation 10:2:5-14.

    1952    Intercultural Relations at Great Whale
            River.  American Anthropologist 54:510-
            522.

1960    The Great Whale River Eskimo: A Focussed Social System. Anthropological Papers of the University of Alaska 9:11-16.

1962    Social Networks in Great Whale River. National Museum of Canada Bulletin No. 178.

1964    Indians of Nouveau Québec. In, Jean Malaurie and Jacques Rousseau (eds.), Le Nouveau-Québec. Paris: Mouton.

1972    Social Disintegration in Five Northern Canadian Communities. Canadian Review of Sociology and Anthropology 2:199-214.

1975    Five Northern Towns. Anthropological Papers of the University of Alaska, 17:No. 1.

Honigmann, John J., and Irma Honigmann
1959    Notes on Great Whale River Ethos. Anthropologica 1:1-16.

1965    Eskimo Townsmen. Ottawa: Canadian Research Centre for Anthropology.

1970    Arctic Townsmen. Ottawa: Canadian Research Centre for Anthropology.

Jenness, Diamond
1928    The People of the Twilight. Chicago: University of Chicago Press.

Johnson, William D.
1962    An Exploratory Study of Ethnic Relations in Great Whale River. Ottawa: Northern Co-ordination and Research Council.

Lieberson, Stanley
1961    A Societal Theory of Race and Ethnic Relations. American Sociological Review 26:902-910.

Québec, Éditeur Officiel du
1976    The James Bay and Northern Québec Agreement. Québec: Québec National Library.

Richardson, Boyce
    1972    James Bay, S. F.: Sieria Club.

    1976    Strangers Devour the Land. New York:
            Alfred A. Knopf.

Robbins, Richard
    1967    The Two Chiefs: Changing Leadership
            Patterns Among the Great Whale River
            Cree. Paper read at the 7th Annual
            Meeting of the Northeastern Anthropologi-
            cal Association, Montreal.

Rogers, Edward S.
    1965    Leadership Among the Indians of Eastern
            Subarctic Canada. Anthropologica 7:
            2:263-284.

    1969    Band Organization Among the Indians of
            Eastern Subarctic Canada. National
            Museums of Canada Bulletin No. 228:
            21-55.

Vallee, Frank G.
    1964    Notes on the Cooperative Movement and
            Community Organization in the Canadian
            Arctic. Arctic Anthropology 2:45-49.

    1967    Pouvungnituk and its Cooperative: A
            Case Study in Community Change. Ottawa:
            Northern Co-ordination and Research
            Council.

    1971    Eskimos of Canada as a Minority Group.
            In, Jean Leonard Elliott (ed.),
            Minority Canadians, Vol. I: Native
            Peoples. Scarborough, Ontario:
            Prentice-Hall.

Willmott, William E.
    1960    The Flexibility of Eskimo Social
            Organization. Anthropologica 2:48-57.

    1961    The Eskimo Community at Port Harrison.
            Ottawa: Northern Co-ordination and
            Research Council.

CHAPTER 9

Indian Dependency and Indian Self-Determination:
Problems and Paradoxes in Canada's Northwest
Territories

June Helm, University of Iowa

FOREWORD

The body of this account was written in 1976, dealing
with events up to October of that year. To now cast
this essay into the past tense would vitiate the sense
of the imperative and continuing nature of the problems and issues that the Native peoples of the Northwest Territories face. Therefore, the text holds to
the temporal frame of the time of writing. The most
significant decisions and events subsequent to 1976
are reviewed briefly in a Postscript.


INTRODUCTION

On March 21, 1974, the Government of Canada by Order-
in-Council appointed a Commissioner to conduct an
inquiry into the social, environmental, and economic
impact of a proposed natural gas pipeline and energy
corridor to extend from the Arctic coast the length
of Mackenzie Valley to Southern Canada. In the
words of the Commissioner, Mr. Justice Berger:

> The influence of the gas pipeline in the
> development of a Mackenzie Valley Transpor-
> tation Corridor and in moulding the social,
> economic, and environmental future of the
> North will be enormous.... The Mackenzie
> Highway is already under construction and
> already reaches beyond the junction of the
> Liard and the Mackenzie at Fort Simpson.
> The [Government of Canada's] Pipeline Guide-
> lines [1972] envisage that, if a gas pipe-
> line is built, an oil pipeline may follow,
> and that the corridor may eventually in-
> clude a railroad, hydro-electric transmis-
> sion lines, and telecommunications facilities
> (Berger 1974:3-4).

In its human dimension, the impending impact involves
some 25,000-30,000 persons who live in the western
sector of Canada's Northwest Territories (NWT), an
area of about half a million square miles.  Of these
persons, about half are white.  Many of the whites
are short-term residents of the NWT, and most of them
(perhaps 80 percent) live in the three largest settlements of the NWT--Yellowknife (the Territorial capi-
tol), Inuvik, and Hay River.  It is, however, on the
other half of the population, the people of Native
heritage, that the brunt of "development" will fall.
For them, it is but the most recent of a set of circumstances imposed from the greater Eurocanadian
world that has massively eroded the self-sufficiency
of Native lifeways within a generation.

The Native population in the "impact region" is composed of three ethnic sectors:  the Inuit (Eskimo),
occupying a few settlements on or near the Arctic
Coast; the Dene, Athapaskan-speaking Indians of the
forested interior; and, also of the interior, the
Metis, the mixed-blood population that, in the NWT
as in the Prairie Provinces, bears a distinctive
cultural heritage and politico-ethnic identity.  Of
these sectors, the Dene are the most numerous in the
impact region--on the order of 6,700 as of 1971.[1]
Most of them live in small settlements of only a few
dozen or a few hundred souls in which they are the
ethnic majority (see map).

Dene, Inuit, and Metis have all experienced and together face the massive "social impact" of the recent
past and near future, and they are reacting to and
struggling with the consequences.  But since all my
research and almost all of my personal relationships
are with Dene, I limit the following account and
assessment to their experiences.


CONTACT HISTORY AND RELATIONS

The subarctic forest, muskeg, and transitional tundra
comprising the Dene peoples' traditional ranges offers no significant agricultural potential, so that
to the present day, contact history has not featured
the encroachment of white landholders.  Only after
World War II did an accelerating rate of immigration
of personnel in mineral extractive industries, small
business and, especially, government, initiate a

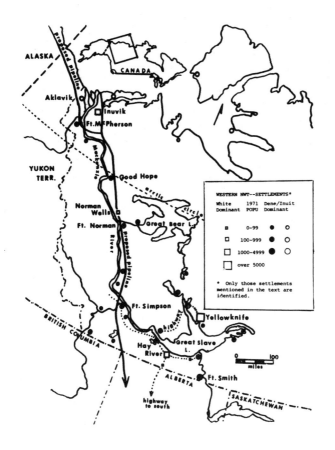

WESTERN NWT--SETTLEMENTS*

| White Dominant | 1971 POPU | Dene/Inuit Dominant |
|---|---|---|
| ▫ | 0-99 | ● ○ |
| ▢ | 100-999 | ● ○ |
| ▢ | 1000-4999 | ● ○ |
| ▢ | over 5000 | |

* Only those settlements mentioned in the text are identified.

ALASKA

CANADA

Aklavik

Inuvik

Ft.McPherson

YUKON TERR.

Good Hope

Norman Wells

Ft. Norman

Great Bear L.

Arctic

Circle

Mackenzie

River

proposed pipeline

Ft. Simpson

Yellowknife

BRITISH COLUMBIA

Hay River

Great Slave L.

highway

ALBERTA

Ft. Smith

highway to south

SASKATCHEWAN

0        100
miles

proposed pipeline

potential swamping by whites of the Native population.[2]

The fur trade was the impetus to white entry into the Mackenzie region in the last decades of the eighteenth century. The fur trade continued to dominate all other monetary enterprises in the NWT until the eve of World War II. In the mid-nineteenth century Roman Catholic and Anglican missionaries arrived and the nominal conversion of most Indians soon followed. In 1869 the Hudson's Bay Company surrendered its territorial rights over Rupert's Land, which includes the present-day NWT. In 1870, those rights were transferred to the new Dominion of Canada. This event carried no immediate consequences for the Native peoples. Only when, at two different periods, it appeared the land held economic potential for white enterprise other than the fur trade was the government concerned to formalize its relationship with the Indians of the NWT--specifically, to make treaties with the Natives along the length of the Mackenzie drainage.

The treaty of 1899 was triggered by the discovery of gold reserves in NWT and by the expectation that masses of gold rushers would pass through the area to the strikes in the Yukon Territory. This treaty, Number 8, included those Dene--Beaver, Chipewyan, Yellowknives, some Slave and Dogrib--who traded or hunted south of Great Slave Lake or along its southern shores. In 1921, Treaty Number 11 was concluded with the Dene groups--Dogrib, Slave, Hare (including Bearlake and Mountain Indians), and Loucheux (Eastern Kutchin)--north of Great Slave Lake, in the Mackenzie River region proper. An oil strike in the latitude of Great Bear Lake (at the site of the present Norman Wells) was the impetus for the governmental decision to establish treaty relations in 1921.

By the texts of both treaties "the said Indians do hereby cede, release, surrender and yield up to the Government ... forever all their rights, titles, privileges whatsoever to the lands...." In both treaties the assignment of band reserves (reservations) in recompense for the cession of Native lands --at the ratio of one square mile per family of five --was specified but never implemented, leaving the government with an outstanding treaty obligation to the Indians. Until World War II the main figures of

federal authority in the North were the few Royal
Canadian Mounted Police who, as the North West
Mounted Police, had established their first perman-
ent post in the NWT in 1903.

Long after Treaty, into the 1940s, governmental assumption of responsibility for the well-being of the
Indians of the NWT was negligible and indirect.  Many
winters brought hardship or famine.  Through the
offices of the Mounties and the Hudson's Bay Company
traders, the government funneled limited funds to
ameliorate extreme cases of destitution.  The Indians were continually prey to introduced diseases,
both epidemic, such as measles or influenza, and
endemic, such as tuberculosis.  Health services were
feeble and, noted a federal official, "provide a
rather seamy story" (Phillips 1967:221).  The Anglican and Roman Catholic churches established a few
hospitals but contested with one another, leaving
some regions completely unserved.  Both churches
resisted government efforts to set medical standards.
Education was also in the hands of the churches; few
children attended the residential schools.

Throughout the contact era, the Dene became ever more
committed to products of European technology:  firearms, ammunition, metal implements, manufactured
clothing and cloth.  However, as of 1940 most Indians
relied on the fish and game of the land for the more
nutritionally significant part of their diet.  Their
purchased comestibles were chiefly flour, lard, sugar
and tea.  They took enough furs to provide themselves
with a modicum of manufactured devices that had become necessities.  The men brought their furs to the
dozen or so trading post settlements, traded for supplies and equipment, and returned to their families
in the "bush" to pursue their livelihood.  In 1940,
the people were mostly monolingual (except for the
Loucheux) and illiterate; most died as they had lived,
largely apart from the presence of whites, and, except for the occupational interests of the trader
and the missionary, generally apart from white concern.

By the humanitarian standards of the twentieth century "liberal," these were a forgotten people in
great need of help while receiving almost none.
From this view, policy changes since World War II
bringing the government into active involvement in
the lives of the Natives of the North may be appraised

as rectifications of past neglect and inequities.

Steps toward minimally adequate health care began in the 1940s with annual tuberculosis X-rays and the establishment of the Charles Camsell Hospital in Edmonton, Alberta, for treating severe TB cases. Two all-Canadian citizen subsidy programs--first the Family Allowance (1944) and then the Old Age Security Pension (1951)--were important to Indian families in providing income for clothing and supplemental food for the children and the elderly, especially after the drop in fur prices during the 1950s. The late 1950s and the 1960s saw vigorous development of a government dayschool program, a housing program which replaced many log cabins with frame dwellings, electrification and oil-heating of many Indian homes, and expanded welfare and health services.

All of these programs combined to encourage or enforce retreat from "bush" life and subsistence; to sedentarize the populations in agglomerates at points-of-service where, as well, they are more effectively "administered"; increasingly to tie the Dene to a "micro-urban" (Smith 1978) lifeway and, for the young especially, to rising consumer expectations.

Beginning in 1967, another set of intermeshing demands and decisions imposed by government and by multinational economic interests exacerbated the stresses building upon and within the Native social body. In the late 1960s, the federal government began to transfer aspects of governance in the NWT from the federal to the territorial level. Congruent with this move was the new Indian policy enunciated in the 1969 Federal White Paper. It was to end the special status of "Indian" vis à vis the federal government and to shift the administration of most programs under Indian Affairs to territorial and provincial governments. This step was promptly assessed as a "termination policy" (Dunning 1969; Duran 1971). It was immediately and vigorously opposed by Indian groups across Canada, and the dissolution of "Indian Status" and of the departmental division of Indian Affairs--to have been completed within five years--has not been carried out.[3]

By 1970 the federal government had begun to fund the nascent national, provincial, and territorial Indian

Brotherhoods as the representative bodies to develop
positions and a data base toward negotiation of Indian "claims." Several young Indians founded the
Indian Brotherhood of the NWT in 1969-1970. To be
assured of government funding, membership was limited
to Treaty Indians. In the background of these political decisions and events affecting the Native peoples
of the NWT, explorations and plans for the development
of hydrocarbon and hydroelectric resources in the
Canadian North received vigorous government encouragement and financial support.


SOCIETAL AUTONOMY AND DEPENDENCY

In pre-contact times the ancestors of the Dene were
probably as independent of alien social and cultural
relations, pressures, and forces as it is possible
to conceive. They relied on no other peoples for
raw materials or items of technology; their world
contained no societal entities to establish dominance
or hegemony over any other. By this absolute standard
of sociocultural autonomy or independence, the Dene's
voluntary involvement in the fur trade marks the first
time in their history when they entered into what came
to be a needful relationship with another sociocultural system. It is this recognition which has led
Asch (1976:81) to say that "...the post-contact economic history of the [NWT Dene] region is dominated
by a single theme: the exchange on the part of native
people of immediate material well-being in return for
long-term economic dependency on external forces."
Certainly, the Dene were in a disadvantaged relationship in that, to advance their material well-being,
they needed the trade goods of the fur trader much
more than the trader's world needed their furs. But
the retreat from their former absolute sociocultural
independence was partial and circumscribed. The Dene
societal groups continued to manage their own affairs
and feed and otherwise provide for the physical well-
being of their members. No doubt the unquestioned
worth of European technology, plus the trader's assured and authoritative cultural arrogance "broke
trail" for the God-given authority assumed by the
missionary. The missionization-Christianization
process may have evoked more resistance, suspicion,
and concern than did the relationship with the fur
trader, but there is little record of it. Certainly
the signing of "Treaty" was carefully and anxiously

weighed by the Indian groups (Fumoleau 1975) who
understood it to be only a mutual pledge of peaceful
relations and a guarantee, rather than surrender, of
intrinsic rights to the land.

With the advantage of hindsight, these processual
relationships can be judged steps in the subjection
of the Dene to the economic, cultural-moral, and
political ascendency of the Eurocanadian system. But
that subjection to the Eurocanadian world was far from
overwhelming. By and large the people still followed
their chosen pursuits, certainly maintained their own
social order, and took care of their own. Only with
the increasing government services and assistance
that began in the 1940s were the Dene of the NWT
pushed and pulled into massive and direct economic
dependence upon and daily political-cultural domination by the national system exactly as they were being "aided" by it.

Twenty-five or even twenty years ago, one could rea-
sonably define the several Dene linguistic/regional/
in-marrying groups on the land as societies in that
they evinced the essentials of a "self-sufficient
structure of action" (Aberle et al 1950). True,
for several generations these little societies had
not been self-sufficient with respect to resources--
which here must be defined as the tools of production
necessary to their evolved hunting-trapping pursuits--
but, then, "to be considered a society, a group need
not be" (Aberle et al 1950:102). The fur trade had
induced a degree of accommodation and adjustment of
the self-sufficient structure of the Dene's relationship to each other and to the land; it had not pre-
empted that structure.

So also with the other pressure points from "Outside."
The Christian missionary exercised or proclaimed authority over aspects of spiritual and moral life, but
basic moral governance was firmly bedded in Native
society. Had the missionary, the Indian agent, the
policeman, the game warden, and the few other agents
of Eurocanadian institutions withdrawn from the land,
leaving only the fur trader, the Dene people would
likely still have had  "the crucial structures necessary for continued existence as an independent entity"
(Aberle et al 1950:102), unless the population eventually lost the biological battle against new diseases.

222

By 1976, however, the Dene of the Northwest Territories had come to look--not only to the anthropolo-
gist but to themselves--like a congeries of dependent
"administered communities ... whose social, political
or economic development is directly determined by
outside agencies" (Weingrod 1962:69). Like reservation populations in the United States, the Dene peoples have become encysted within an encompassing,
dominating system, their lives and livelihoods in
critical ways shaped and controlled by alien, largely
unheeding forces.


THE DENE TESTIFY

From March 1975 to October 1976, Mr. Justice Berger,
as Commissioner of the Mackenzie Valley Pipeline
Inquiry, took testimony relating to the potential
environmental, economic, and social impact of the
construction and operation of a pipeline and energy
corridor through the Northwest Territories (See Gamble
1978 for a summary of the Inquiry process). Formal
hearings involved sworn testimony and submissions from
the applicant pipeline companies, an environmental
organization, white business and other special interest groups, and from the several Native organizations
of the NWT.[4] Of special interest, however, are the
informal Community Hearings, which were held in almost every community in the western NWT and at which
all local persons were invited to speak. This record
runs to over 6,000 pages of transcript.

The Community Hearings provided a forum for the enun-
ciation of Dene experiences, values, concerns, and
fears by the Dene themselves. Beyond specific questions about and positions on the proposed pipeline,
the Dene spoke to several broader themes: personal,
cultural, and regional histories; accounts of life
on the land and love of the land; anxieties over and
evidence of damage to the renewable resources of the
land by "development" activities; knowledge of, experiences with, and attitudes toward white culture
and society in general and government in particular;
economic worries; present and anticipated social problems such as alcohol abuse; circumstances and under-
standings at the signings of Treaty; inherent rights
as human beings; Indian aboriginal rights; and affirmation of the Brotherhood position: "No development
without settlement of Indian land claims." Many of

the testimonies richly reveal Dene perceptions of
the erosion of the self-sufficient structure of action of their community-societies.

## "The Olden Days"

A Treaty Indian in his mid-fifties testifies, through
an interpreter, at the Community Hearing held at the
small Indian enclave in the town of Hay River:

> [The people] used to make their living off the
> land.... [W]hen they wanted to go some place
> or they want to go in the bush, they never
> used to wait for somebody to help them....

> [I]n them days there used to be about 20 or
> 25 families get together, those married people
> used to get together and they used to take
> their family out in the bush and that's where
> they used to make their living, right off the
> bush.

> [I]n those bunch there used to be about four
> or five good hunters and those five good
> hunters used to be a good Welfare to [their]
> own people. He [the hunter] used to be a
> good Welfare because he's keeping everybody
> well-fed because they're doing the hunting
> for them (MVPI-CH Vol. 6:499).

Hay River is now a town of over 3,000 persons, 90
percent of them "Others." A kinsman of the first
speaker describes what it was like before World War
II, before Hay River became the terminus of the
gravel "all-weather highway" from the south.

> There's a priest and there's Hudson's Bay man-
> ager, that's all the white man used to be in
> Hay River. You never heard no people complain-
> ing about being broke all summer. Right from
> springtime till in the fall, people used to
> have money all the time and the people, they
> used to live real good. Not like today.

> They never used to have Welfare in them days.
> If you were going to take your family in the
> bush, you used to go to Hudson's Bay Store
> and that's where you'd get all your supplies
> from.

I look at it today now. If anybody wanted to
go in the bush, well he's got to go across
and see the Welfare and they got to look
around so somebody can pay for their charter
plane. The only way the people can take
their family in the bush these days is somebody's got to pay for their charter plane,
the plane's got to make two trips out in the
bush before they can move.

If you want to know what done that to the
people, I'll let you know right now. White
man done that to the people. White man made
the people more poor than what they used to
be in the olden days (MVPI-CH Vol. 6:491-
492, through interpreter).

Fred Andrew, a well-known "old-timer" of Fort Norman,
says:

I was brought up real pitiful, real poor. I
am a Mountain Indian. My dad must have really
loved me because he hunted for me, he went out
and got rabbits for me, and fish for me. That
is how he brought me up.

.... My dad used to tell me when I was young,
watch other people, how they work. And if
they work good, follow them. Do as I tell you
now and you will live to have a grey hair.
Now I think about my dad, and I am proud of
him for talking to me like that when now I
know my hair is all grey. And many times I
think about how my dad used to talk to me.

.... Now the kids are going to school. They're
growing up a different life from what I grew
up. Even if an older person went to talk to
them, they would not take that, they would
not listen (MVPI-CH Vol. 10:887-889), through
interpreter).

Whiteman's Education and the Cultural Gap

A grandmother of Fort Good Hope echoes this theme:

I teached all my children how to live in
the bush. They know how to make snow-
shoes, how to make their living in the

225

bush. They [the people] are talking about
their childrens going to school today. It's
true. When a parent raised a child, this
child respected his mother. Today, the
childrens that are going to school outside
the community, when they come back they
have no respect for their mother or their
dad; they have no respect for nothing
(MVPI-CH Vol. 19:1905, through interpreter).

Another grandmother, from Fort Norman, issues a
poignant appeal:

[W]hen I heard ... my grandchild, talking,
and when he said "I don't know anything
of their way of life in the bush," it
brought tears to my eyes, but in a way it
is our fault. When they go to school and
come back [for] two months [in the summer],
we could take them out in the bush and
live out there with them and teach them
our way of life, but we never do that.

.... I am speaking to you people that's
in here, the Native people, the father
and mother of your childrens. Speak to
your children in your old tongue, teach
them the way of life at home, it is good
to speak English and do the things that
whitemen do, but it is good to be our own
self in our own language and live the way
we used to in the land (MVPI-CH Vol. 10:
941-943, through interpreter).

Youth who have gone through the schooling system of
the 1960s and 1970s frequently express resentment
and anger:

Until I was eight years old I have lived
with my parents out in the bush. During
those early few years of my life I have
inherited my language and culture, thus
I inherited the Dene way of life....

Then in the summer of 1962 I was persuaded
by teachers to attend school. My sister
and brother and myself boarded a plane to
attend the Sir Alexander Mackenzie School
and was a resident at Grollier Hall, a

Roman Catholic hostel at Inuvik. At that
time I did not know any words in English
or other foreign languages. Most of the
punishments, discomforts and frustrations
imposed upon me were because of my language
and culture. I think partly because of the
colour of my skin. I was too stubborn to
stop being a Dene.

I attended school there for two years during
which time I learned very little of value.
I then decided to remain home for the '64/'65
school year to get away from the whiteman's
system. Even then I learned that my decision
was not to go on undebated because my parents
were threatened by teachers and local government people, that if I stayed, they would
forfeit any more Government aid (MVPI-CH
Vol. 18:1820).

Between these youth and the older Dene, "the generation gap becomes a cultural gap" (Smith 1978). A
young Slavey Indian documents this change from his
own life:

I'm a young native Indian [born 1951]. I've
got an education, I've got a job with the
government, and there is one thing that
people, like O.K., most of the native people
say, "O.K, we got to grow up our children
so that we can use them when they grow up
and they can fight for us."

I grew up here in Hay River. I went to
school until I was about 16, and then I
quit, then about three years later I went
back to Fort Smith for the Adult Education
program and I got my Grade 11, .... and I
worked in Smith for one year.

But since I was about 16-17 years old I
been travelling around trying to figure
out, you know, where I'm at, what I can
do for my people; and so I thought like
if I got this education then I would be
able to do something for them. But--and
then so I come back to Hay River, I came
back here last year after spending about
five years out of Hay River and thinking

227

that, "Here are my people and I'm going to
try and help them through education."

So I come back and I find that people don't
accept me as I am. They expected me to
come back as the way I was five years ago,
not the way --they really can't accept me
as I am because they either can't accept
the changes I went through or it's something else. I can't understand what it is.

So I'm not really accepted back into the
culture, maybe because I lost the knowledge
of it. So now I'm sort of -- and then I
can't really get into the white society
because I'm the wrong color. Like, there's
very very few white people that will be
friends with native people. Any of these
white people that are friends with native
people, it's, you know, it's like a pearl
in a pile of gravel.

For myself, I find it very hard to identify
with anybody because I have nobody to turn
to. My people don't accept me any more
because I got an education, and the white
people won't accept me because I'm not the
right color. So like, a lot of people keep
saying, "O.K., we've got to educate these
native--these young native people so that
they can become something." But what good
is it if the person has no identity (MVPI-
CH Vol. 6:557-558)?

The personal history of one woman now in her mid-
thirties encapsulates experiences common to her
generation. She, like a number of the Dene testi-
fying, offers analysis, and indictment, of the
package of dependency delivered to the northern
natives.

The school was build here [Ft. Good Hope]
in 1952. That year I was nine years old.
I never spoke nor understood no English at
all. When I started going to school I
didn't like going to school at all because
it was a great change compared to living
in the bush with my parents. One reason
I didn't like the school was because I
couldn't speak English.

.... When you are in the bush like a family everybody takes part in doing the everyday chores. My dad would go to visit his trap-lines by dog team. There was no such things as skidoos [snowmobiles], and then my mother would be busy tanning hides and us children would cut wood or haul some clean snow for cooking and drinking water. There was no danger of pollution in those days.

[Tuberculosis] got the best of my father and I am proud at this moment to say that my father is a real -- or was a real Dene. Because he made his living off the land for us. There was no Welfare at that time. He died in 1953 but left a memory for me and my brother to be a true Dene and we are still and we'd like to keep it that way.

.... [The witness, her mother, and her brother had also contracted TB.] So after a year in the hospital I went to the mission school as mother and brother had to go to the [Charles Camsell] hospital in Edmonton for better medical treatment in order to survive the deadly sickness.

I went to school in Aklavik for three years and four years here [Fort Good Hope]. All that time I never saw ... my mother and brother for five years. I was very lonely but [back at Good Hope] I was still happy because I was still living in the bush, a life on the Dene land with my uncle and aunt, they took care of me.

I went to the bush and the fish camp. Those days everybody was out in the bush where they belonged. Very few people stayed in town. Then in 1958 the Government program slowly crept into this community. Like the hostels, whiteman's education, low rental houses,[5] and, the worst of them all, alcohol and Welfare.

You think the Dene beg on their knees for those programs? No way. The so-called Government threw it at us and we accepted their trick.

.... Mr. Berger, I am the social worker for
this community. I started to work on March
the 19th, 1974.... After I worked a year,
let me tell you I have never seen anything
like it. This program was made up in the
whiteman's way. We Dene people have no say
in it. Everything about social development
is policy here, policy there, and the boss,
the so-called whiteman or Government in
Inuvik whom I am working for, I think expect
they could give me orders. I ignore them
because I am a Dene and I know the Dene
problems. I have no intentions to hurt and
destroy my people. They have been hurt too
many times in the past and the present by
the Government. I tell them, you are in
Inuvik, you do your own thing, and I'll do
mine (MVPI-CH Vol. 20:1939-1943).

The young Chief of the Fort Norman Band points out
that the recent innovation of "local government"
undermines the Indian band council system and is
illusory besides:

I was ... one of the very few fortunate
native people [in that] I was able to
secure a job with the Territorial Government ... [as] Settlement Secretary. That--
one of the terms of reference of that particular job was to work for the Territorial
Government. Pardon me, I mean work for the
Settlement Council but get paid by the
Territorial Government. That by itself
indicates the type of struggle [confusion]
that can exist in a position such as this.

It was quite obvious also that this whole
Settlement Council system has never worked
and never will work because it is a form
of tokenism to the Territorial Government.
And an Advisory Board, whose advice [is] not
usually taken....

[I]t seems like one of the aims of the Territorial Government was to creat a conflict
among the native communities that already
had an existing governing body, such as
Band Councils, by introducing the Settlement Council....

230

The frustrations that I found [in] the position was that I was told that I was working
for the people. But I was continuously
getting orders from the Regional Office.
They were the ones that finally decided
what would happen and what would not happen
(MVPI-CH Vol. 10:875-876).

The proliferation of installations for the transient
white bureaucratic elite, in what were once fur post
and mission stations, renders visible the subordination of the Indian community to the national system
and its agents:

I am a Treaty Indian from Fort McPherson.
I have worked as a social worker here in
Fort McPherson here for the past five and
a half years....

I am not an old man, but I have seen many
changes in my life. Fifteen years ago,
most of what you see as Fort McPherson did
not exist. Take a look around the community
now. And you will start to get an idea of
what has happened to the Indian people here
over the past few years.

Look at the housing where transient Government staff live. And look at the housing
where the Indian people live. Look at which
houses are connected to the utilidor. Look
at how the school and hostel, the R.C.M.P.
and government staff houses are right in the
center of town. Dividing the Indian people
into two sides.

Look at where the Bay [Hudson's Bay Company]
store is, right on top of the highest point
of land.

Mr. Berger, do you think that this is the
way the Indian people chose to have this
community? Do you think the people here
had any voice in planning this community?
(MVPI-CH Vol. 12:1078)

Scores of testimonies bear witness to the erosion
of societal self-sufficiency and self-determination;

231

this final selection from a young Treaty Indian of Fort Norman captures the range of issues.

> There are so many pressures on the people
> nowadays, and everything has to be done
> right away. The pipeline, the gasoline,
> the [proposed Great Bear River hydroelectric]
> dam. The government wants the people to
> get snowed under.
>
> If we did have enough time on our own, we
> could work it out together on our own feet.
> If we had as much time now as the govern-
> ment has, to try to brainwash us, we could
> work it out and get ourselves back together.
>
> Now the government tells us that they want
> the pipeline right now. Right this day
> Arctic Gas is out drilling along the pro-
> posed route. The Government must still
> think we are brainwashed because they
> think we still agree with the pipeline.
>
> There is no way.
>
> I remember a few years ago, people lived
> in their homes, they got their own wood and
> hauled their own water. People were happier
> then. When they didn't have to depend on
> the government all of the time. We were
> happier then and we could do it again.
>
> But look what has happened. Now the govern-
> ment gives the people everything, pays for
> the water and the fuel and the houses, the
> education. It gives the people everything,
> everything but one thing. The right to
> live their own lives.
>
> And that is the only thing that we really
> want, is to control our lives, our own
> land (MVPI-CH Vol. 10:597).

Some of the concern expressed in these testimonies over the loss of a self-sufficient system of action takes the form of a seemingly too-rosy retrospective view of living off the land. But Dene are aware that the actualities of the hunting-trapping life involve many hardships and preclude many comforts.

232

One trapper from Fort Norman asks:

> Why should our kids get educated and go sit
> on the lake and set a fish net and freeze
> their fingers when they have got education?
> Why should they do it?.... Nobody's going
> to ... put on a pair of snowshoes and tramp
> snow down and set traps in forty or fifty
> below weather when he has got education
> (MVPI-CH Vol. 10:963).

The point is, of course, not that most Dene reject
the comforts and entertainments of monetized urbanism
per se (for they are like most of the world in this
respect) but that many have come to recognize that,
to date, the price has been loss of decision and control over their own lives. Life on the land symbol-
izes a more autonomous, less harassed existence. In
the judgment of the young Chief from Fort Smith:

> I think the feeling of the people you [Mr.
> Berger] have talked to throughout these
> communities say that they want some kind
> of development but a controlled develop-
> ment; not something that is imposed by
> somebody else.... [T]hey're saying that
> for once ... we've got to have a chance
> to decide what we want for ourselves
> (MVPI-CH Vol. 33:3230).

CONCLUSION

As the Dene look to the future, self-determination--
economic, cultural, political--is the core issue.
On October 25, 1976, the Indian Brotherhood of the
NWT submitted to the federal government a position
paper in the form of an "Agreement in Principle
Between the Dene Nation and Her Majesty the Queen,
in right of Canada" (published in Watkins 1977:182-
187). In the scope and inclusiveness of the formu-
lations in this statement, the Dene by-passed the
constraints of the existent Canadian political structure, rejected "the tradition in Canada that [Native]
rights must be extinguished," and drove to the heart
of the economic, social and cultural issues they
deem vital to their continuation as "a People."

In the name of "the Dene Nation," the Brotherhood

called upon the Government of Canada to negotiate with the Dene according to principles set forth in the Agreement. These principles include the right to recognition, self-determination, and self-definition as Dene; the right to practice and preserve their languages, traditions and values; the right to develop their own institutions and enjoy their rights as a People in the framework of their own institutions; the right to retain ownership of so much of their traditional lands, and under such terms, as to insure social and economic independence and self-reliance. To these ends the Agreement calls for "within [the] Confederation [of Canada], a Dene government with jurisdiction over a geographical area and over subject matters now within the jurisdiction of either the Government of Canada or the Government of the Northwest Territories."

In essence, the Agreement in Principle proposes for the Dene people collectively an extent of self-governance over their land, lives, and fortunes unparalleled in the history of Indian "claim settlements." The mode, means, and procedures by which this self-governance would be realized are not specified. If attained--in whatever specific form--the paradox remains, however, that Dene self-determination will necessarily be phrased within the context of the nation-state in which the Dene are embedded. Dene government will have to be structured as a countervailing system, not as a free choice of polity. The formation and structure of the NWT Brotherhood itself reflects the working of these forces. Created in response to the pressures and demands of the national system, the Brotherhood's organization and programs have been developed in reaction to that system and in some ways constrained by it as well. As one consequence, a "class" of Brotherhood officers and activists, mostly young and with advanced schooling, emerged from the Dene populace. In time, within that group disaccord regarding strategy and procedures developed and culminated in a rupture over leadership.

The Dene Nation is itself an emergent polity construct conceived as a counterpoise to the forces of the national system. In the internal affairs of traditional life, there was no overarching Dene polity nor tribal polities in the sense of coordinated political authority within the several major linguistic-

territorial sectors. Each small hunting group or
aggregation of such groups in temporary gatherings
were self-governing under a consensually recognized
leader. Groups of families formed small mobile communities upon the land; at the wider level, regional
societies were committed to mutual sharing and to
egalitarian consensuality. These families were free
to alter their social and community alliances when
and as they saw fit. In critical contrast to the
present day, few issues of consequence had to be
faced or decided upon by a group as a whole. After
Treaty, the government required that a "chief" and
"councillors" be elected or consensually selected to
represent the official "Indian Band" identified with
each trading post. But, as these "officials" were
powerless vis-à-vis government, they and their constituencies could make no decisions affecting "Indian
policy" for the NWT, which in any event was at best
a policy of "benign neglect."

The testimonies at the Community Hearings have docu-
mented the extent to which in the last 25 years decisions critically affecting Indian life have been
made and implemented by an alien society. Now, with
recent changes in the national political climate,
the Dene are called upon--as a single, total entity--
to organize and represent themselves as an interest
group in the face of the interlocked imperatives of
the government, the "energy crisis," and multinational
corporations. In creating a Dene polity, they are
required to make decisions regarding internal structure, strategy, and goals so they can be pressed further to respond to demands of the greater systems
external to them and yet in which they are enmeshed.

How shall all those decisions be made? Who shall
set policy and make decisions? What shall be the
mode, means, and procedures of self-governance if
some kind or degree of a "Dene government" comes
into being? What will be the economic support-base
for such a "government" and how will that base be
structured and administered? (Brotherhood leaders
are aware that the Alaska Settlement--the best "claims
settlement" so far--came "down clearly on the side
of money, not land" and that the economic and administrative structure of village and regional corporations
with shareholders and an emerging managerial class
"was designed to bring the natives into the mainstream of American capitalism" [Forrest 1976:18]).

Indians active in the Brotherhood or attentive to problems of the present-day and future political scene are aware of the paradox that achievement of a substantial degree of Indian economic and political self-determination threatens the sociopolitical autonomy, self-sufficiency, and consensuality in Dene life that traditionally was lodged in the local group and local community. The Brotherhood espouses the principle of full participation and agreement by all Dene in the formulation of policy. Yet in the General Assemblies held by the Brotherhood, decisions are reached by the majority vote of a few score delegates drawn primarily from the elected leaders of the government-defined "Indian Bands," that is, "Band Chiefs" and "Band Councillors."

In seeking strength through unification, can the ancient social values and principles based in the small scale, intimate society be sustained, or at least satisfactorily transmuted, rather than obliterated? A young Dene activist who resigned from the NWT Legislative Assembly in frustration with the Eurocanadian governmental system with its imposed time tables, political hierarchism, and parliamentary rule, has pinpointed the issue:

> See the way people make decisions when a group goes hunting. They sit around in the evening and drink tea and talk about everything. They talk about the weather, they talk about where the moose might be, they talk about times they've hunted in the past. Everybody talks, everybody listens to everybody else.
>
> You never tell anybody that they're "out of order." Its like a group of people who live in the bush. People realize what they need and everybody talks about it. It comes out through conversation. There's no formal decisions. Nobody makes any motions. People just talk until there's a general agreement, nobody gives orders to anybody else.
>
> It should be the same with all Dene decisions. People should be allowed to get together to decide what they want, not everybody wants the same thing; that's

236

fine. A true Government would be people
themselves deciding what they want and
then helping each other get what they
want.

.... If we go through a whole Dene movement and we end up with native people just
giving orders to their own people, we're
not better off than now, when white people
order us around (The Native Press, October
22, 1975:12).


POSTSCRIPT 1979

On April 15, 1977, Mr. Justice Berger, Commissioner
of the Mackenzie Valley Pipeline Inquiry, submitted
his recommendations to the Minister of Indian Affairs
and Northern Development. They stated, in part, that

There should be no pipeline across the
Northern Yukon. It would entail irreparable
environmental losses of national and international importance. And a Mackenzie Valley
pipeline should be postponed for ten years.
If it is built now, it would bring limited
benefits, its social impact would be devas-
tating, and it would frustrate the goals of
native claims. Postponement will allow
sufficient time for native claims to be
settled, and for new programs and new institutions to be established (Berger 1977:
xxvi-xxvii).

Subsequently, the National Energy Board of Canada
also recommended against the construction of the
Mackenzie Valley pipeline. Bowing to these recommendations, the Canadian government and the pipeline
interests turned their efforts toward establishing
an Alaska Highway pipeline route.

For the concerned Native organizations, the basic
issue had always been not the pipeline but the claims
to the land. In regard to land claims, from the beginning the two collaborating Inuit-based organizations, The Committee for Original Peoples Entitlement
(COPE) and Inuit Tapirisat of Canada (ITC), pursued
a course apart from the coalition of the two Indian-

heritage organizations of the Northwest Territories, the Indian Brotherhood and the Metis Association. By the beginning of 1977 both the COPE-ITC coalition and Dene-Metis coalition had collapsed, the organizations undergoing a degree of internal conflict and factionalism as well (Gribbons 1977).  The new leaderships that emerged in each of the organizations pursued land claims of differing conception and scope independently of one another.  Of the Indian-heritage organizations, the Metis Association pushed for economic development within the established political framework while the Indian group continued to insist on a radical political restructuring that would realize Dene self-determination and self-governance as set forth in the Agreement in Principle document of 1976.  The strength of that intent is reflected in the change of title from Indian Brotherhood to Dene Nation, as the organization is now known.  By the spring of 1979, negotiations on specific land selections in the Western Arctic made by COPE were under way between that organization and the government. By mid-year of 1979, the Dene Nation and the Metis Association were attempting to achieve a political rapprochement that would afford them a unified bargaining position <u>vis-à-vis</u> the COPE claims and which would meet the government's insistence (DINA 1978) that they "agree on a mechanism for conducting joint negotiations with the federal government on their overlapping claims."


FOOTNOTES

1.  Population statements are here based mainly on 1971 data compiled by Gemini North (1974) in a study carried out for Canadian Arctic Gas Pipeline Limited, but I have added to those data my estimate of the 1971 populations of the few communities that did not fall within the scope of the Gemini report.  For the entire NWT, the 1971 census figure was 34,805; the additional population is in coastal Arctic settlements, the majority are Inuit, the remainder white. The population of the NWT and in the impact region has increased since 1971, but as exact figures and ethnic proportions are not available, I here use the 1971 figures.

The Gemini North study faced the same problem that

other inquirers into ethnicity in the NWT must face: those individuals who do not have relations as "Treaty Indians" with the federal government, or who are not identified by the government as Inuit, are lumped under a general category "Other" in the census. Included in "Other" are not only whites but also the bulk of the Metis. (Some Metis have through certain historical circumstances been accorded "Treaty Indian" status.) Also included are Non-Status Indians and Inuit, relatively few in number, who, through particular individual circumstances, are "enfranchised," that is, without any special relationship with the federal government. (For example, a few Dene men "went off Treaty" in order to escape the pre-1959 discriminatory liquor law and/or other invidious definitions of "Indian status"; they and their descendants are "Others.") These Native persons cannot be isolated from "Others" in government census figures. I estimate the Metis and Non-Status Natives at approximately 3,000-3,500 for the impact region, possibly 3,500-4,500 for the entire NWT. An official of the Metis Association provides an estimate of 7,700 for the Metis in the NWT as a whole (Gemini North 1974, V. 2:71). One estimate of 10,000 (Hoople and Newberry, n.d., map p. 20-21) is assuredly too high.

2. In 1941, the population of the NWT was 12,028, of which Treaty Indians composed 36 percent, Inuit 45 percent, and "Other" (including Metis and Non-Status Indians as well as whites) 19 percent. In 1971, the ethnic proportions of the total NWT population of 34,805 were: Treaty Indians, 20.6 percent, Inuit, 32.7 percent, and "Other" 46.7 percent. In Gemini North's "Study Region" (which excludes two settlements that I include in the Dene "impact region") the shift in ethnic proportions has been from 76 percent Indian, 12 percent Inuit, and 12 percent "Other" in 1941 to 26 percent Indian, 7 percent Inuit, and 67 percent "Other" in 1971 (Gemini North 1974, V. 2:89).

3. Actually, Indian Affairs had in 1968 turned most of its responsibilities to Treaty Indians of the NWT over to the Territorial Government, apparently "getting a jump on" implementing the as-yet-unannounced 1969 Indian Policy statement. Finally responding to sus-

tained Indian protest, the federal government in 1972 reopened the Indian Affairs Office in Yellowknife.

4. The competing pipeline companies were Canadian Arctic Gas Pipeline Ltd. (a consortium of U.S. and Canadian-based firms) whose project involved bringing natural gas from Alaska's North Slope across the northern Yukon Territory, thence down the Mackenzie Corridor, and Foothills Pipe Line Ltd., arguing for an all-Canadian gas supply and sales. Canadian Arctic Resources Committee (CARC) was the major environmental group, organized in 1971 in reaction to early U.S.-Canadian negotiations around the North Slope-Mackenzie Corridor pipeline. Besides the Indian Brotherhood of the NWT, native organizations included Inuit Tapirisat of Canada (ITC), the Eskimo-wide organization incorporated in 1971, its ally in the Mackenzie Delta, Committee for Original Peoples Entitlement (COPE), organized in 1970, and the NWT Metis Association, formed in 1972. White interest groups included the NWT Chamber of Commerce, Association of Municipalities, and Mental Health Association.

5. "The governmental rental housing programme has been an important means of increasing the dependent status of native people.... Briefly, it has changed the status of virtually every native person from home owner to tenant" (Usher 1976:10).

REFERENCES CITED

Aberle, D.F., A. K. Cohen, A. K. Davis,
   M. J. Levy, F. X. Sutton
      1950    The Functional Prerequisites of a
              Society.  Ethics 60:100-111.

Asch, Michael
      1976    Past and Present Land-Use by Slavey
              Indians of the Mackenzie District.
              Dene Rights, Supporting Research and
              Documents: Vol. II, The Dene and their
              Land. Part III:66-109.  Indian Brother-
              hood of the Northwest Territories.

240

Berger, Mr. Justice Thomas R.
  1974    Preliminary Rulings. Issued by the
          Commissioner, Mackenzie Valley Pipeline
          Inquiry, Yellowknife, NWT, July 12.
          Mimeo.

  1977    Northern Frontier, Northern Homeland:
          The Report of the Mackenzie Valley Pipe-
          line Inquiry. Vol. I. Ottawa:  Supply
          and Services Canada.

DINA
  1978    Department of Indian and Northern Affairs
          Communique of September 27.  Reprinted
          in The Musk Ox (1978) 22:90-93.

Dunning, R. W.
  1969    Indian Policy:  A Proposal for Autonomy.
          The Canadian Forum 49(587):206-207.

Duran, James A., Jr.
  1971    Canadian Indian Policy:  A Year of Debate.
          The Indian Historian 4(3):34-36.

Forrest, Ann
  1976    Development and Land Rights:  The Case
          of Alaska.  Dene Rights, Supporting Re-
          search and Documents: Vol. VII, Compara-
          tive Experience: 1-18.  Indian Brotherhood
          of the Northwest Territories.

Fumoleau, Rene
  1975    As Long as This Land Shall Last.
          Toronto:  McClelland and Stewart, Ltd.

Gamble, D. J.
  1978    The Berger Inquiry:  An Impact Assessment
          Process.  Science 199:946-952.

Gemini North, Ltd.
  1974    Social and Economic Impact of Proposed
          Arctic Gas Pipeline in Northern Canada.
          Vol. 2.  Canadian Arctic Gas Pipeline, Ltd.

Gribbons, Collin
  1977    The Berger Report:  It Doesn't Mean We've
          Won.  The Native Perspective 2(2):9-10.
          Ottawa:  National Association of Friend-
          ship Centres.

Hoople, Joanne and J. W. E. Newberry
    n.d.    And What About Canada's Native Peoples?
            Ottawa:  Canadian Council for Interna-
            tional Cooperation.

MVPI-CH
    1975-   Mackenzie Valley Pipeline Inquiry:
    1976    Proceedings at Community Hearings.
            Burnaby, B.C.:  Allwest Reporting Ltd.

Native Press, The
    1975    Bi-Monthly Publication of the Native
            Communications Society of the Western
            NWT.  Yellowknife, NWT.

Phillips, R. A. J.
    1967    Canada's North.  Toronto:  Macmillan.

Smith, J. G. E.
    1978    The Emergence of the Micro-Urban Village
            among the Caribou Eater Chipewyan.
            Human Organization 37:38-49.

Usher, Peter J.
    1976    Overview Evidence (Panel Two):  Evidence
            Presented on Behalf of COPE.  Mackenzie
            Valley Pipeline Inquiry, Phase Four.
            Mimeo.

Watkins, Mel, editor
    1977    Dene Nation--The Colony Within.  Toronto:
            University of Toronto Press.

Weingrod, Alex
    1962    Administered Communities:  Some Charac-
            teristics of New Immigrant Villages in
            Israel.  Economic Development and Cul-
            tural Change 2:69-84.

CHAPTER 10

The Politics of Inuit Alliance Movements
in the Canadian Arctic

Ann McElroy, State University of New York at Buffalo


The development of political unification among eastern Arctic Eskimos, a people who call themselves
Inuit, is a recent phenomenon in Canadian history.
This unification involves alliances among Inuit in
the Northwest Territories, Arctic Quebec, northern
Manitoba, and the Mackenzie region.  It represents
a major change in the political organization and
identity of Canada's 17,000 Inuit.

The Inuit have had an ambiguous political identity
throughout the stages of northern exploration, settlement, and modernization.  They are technically
defined as Indians under the legislative jurisdiction
of the Canadian Federal Government (Cumming and Mickenberg 1972:7), but they are excluded from coverage
by the Indian Act of 1874 which legally defines the
category of "native person" as one entitled to interest in reserve lands.  Like the Métis of Canada, the
Inuit do not live on reserves and are not organized
into tribal bands (Lurie 1971:467).  They have signed
no treaties with one exception in Labrador in 1769
(Cumming and Mickenberg 1972:13).  While the Canadian
Government does recognize treaty rights, it is uncertain whether aboriginal rights based on use and original occupation of lands will be recognized.  Settlement of the issue of aboriginal title becomes increasingly important as pressures mount for exploitation
of natural resources.

While northern development has been a major factor
in the mobilization of Native organizations, the
significance of Inuit political unification goes
beyond resource management and land rights.  Inuit
are indeed concerned about the potential ecological
and social impact of development, but they are also
dissatisfied with current employment, educational,
and health conditions in their communities.  As they
become aware of structural limitations on their participation in decision-making about proposals to
explore for oil and gas and to construct pipelines,
they are beginning to understand that political

243

changes must precede desired changes in the quality
of their lives. To bring about these changes, they
must create new rules of conduct in interethnic relations, not only in terms of formal negotiations at
council meetings and land claims hearings, but also
in day-to-day interpersonal transactions.

Until the construction of DEW-line sites, air bases,
and permanent settlements after the Second World War,
relations between Inuit and the outside world had
been mediated through particularistic relations with
explorers, missionaries, and traders. Awareness of
the scope and complexity of Canadian society, and
particularly awareness of their status and rights
as Canadians, was filtered and refracted in interactions and communication with individual Eurocanadians. The politics of contact resembled the dyadic
linkages by which Inuit had traditionally created
expedient alliances through spouse exchange, infant
betrothal, meat-sharing partnerships, and adoption
(Balikci 1970; Boas 1964; Graburn 1969; Van den
Steenhoven 1959). Liaisons were formed between individual households and southerners, and in the early
stages of contact between 1840 and 1900 these relationships tended to be interdependent. As Lantis
(1966:92) has pointed out: "...essential in the
early days was mutual assistance between Caucasian
and Eskimo or Indian in fighting the common enemy:
weather and the scarcity of food and fuel."

The dyadic model for interethnic relations was retained during the gradual process of acculturation
and movement into permanent villages and towns during the twentieth century. As Inuit began to encounter increasing numbers of Eurocanadians with
specialized roles such as nurses, teachers, social
workers, administrators, construction laborers,
store clerks, they continued to interact with these
agents of change on a personal level. The two ethnic groups rarely found themselves in organized opposition to one another, even with the formation of
community councils and the election of Inuit to
territorial government positions.

In an early survey of attitudes among Frobisher Bay
Inuit by Yatsushiro (1960), 61 percent thought that
"Eskimos are treated fairly in their jobs" and 77
percent affirmed that "Eskimos are living a better
life today than twenty years ago." An informant of

the Honigmanns (1968:173) also spoke positively about Eurocanadians: "Those who come after us will gradually come to do the work now done by white men -- we will be able to do some because the whites are good teachers. The whites, most of them, do not get angry with the Eskimos...." Still, a system of interpersonal politics developed which on occasion affected the status and rights of Inuit as a class. John and Irma Honigmann's ethnography (1965) of Frobisher Bay gives examples of the informal segregation and discriminatory practices Inuit perceive as arbitrary and unjust.

Organized protest of Inuit against conditions in the settlements signifies the beginning of a break from customary patterns established earlier. This change is the product of several converging trends. First, as the populations of these settlements grow due to a high birth rate as well as immigration of Natives and southerners, job opportunities and housing have become limited and class stratification has increased. Native individuals with some education, especially young people selected for training in special programs, have become disillusioned as they see their aspirations for equality with Eurocanadians blocked.

Second, the sense of alarm created by increasing government interest in developing and exploiting exportable resources has been reinforced through the mass media. Some settlements receive television transmission via satellites, and most have radio transmission. Through newsletters, newspapers, and magazines, Inuit are becoming aware of controversial issues such as the James Bay Development project, the effects of the Alaska pipeline construction, off-shore drilling in the western Canadian Arctic, and the demands for land claims settlements made to the Mackenzie Valley Pipeline Inquiry headed by Justice Berger (ITC Annual Report 1976:29-30).

Third, individual expressions of discontent and concern about northern development have been supported and legitimized through the formation of several national and regional organizations. In 1970 COPE (Committee of the Original Peoples' Entitlement) was established in the western Arctic, and in 1971 Inuit Tapirisat of Canada (ITC) was formed. ITC has been responsible for much of the movement toward national unification of Inuit, while COPE, with Inuit, Indian,

and Metis membership, tends to focus on pressing regional concerns.

Inuit Tapirisat, the regional associations, and special-purpose groups do not present themselves as
separatist movements, although they have proposed
segmentation of the existing Northwest Territories
through creation of a new jurisdictional area called
Nunavut, "our land" (ITC press release, February 12,
1975). The Northwest Territories has recently been
divided into two electoral districts, one of which
is called Nunatsiaq, translated as "beautiful land."
Inuit Tapirisat has approved this move because it
will provide for two members of parliament from the
Northwest Territories in the 1978 Federal elections.

ITC denies being a political organization in the
narrow sense of the word. In reference to the 1978
Federal elections, the editors of ITC News (December
1976-January 1977:2) write:

>      Inuit Tapirisat is a non-political organiza-
>      tion, so we won't be telling you to support
>      any national party or any particular candi-
>      date. But we do suggest that you start
>      thinking now about the kind of person you
>      want to represent you in Ottawa. This is
>      extremely important, because for the first
>      time the people of Nunatsiaq, or Nunavut,
>      will have some say in making the Canadian
>      laws that affect their lives.

To readers familiar with Native American protest
movements in the United States, such as the dramatic
confrontations of Alcatraz Island, Wounded Knee, and
the Washington fish-ins, the description of Inuit
Tapirisat's activism will seem enigmatically moderate. The politics of this organization are explicitly a politics of negotiation, not confrontation,
and the reasons may be sought in analysis of the
history of interethnic relations.


AN INTERACTIONAL MODEL OF ANALYSIS

In seeking structural antecedents for the dimensions
of culture change, one has the conventional option
of focusing on the values, personality traits, and
patterns of interpersonal relations specific to a
single cultural system. In such an approach, the

246

pertinent question would be: what is it about traditional Inuit society which shapes and colors its style of political adjustment to contemporary conditions? It may be more productive, however, to look at the interactional dynamics of contact, that is to say the development of relationships between Inuit and Eurocanadians over the course of history. In this view, one sees individuals in contact as creating an interactional field in which decisions are negotiated, options presented and chosen, and attitudes communicated. The field may be integrated and function smoothly, or it may be full of contradictions and in a condition of essential tension. In this condition, messages become distorted, and considerable energy and reorganization must be devoted to negotiation of understanding and a working agenda. A dissonant interactional field may be more conducive to change than an integrated one, and the new political activism may be an indicator of the degree of tension involved in creating bicultural systems in the northern settlements.

This study, then, will be primarily historical in focus, tracing the stages and dynamics of contact and acculturation which Inuit of the eastern Arctic have experienced. The interpersonal politics, that is the establishment of relational dimensions, of each stage are to be understood not only in terms of the motives and values of persons in contact, but also in terms of the ecological pressures induced by their technological exchanges and socioeconomic arrangements. Many frameworks are available for analysis of the development and role of Inuit Tapirisat, and the present study chooses to construct a diachronic perspective against which the particular stance and strategies of the organization may be clarified. A description of Inuit Tapirisat's history and present policies will follow an account of the various stages of contact and modernization in the eastern Arctic.

The research for this analysis was carried out between 1967 and 1974, during which the author spent 14 months of field work in the Baffin Island communities of Frobisher Bay and Pangnirtung studying the psychological dynamics of culture contact and modernization. Interviews with officers of Inuit Tapirisat in 1971 and 1972 led to an article presenting preliminary analysis of the structure and potential of the organization (McElroy 1972). The impact of ITC on the communities of Frobisher Bay and Pangnirtung was assessed during a follow-up visit to Baffin Island in 1974. The reports, press releases, and publications of the organization have provided current information.


EARLY CONTACTS:  EXPLORERS AND WHALERS

The first recorded contacts between Europeans and Inuit occurred in the sixteenth century as British expeditions seeking gold and a northwest passage to Asia explored the coasts of Baffin Island and the Hudson Strait. Most of these encounters involved suspicion and treachery on both sides. Initially peaceful trade between Baffin Island Nugumiut and the crew of Frobisher's expedition in 1576 escalated into violence when four crewmen who went ashore disappeared. Presumably the men were killed, and three Inuit were kidnapped and taken as hostages to England, where they died. In the early seventeenth century the explorer Knight and three of his crew were killed by Inuit in the Hudson Strait area. Four of Hudson's crew met a similar fate in 1610 (Graburn 1969:77-78). These accounts belie the peaceful and hospitable Inuit stereotype which grew out of favorable accounts by whalers and explorers in the mid-nineteenth century.

At the time of these encounters, the Inuit of the eastern Arctic were seasonally nomadic exploiting both land and sea resources. They depended primarily on fish and caribou in summer and autumn and on sea mammals in winter and spring. Ice-fishing, the collecting of eggs, berries, and mussels, and some fowl and small-game hunting supplemented and varied the diet. They traveled and camped in small bands of several extended families, ranging in size from about 15 to 75. Band membership was flexible, and leadership was achieved and situational. Whenever friction between individuals or food shortages developed, nuclear or extended units left a camp to seek more favorable conditions. Maintenance of alliances with individuals in other bands allowed easy movement (Balikci 1970; Boas 1964).

Incursions of whalers and explorers in the nineteenth century did not change subsistence patterns greatly,

248

but they did provide seasonal employment for some camps and did begin to create a need for imported goods. Hall's journal (1970) notes that by 1860 the Nugumiut of southern Baffin Island had become accustomed to working as boat crews for whalers. The Inuit provided land food, skin clothing and boots, and services as guides. In return they received rations, cloth, firearms, tea and tobacco, and metal goods. Even as late as 1883, after the whaling industry began to decline, Boas (1964:17, 59) observed that Oqomiut of the Cumberland Sound region continued to be involved with whalers, seeking occasional employment as boat crews.

In contrast to the hostility characterizing earlier encounters, the relationships between Inuit and Europeans during the nineteenth century were primarily cooperative. Natives worked for whalers voluntarily, willingly served as guides and interpreters, and shared their food and women in return for trade goods. Hall's accounts do reveal certain points of tension, however, notably open conflicts between angakot [shamans] and white men. Certain passages also suggest conflict between whalers and Inuit men over the issue of their right to work autonomously, according to their own schedules, and to be free to hunt when they chose. In contrast, Hall is full of praise for the diligence, reliability, and submission of Inuit women, and one wonders whether the issue of male autonomy and female subordination affected inter-ethnic relations at this time (cf. McElroy 1975, 1977 for analysis of this issue).

## TRADERS AND SUBSISTENCE PATTERN CHANGES

According to Graburn and Strong (1973:192), the period of contact with whalers did not disrupt the social organization or ecology significantly although exposure to venereal disease, tuberculosis, measles, diphtheria, and other communicable diseases did affect the health of the population. But the period to follow, that of extensive fox trapping and regular trade with the Hudson's Bay Company and competitors, involved a "fundamental revolution" with "unanticipated and irreversible consequences" (Graburn and Strong 1973).

The earliest HBC post to deal with Inuit was established in 1749 at Richmond Gulf in northern Quebec, but it closed after seven years because of hostile relations between Indians and Inuit (Graburn 1969: 79-82). A post was kept open at Great Whale River for 44 years and then reopened in 1837. The Fort Chimo post was established from 1830-1842 and again in 1866, and Inuit living 400 miles to the north traveled to the post with furs each spring. Trading posts were established on Baffin Island considerably later: at Lake Harbour in 1911, at Ward Inlet, near Frobisher Bay, in 1914, and at Pangnirtung in 1921 (Haller 1966; Higgins 1967; MacBain 1970). Revillon Frères stores opened during this period at Baker Lake in the Keewatin and at Repulse Bay in the Foxe Basin area. One private individual opened a post at Pond Inlet on northern Baffin Island (Jenness 1964:23).

The presence of trading posts tended to stabilize band membership and to change seasonal subsistence patterns. The trading companies extended credit to trappers, providing them with food, guns, ammunition, and traps; in the spring the debts were paid off with furs. Larger dog teams were needed for inland trap lines, and Inuit began to rely on rifles to provide adequate food for dogs. Family members did not always accompany trappers inland, and camps became more permanent. Periodic famines due to decline in the size of caribou herds increased dependence on imported rations from traders (Graburn and Strong 1973:192). These rations were high-carbohydrate foods of little nutritional value to a population adapted to a high-protein diet, and health continued to decline.

The traditional pattern of leadership had corresponded to band flexibility. Leaders were those individuals, men or women, esteemed for their wisdom and skill in procuring food, processing skins and tools, and creating alliances. Leadership was achieved by action and influence, or in the case of shamans, through the ability to intimidate and manipulate people. Isumatat, "advisors" or "thinkers," led on the basis of providing economic benefits to the group, according to Graburn and Strong (1973: 163). They had authority over their families but could only advise and never coerce other individuals to follow them. While these leaders inspired a certain degree of fear and jealousy and thus competition, their need for group support in economic activities usually inhibited abuse of personal power.

The traders took advantage of this pattern of leadership by singling out certain individuals as middlemen, reinforcing their influence through economic benefits. For example, in the Port Harrison region of northern Quebec, Willmott (1968:153) found that,

> a man's position of leadership was assured by the [trading company's] policy of presenting Peterhead boats and whaleboats to spokesmen in order to assure their loyalty. Since these boats then became the primary means of summer transportation and hunting, the owner [umialik] controlled the movements of the camp and assumed a position of considerable power. Three of the six camps around port Harrison have powerful leaders who own large boats, and each has a stable population with a strong feeling of differentiation from the other camps.

On Baffin Island, whole families gained material advantage and prestige through affiliation with traders. Traders preferred to employ the kin of individuals they knew well. In some cases private traders in the Cumberland Sound region formed liaisons with Inuit women, including several common-law marriages. In Pond Inlet it was customary for the daughters of Native employees to work as housekeepers and cooks for HBC personnel, frequently providing sexual relations (Matthiasson 1979:62). Vallee (1968:116-117) has noted that similar patron-client relationships developed between Inuit families and contact agents near Baker Lake:

> Traditionally the Kabloona [white] patron, whether Hudson's Bay company trader, missionary, or Royal Canadian Mounted Police, showed diffuse interest in their Eskimo employee and his family, doing special favours for them, offering them advice, scolding them for untoward behaviour, even when this had nothing to do with the job.

There is no question the traders were influential and respected by the Inuit, who called them angiyukat,

251

"bosses," literally "big men." They had tight economic control over the trading transaction. No cash was paid out and tokens or simply credit were allotted. The traders and their clerks, mostly youths from the British Isles and the Maritimes, spoke Inuttitut fluently. From both the whalers and the traders Inuit adopted many customs: jigs and reels, accordions and mouth organs, folk tunes, and a great love of tea, tobacco, and bannock, a pan-bread.

## CONTACT WITH MISSIONARIES

The presence of missionaries brought additional impacts on Inuit culture, not only ideological but also in marriage and family patterns. Moravian missionaries arrived in Labrador in 1770 and attracted Inuit seeking trade (Graburn 1969:80-84). In 1873 a Roman Catholic mission was established at Fort Chimo, and between 1876 and 1890 E. J. Peck founded a series of Anglican missions for Indians and Inuit in the area. Peck developed a syllabic writing system for the Cree and Inuit and translated the Bible, the Anglican prayer book, and hymns.

Peck traveled to Cumberland Sound in 1894. His strategic provisions of rations, medical supplies, and magic lantern shows facilitated Native acceptance of his teachings. In general only the angakot opposed the missionaries directly, although Inuit passively resisted missionary demands to abandon their winter ceremonials, their seclusion of the dying, and partying with ship crews (Fleming 1932; Lewis 1905).

Among the changes which missionaries brought were a decrease in female infanticide, polygamy, infant betrothal, and spouse exchange. Inuit traditionally had a flexible marriage system involving trial marriages to test fertility and compatibility; the wife's autonomy was supported by her kin, and any mistreatment by the husband provided sufficient grounds for "divorce" and remarriage (Boas 1964:170-171). Polygamy was acceptable, most commonly to sisters. Spouse exchange could be initiated either by the husband or the wife (Balikci 1970:141-142; Boas 1964:171). One of the major forms of birth spacing was the practice of infanticide, and infant betrothal not only allowed long-term alliances between prospective in-laws but also the survival of more female infants than

252

might otherwise be the case (Balikci 1970:147-153;
Boas 1964:170-172; Freeman 1971).

All these practices offended the missionaries, who
withheld baptism and approval as well as materially
advantageous patronage from those who persisted in
them.  The moral conviction and oratorical skills
of missionaries impressed the Inuit, and Graburn
(1969:121-122) suggests the missionary resembled the
shaman and easily took over his role.  It has also
been suggested that the missionary liberated the
Inuit from a great many taboos and a fearful cosmol-
ogy, but Jenness (1964:26) writes that the Inuit,

> regarded the missionary prayers as magic
> spells, his hymns as incantations similar
> to those they had chanted in their dance-
> houses during days of stress and hunger, and
> the new command "Remember the Sabbath day,
> to keep it holy" as a new taboo that silenced
> their guns each Sunday from morning until
> evening, even when the cooking-pots were
> empty and a flock of ducks settled on the
> water near the camp.

Once the majority of the population was converted
and the missionary and his Native catechists were
accepted as moral authorities, the doctrine and ad-
monitions of the church were followed literally and
rigidly.  The Victorian attitudes of the missionaries
were emulated fervently by ayogeseyee (catechists or
lay preachers), the religion taking on an intensely
moralistic stance.  "Hell-fire and damnation" sermons
were preached against use of alcohol, gambling, enjoyment of sexuality, exposure of the body, the wearing of trousers by women, common-law marriages, and
traditional songs, legends, and myths.  Conservative
church-goers still try to adhere to these principles,
especially in smaller settlements.  In larger hamlets
such as Frobisher Bay, standards have relaxed somewhat, but Inuit active in the church are ambivalent
about drinking and gambling and tend to have repressive attitudes about sexuality.  Perhaps one of the
greatest missionary effects was to inculcate a sense
of sinfulness and guilt about pleasure.  This guilt
is often expressed as vindictive hostility toward
those persons, including Eurocanadians, who do not
uphold high moral standards.  In sum, the missionaries were the first contact agents who held con-

sistently disapproving attitudes toward most of Inuit
culture, especially toward patterns developed in interaction with easy-going whaling crews.  These attitudes likely planted the first seeds of anxiety about
the relative value of the Inuttitut way of life which
police, nurses, and teachers later reinforced in their
efforts to bring civilization to the Arctic.


GOVERNMENT SERVICES AND TOWN SETTLEMENT

Although Canada claimed all arctic islands in 1880,
no government representatives occupied the area until
1903.  Not until the 1920s were Royal Canadian Mounted
Police posts established in the eastern Arctic.  These
police conducted censuses, administered medicines and
rations, searched for missing persons, and tried to
enforce the law, including an interesting campaign
against infanticide using material inducements rather
than punishment (Jenness 1964:17-22).

The health of the Inuit deteriorated during the first
half of the twentieth century.  Epidemics and famines
continued through the 1950s in some regions.  Infant
mortality remained consistently high even after infanticide ceased; rates were 200 per 1,000 live
births as late as 1961, and 105 in 1970, four to five
times as high as the rate for Canada as a whole (Hobart 1975:37).  According to Jenness (1964:30-31),
the Federal Government was aware of the poor conditions in Inuit camps by the 1920s, but the ambiguous
status of the Inuit perpetuated a laissez-faire attitude toward intervention.  The Government relied on
missionaries to provide education, medical services,
and some social welfare (Rea 1968:37).  In 1928 the
Anglican church built a hospital in Pangnirtung which
still functions today, and the Department of the
Interior paid a doctor and nurse, with grants for
each patient (Jenness 1964:44).

The economic depression of the 1930s created a crisis
in the Arctic, as elsewhere; fur prices dropped,
deaths due to epidemics and starvation mounted, and
missions and trading posts could hardly remain open.
Probably the extreme hardship of this period, which
many Inuit today experienced in early childhood, increased the emotional and material dependence of the
Native population on Eurocanadian institutions.  In

254

the 1940s and early 1950s, when military installations were being constructed, increased public concern about the condition of the Inuit prompted the Federal Government to provide services to families camping near the installations. Government officials were uncertain as to the wisdom of encouraging Natives to settle near the bases, DEW-line sites, and meteorological stations, however (Jenness 1964:75-76). These officials worried that Inuit would become overly dependent on government assistance and wage employment, losing their hunting skills and ability to return to the land. The living conditions of Inuit camping near the bases embarrassed the government, and it was apparent Federal subsidization was essential for adequate housing, education, and medical services, not to mention job training for an essentially monolingual population.

Despite the lack of jobs and adequate housing, the Native population of Frobisher Bay grew rapidly, from 258 in 1956 to 624 in 1958, 906 in 1963, and 1,174 in 1969, stabilizing at around 1,500 in the 1970s. By the time of John and Irma Honigmann's study in 1963 (Honigmann 1975:15), modern housing was provided at reasonable subsidized rents, about 20 percent of the Native people were steadily employed, and children were being educated in standard southern curricula. By 1967 it was clear that Frobisher Bay was a permanent community, at least for the Inuit residents; the thousand or so Eurocanadians, mostly government employees and their families, were more transient. The region lacked exportable resources, and hopes the town might become an important fueling stop for transatlantic flights ended with the advent of jet aircraft. The main justification for the expensive maintenance of the community was that it provided important administrative, educational, and medical functions.

Only a few other communities in the eastern Arctic resemble Frobisher Bay in terms of the rapidity of growth, the heterogeneity of life-styles, and the larger proportion of Eurocanadians. Most communities are considerably smaller, with populations between 300 and 700 who are predominantly Native. These settlements grew around trading posts and missions. Economic incentives, including family allowances, old age pensions, aid to the disabled, and social assistance, and the need for medical care have been

primary reasons Inuit have established permanent
residence at these centers.  For example, the Caribou Eskimo moved into Eskimo Point, Rankin Inlet,
and other Keewatin villages after a period of severe
famine requiring extensive government rehabilitation
in the 1950s (Van Stone and Oswalt 1959).  Pangnirtung did not develop as a community until the mid-
1960s when an epidemic decimated the dogs and immo-
bilized the Cumberland Sound population.  The establishment of Federal day schools in most settlements
has also induced year-round sedentism.


THE MODERN PERIOD

Until the late 1960s, administration of northern
communities was the responsibility of the Federal
Department of Indian Affairs and Northern Development.  With the recent shift to territorial (and in
northern Quebec, to provincial) administration, emphasis has increased on local govenment and financial
administration through hamlet and village councils.
In both large and small settlements, Inuit serve on
community councils, juries, and school advisory
boards.  Inuit also manage, with financial guidance
and advice from territorial staff, crafts and fishing
cooperatives, housing administrations, janitorial and
municipal services businesses, and recreational associations.

The settlements are in many ways socioeconomic repli-
cas of small southern Canadian towns, in spite of the
harsh arctic environment and continued involvement
of Inuit in hunting and fishing.  Inuit are employed
in a variety of occupations:  bus, taxi, and truck
drivers, construction workers, power plant technicians, telephone operators, carpenters, secretaries,
nurse's aides, dental hygienists, in weaving and
knitting industries, as hotel maids and cooks, hostel
superintendents, interpreters, and airline ticket
agents.  Many of the Inuit keep busy schedules, attending council and co-op meetings, going to church
services two or three times a week, playing bingo
and going to movies, organizing square dances and
community games, taking adult education classes,
coaching an ice hockey team, planning weekend hunting trips.  When one recalls that these Inuit have
lived in towns only 20 years, and in some cases only
10, the rate of acculturation and extent of active

participation in town institutions is striking.
Honigmann (1975:59) suggests that three factors
encourage the high degree of Inuit involvement in
town life in Frobisher Bay: 1) the ethnic homogene-
ity of the Native population; 2) the comparatively
large proportion of Natives; and 3) the transience
and lack of commitment of Eurocanadian residents to
the town. "Hence non-natives do not monopolize community enterprise and associational positions the
way 'northerners' do in the Mackenzie Delta."

To avoid presenting a distorted view of the extent
of involvement and leadership by Inuit in the settlements, the above description must be qualified.
First, considerable diversity occurs in the life-
styles among Frobisher Bay Natives, just as in the
Mackenzie Delta administrative center of Inuvik
(Honigmann and Honigmann 1970). Some individuals
and families are highly acculturated, able to cope
bilingually and biculturally with the complex and
novel environment of the arctic town. Others are
far more traditional, especially older persons who
have had to make a radical transition in their lives.
Second, involvement in community councils, cooperatives, and school boards does not necessarily mean
that an Inuk is a political activist or supportive
of organizations such as Inuit Tapirisat of Canada.
Some of the local leaders in Frobisher Bay, Pangnirtung, Great Whale River, and other communities have
a large stake in the security which cooperation with
Eurocanadians has brought. They are reluctant to
jeopardize their positions through political opposition.

Nevertheless, the experience gained in running cooperatives, housing administrations, and small businesses has increased the assertiveness of Inuit, who
tend to be sensitive and self-critical about their
difficulties in using English and in understanding
the bureaucratic procedures recommended by their
Eurocanadian advisors. This experience may be a
necessary antecedent to local self-government.
Graburn and Strong (1973:202-203) feel that the
Cooperative Federation of northern Quebec "has provided a prototype organization for political consciousness and action among Eskimos." The annual
or biannual conventions held by cooperatives leaders,
in which "policies and aspirations that go far beyond
the running of cooperative stores" are discussed,

257

have laid a foundation for "the beginning of regional self-determination for Eskimo communities
within the provincial and national political framework of Canada."


## INTERETHNIC RELATIONS IN MODERNIZING COMMUNITIES

It is difficult to summarize the interpersonal politics of the modernizing period neatly because there
is no one type of town-living Inuk, nor is there one
type of Eurocanadian resident.  The Eurocanadians,
in fact, represent diverse linguistic and regional
backgrounds.  Most are French or English Canadians,
but a number are Blacks from the Caribbean, persons
of Central European background, and a few East Indians and Pakistanis.  Thus, it is necessary to describe the complexity of the interactional field in
some detail through examples from the communities
of Frobisher Bay and Pangnirtung.

Some Inuit, especially older people and unemployed
women, speak little English and live isolated lives
heavily dependent on traditional subsistence.  These
persons contact Eurocanadians mostly at nursing stations and HBC stores.  They tend to have stereotyped
views of Eurocanadians, alternately perceiving them
as infallible and powerful or as inept and childishly
aggressive.  More than anything else they see whites
as unpredictable and thus frightening.  One Inuk, for
example, has written (Inuit Today, March-April 1977:
79):

> I myself, even now, am afraid of white people
> sometimes, even though I know there is no
> reason to be.  Why is it that I cannot get
> over my fear of them?  They don't do me any
> harm.  But if I do something they consider
> to be wrong, or if anyone makes any trouble,
> yes, then they can become very frightening.

Other Inuit, particularly young adults and adoles-
cents, are fully bilingual and have active involvement with Eurocanadians through work, recreation,
and significantly in the larger settlements, through
encounters with law enforcement agents.  These individuals are more aware of the diversity in the personalities, roles, and attitudes of Eurocanadians
and thus stereotype them less.  Some maintain genuine

friendships with peers and co-workers while continuing to have hostile and somewhat fearful attitudes toward authority figures. Others are shy and inhibited in dealing with all Eurocanadians; yet they are basically positive and likely to copy their mannerisms. Other individuals have an unremitting hostility or ambivalence toward all Eurocanadians, seeking recognition through aggressive or promiscuous behavior but also ridiculing and criticizing them in private.

Similarly, Eurocanadians differ in the extent of contact and the degree of positive interactions with Inuit. Some are very positive in their attitudes, avoid stereotyping, and actively initiate contact. They attend bingo games, movies, and dances, join bi-ethnic sports teams, arrange to accompany Inuit on fishing and hunting trips, and invite Inuit to their homes. Others, probably the majority, encounter Inuit only on the job or in schools and often take on a tutorial and socializing role. These individuals tend to classify Inuit in terms of the ease of interaction which they experience as well as the extent to which Inuit individuals meet their approval. Their attitudes range from a patronizing determination to help the Inuit to improve their lives to a romantic sense of regret that the Inuit have been "ruined by civilization." Locked into these attitudes by their roles and motives for coming north, these Eurocanadians are most frustrated in their dealings with Inuit, who fail to be grateful and enthusiastic about their efforts. And some Eurocanadians, particularly housewives and persons whose jobs do not involve frequent contact with Inuit, remain isolated. These individuals tend to have the most critical views of Inuit, seeing them as unhygienic, promiscuous or alcoholic, and above all, childish.

In general, few Eurocanadians speak any Inuttitut other than a few popular phrases; exceptions include HBC clerks, some Anglican ministers, and those administrators who have learned the language through previous work as HBC clerks or as missionaries. Obviously, then, the language of contact is English, or to a limited extent in northern Quebec, French. Since few Inuit learn English as their first language, verbal communication is not always smooth or complete. Of course, much non-verbal communication occurs between ethnic groups, often conveying tension, mistrust, and even fear which neither group intends.

Interpersonal politics include the informal rules, and "negotiations" about the rules, which define power and status relations in a community. In complex settlements such as Frobisher Bay, the rules are ambiguous and rapidly changing. They include such patterns as the fact that Inuit who appear intoxicated in public can expect to be held in "protective custody" by the police overnight while Eurocanadians in a similar state will be told to go home and sober up. Little disapproval is expressed when Eurocanadian youths develop romantic or sexual relationships with Inuit girls, but negative pressure is put on the Inuk who becomes similarly involved with a Eurocanadian girl. Interethnic marriages are accepted by both groups, but only if it involves a female Inuk "marrying up."

Clearly, gender is an important factor in interethnic relations, and interaction on the job is considerably smoother between female Native employees and their supervisors than between male co-workers. Inuit males tend to be sensitive about criticism and pressure on the job, perhaps because negative feedback insults their pride and threatens their need for autonomy. The types of jobs open to males require close attention to technical details, and criticism is considered by supervisors to be a necessary part of training. The employment rate of young males in the settlements, approximately 50 percent, has not risen over the last ten years. Male employees turn over at a high rate, whereas increasing numbers of young women are finding jobs in public-service capacities.

Not all informal rules of conduct put Inuit at a disadvantage. Because Inuit are uncomfortable about refusing a request or criticizing a suggestion, they may agree to a proposal or commitment which they privately dislike or do not intend to honor. The passive resistance which follows is often frustrating to Eurocanadians; yet the absence of an open refusal or disagreement makes it difficult to assess the situation. Liberal Eurocanadians often decide that Inuk who forgot an appointment or who did not make a parka on time, for example, simply did not understand the arrangement. More critical individuals conclude that the Inuk is simply unreliable or hostile.

One pattern most perplexing to Eurocanadians is that
Inuit tend to withdraw from stressful situations.
Withdrawal may involve the Inuk leaving the scene
rather than expressing anger or anxiety, but more
often it is a psychological withdrawal expressed by
becoming very quiet, noncommittal, and uninvolved.
The more Eurocanadians push and the louder they speak,
the more withdrawn the Inuk becomes, making the conduct of business in classroom or office difficult.
Even in situations involving little stress and ideally
promoting congeniality, such as a dinner party or community dance, the silence and passive composure of
Inuit are distressing to Eurocanadians who do not
understand the politeness and caution implicit in
such demeanor.

These few examples indicate that power, especially
in a psychological sense, is by no means confined to
the issues of who gets and keeps jobs, how housing
is allocated, enforcement of the law, and double
standards of sexual morality, although these are the
more obvious arenas in which the subordinate status
of Inuit is evident. Power and esteem are also negotiated on a day-to-day basis in terms of agreements
kept or broken, smooth communication, whether people
freely touch one another or keep their distance, and
how they express their approval or disapproval of
each other's life-style and behavior. Rightly or
wrongly, many Inuit perceive that Eurocanadians
consider them to be inferior in their education,
their ability to use English, and their clothing or
furniture. Inuit resent this perceived attribution
of inferiority, but until recently their resentment
has come out sideways, without direct confrontation.


THE FOUNDING OF INUIT TAPIRISAT OF CANADA

Tapirisat is officially translated by ITC as "brotherhood." Various informants have suggested that the
term also means "allies" or "partners." Inuit Tapirisat was established at a conference held at Carleton
University in August of 1971. It was organized by
Inuit themselves, with support from the Indian-Eskimo
Association of Canada, a non-partisan and primarily
non-Native organization which changed its name in
1972 to the Canadian Association in Support of Native
Peoples. An employee of IEA, Tagak Curley, along
with six Inuit delegates to an IEA board meeting,

had requested support for the founding conference in February 1971.

The idea of forming a national organization of Inuit grew out of many meetings with community council members, co-op leaders, and representatives of COPE. These Inuit leaders were concerned about the isolation and lack of communication among the various "grass-roots" movements in the North struggling to organize community support for expression of grievances. The range of concerns among local leaders, many of them young and politically inexperienced, included revision of the assimilationist school curriculum, the current exploitation of interpreters, the need to preserve traditional myths and songs, and the effects of increasing jet and supersonic aircraft, use of dynamite, leakage of oil, and raw sewage disposal on local ecosystems.

Underlying these specific concerns was a general urgency about the lack of Inuit decisions on northern development being reported in the media. For example, Panarctic Oils, Ltd. had spent more than a hundred million dollars on exploration and drilling in the North in 1970. The magnitude of this investment was perturbing, particularly in view of the fact that Inuit had not been consulted, and the issue of land title was still open. Leaders who met with IEA representatives in February 1971 "expressed a feeling of urgency for the Inuit to become aware of their legal rights if they are to be a part of northern development rather than its casualties" (IEA Bulletin, March 17, 1971:1).

Twenty-three delegates, six women and seventeen men, all of them under the age of 40, attended the week-long conference in Ottawa. They represented communities in the eastern and central districts of the Northwest Territories, northern Manitoba, and Arctic Quebec. Nine men and one woman were elected to the Board of Directors, corporation by-laws were drawn up, and six formal objectives were established, as follows (Inuit Monthly, December 1971:1):

> 1) to help preserve Inuit (Eskimo culture and language and promote dignity and pride in Inuit heritage;

262

2) to unite all Inuit of the Northwest Territories, Arctic Quebec, Labrador and Manitoba, and to represent them with regard
   to all matters affecting their affairs;

3) to protect the rights of Inuit hunters
   and trappers in the Canadian North and
   to promote the formation of a Hunters
   and Trappers Association in each Inuit
   community;

4) to improve communication among the Inuit
   communities of the Canadian North by use
   of all available sources of communication;

5) to assist the Inuit to become aware of
   their own situation, government plans,
   aboriginal rights, legal matters, and
   educational opportunities so that they
   may determine those things of a social,
   economic, educational, and political
   nature which will affect them and future
   generations.

6) to assist the Inuit in their right to
   full participation in and sense of belonging to Canadian society and to promote public awareness of those rights.

National headquarters was established in Ottawa,
and regional offices and field stations on Baffin
Island, in the Keewatin, in Northern Quebec, and
in Cambridge Bay. Financial support was provided
by IEA, the Canindis Foundation, the World Council
of Churches, and the Federal Government.


ACTIVITIES AND ORGANIZATION OF ITC

From the beginning the scope of ITC's activities has
been ambitious and greatly demanding of the energy
of its small staff, about 30 Inuit and Eurocanadians
at the head office. The original newsletter has developed into an impressive 80-page bilingual magazine,
with features including news, editorials, letters,
book reviews, autobiographies, poetry, conference
proceedings, information about other Native organizations, announcements of employment opportunities,
and many photographs and cartoons. The officers

and staff of ITC have intervened in grievances of
Inuit workers, provided assistance and guidance in
legal problems, represented communities protesting
off-shore drilling and use of dynamite, and attended
national meetings of other organizations such as
COPE and the Native Council of Canada as well as
coordinating annual ITC meetings in northern settlements. ITC representatives working out of settlement
officers have provided employment and legal counsel
to Native residents and have helped to maintain communication between the various settlement offices
and with the national office.

The internal organization of Inuit Tapirisat reflects
models provided by western organizations and bureau-
cracies. ITC has established a number of committees
and formed liaisons with regional affiliates and
special-purpose commissions. The regional affiliates
are the Baffin Region Inuit Association, the Keewatin
Inuit Association, the Kitikmeot Inuit Association
(serving the northern Mackenzie district around
Bathurst Inlet), the Labrador Inuit Association, and
the Northern Quebec Inuit Association. Each of these
associations holds annual meetings and elections,
sends representatives to the annual ITC general assembly, and reports on local activities and concerns
for publication in Inuit Today, ITC's newsmagazine.

The committees and programs that ITC has organized
include the Inuit Non-Profit Housing Corporation,
which has initiated pilot projects for house design
and construction in five communities; the Inuit
Development Corporation, which assists small community-owned businesses managed by local Inuit; the
liaison and research program, funded by the Secretary
of State, which attempts to improve communication
between government departments and Inuit; the com-
munications research project, which works for improved
television, radio, and telephone service in the North;
and the very active information and public relations
program, whose staff has spoken at a variety of conferences in Canada, produced posters and T-shirts,
helped to organize and publicize the Nunavut land
claims proposal, and prepared two documentary films
about Inuit.

A newly established organization until quite recently
affiliated with ITC is the Inuit Cultural Institute
(ICI), directed by Inuit Tapirisat's first president,

Tagak Curley. ICI's programs correspond closely to Curley's initial interest in emphasizing Inuit identity through educational activities. These programs include the National Inuit Council on Education (NICE), an advisory group working with the director "to develop a truly Inuit approach to education" (ITC Annual Report 1976:21). In addition, ICI sponsors the Inuit Language Commission which has prepared a new Inuttitut writing system and will develop a dictionary and taped material. A resource library and printing system are being organized at Eskimo Point and will include audiovisual materials, books, and articles about Inuit. Various workshops have also been planned for 1977: a "cross-cultural learning experience" for Eurocanadian government staff members "to give them an awareness of the cultural differences between Inuit and Kabloona"; a workshop to discuss development of an Inuit history course to be taught to Native schoolchildren; and a workshop to "explore methods to implement the Man and the Biosphere (MAB) 'Principles for Conduct of Scientists in the North'" (ITC Annual Report 1976:22-23).

With this proliferation of committees and programs, considerable effort and financing are needed to coordinate ITC's activities. Yet coordination is difficult because many programs operate in the settlements while the head office is in Ottawa. Thus, a fair amount of time is spent organizing conferences and workshops, which are often held in northern settlements to allow the residents to participate and to voice their concerns. The problems faced in arranging air transportation and support facilities are formidable.

The leaders and active members of Inuit Tapirisat are mostly young people between 20 and 35 although recently older individuals are taking positions as heads of regional associations. The level of formal education varies among the leaders, although most are bilingual. Some have completed a secondary school education or have received extensive vocational training. Older individuals usually have had little formal schooling; nevertheless, they are literate in the syllabic system or in the Roman orthography system of writing used in Labrador and parts of western and central Arctic.

265

The background of the 1977-term president of ITC, Michael Amarook, is similar to that of many other leaders. He comes from Baker Lake, is 35 years old, and has nine children. He has worked as a full-time hunter, an interpreter and translator, a director of print-making in a crafts shop, a co-op manager, and a regional land claims officer. He has had no formal schooling.

Each of the three presidents of ITC in the years 1971-1977 have been low-keyed, almost self-effacing individuals decidedly non-charismatic in their style of leadership. While Tagak Curley and James Arvaluk maintain a "mod," sophisticated appearance with full moustaches, longish hair, pilot-style eyeglasses, and stylish clothes, Michael Amarook appears to be a more traditional person. He works in shirt sleeves and poses for his official photograph in a Scandinavian pullover. His hair is short and he has only a shadow of a moustache. He began his speech to the general assembly (Inuit Today, March-April 1977:29) by stating he had decided to run for presidency of ITC because he was an Inummarrit, a "real Eskimo"--a concept of considerable significance to Inuit who use the term to describe one skilled in traditional subsistence techniques and loyal to traditional values.

One of the interesting characteristics of the structure of Inuit Tapirisat is the low profile of women in the organization. Since its initial founding, men have dominated, particularly in elected and executive positions. Women are active in the organization but more in terms of managing internal business matters, such as editing Inuit Today, accounting, and secretarial work. The one Native woman on the Board of Directors serves as secretary-treasurer.

## LAND CLAIMS AND THE BEGINNING OF INTERNAL FACTIONALISM

The land claims issue continues to be a major concern and one of the most controversial activities of ITC. In 1972 it received a Federal grant to prepare a position paper on land claims and northern development. Further studies, funded by loans from the Department of Indian Affairs and Northern Development, have been conducted to collect data on original and present Inuit occupancy and use of northern lands. These data are considered necessary as a first step in negotiations about land claims settlements according to the legal theory of aboriginal rights in English and Canadian law. Cumming and Mickenberg (1972: 3:160-164) define aboriginal rights as "those rights which native people retain as a result of their original possession of the soil." Because Inuit as well as many Indian groups did not possess territory in a conventional sense, in this context aboriginal rights are defined as "those property rights which inure to native people by virtue of their occupation upon certain lands from time immemorial." Aboriginal title has not yet been specifically recognized for the Inuit by the government or the courts. Until it is recognized, there is danger that extinction of title might proceed from any Territorial or Federal legislation transferring lands from the public (Crown) domain to other sectors.

The land claims project has an interesting history which reflects the importance of consensus and local support in the operation of ITC. Early in 1975 ITC presented an official proposal for settlement of Northwest Territories land claims to the Federal Government. After the proposal was submitted, field workers of the land claims committee visited communities to explain the proposal at public meetings and to organize local claims committees. In September 1975, ITC decided to withdraw the proposal for revisions. This decision was made in response to feedback at the community level. There are at least two explanations why this feedback was negative. John Amagoalik, the ITC land claims director, has stated (Inuit Today, March-April 1977:45):

> ...land claims fieldworkers started travelling to the communities to explain the proposal to the Inuit and what it would mean to them. We then began to realize that the Inuit did not fully understand the proposal, and it was very hard to explain fully because it is a legal document written in lawyer's language. We knew then that Inuit would need more time to absorb the proposal and its full meaning.... It would be wrong for Inuit to agree to something they don't fully understand. So when we, the land claims staff, became aware of the situation, we decided to withdraw the proposal.... We did this so that we could take the proposal

back to the Inuit and explain it until they understood it fully.

A second reason for the withdrawal is that local input had not been sufficient from the beginning. The ITC Annual Report (1976:7) states:  "From the field work we found that many Inuit were concerned that some parts of the proposal did not represent their views, and that they had not had enough participation in producing the Nunavut proposal.  They wanted some major changes."

At the 5th annual ITC general assembly held at Fort Chimo in January 1977, John Amagoalik proposed that a new land-claims commission with full-time workers be established to function independently of the ITC Board of Directors.  This proposal met with approval, and the organization to be established consists of three members from each of three regions, with election of officers at the annual land claims conference.  The commission, affiliated with ITC but with its own Board of Directors, is responsible for drafting the new claims settlement proposal.

The internal dynamics which have led to the splitting off of the land claims workers from Inuit Tapirisat are not clear.  Amagoalik has written (Inuit Today, March-April 1977:1) that the main reason,

> was to speed up the land claims process.  It was felt that the ITC board of directors did not have enough time to deal with land claims while they had so many other issues to deal with.  It was also felt that some regional issues were being neglected because the board spent so much time on land claims in the N.W.T.

This statement obviously confounds the issue; is the criticism that the Board has spent too little time, or too much time, on land claims?

James Arvaluk, whose term of office as president of the organization ended in 1977, has written the following about the progress of claims settlements (1976 Annual Report:1):

> We cannot point to any dramatic or spectacular achievements.  We still do not

268

have an agreement in principle with the
government of Canada.  But it has been a
year of quiet progress.... It may be said
that we are not moving quickly enough to
satisfy some people.... We have to move
as quickly as possible to protect our land
and resources while there is still something
left to claim, but at the same time it is
vital that our decisions are the right ones,
because our children and their children will
have to live with them forever.

The independent establishment of the new land claims
commission is not the only example of divergence in
goals and disagreements about methods among ITC's
members and affiliates.  The members of COPE have
decided to proceed independently in pursuing their
own land claims policy.  The official stance of ITC
on this decision is one of support; James Arvaluk
(1976 Annual Report:2) has written:  "It is perfectly
understandable that the Western Arctic people are in
a hurry.  They are under extreme pressure, due to
oil and gas development and the proposed Mackenzie
Valley pipeline."  But in his election campaign,
Michael Amarook stated a different position (Inuit
Today, March-April 1977:31):

The first thing I will think about is COPE's
split with ITC on land claims.  I was shocked
to hear that they had decided to go it on
their own on this very important issue.  If
I am elected, I will try to get COPE to re-
join the other N.W.T. regions to work out a
land claims settlement through the new commission.  I will work to unite all Inuit in
the North.

The conflict with COPE escalated because of rumors
that ITC was involved in circulating petitions in
the western Arctic sponsored by councillor John Steen
which urged COPE to work with ITC on land claims.
Amarook has affirmed that ITC is "maintaining a
strictly neutral position in what appears to be an
internal problem among Inuit of the western region"
(Inuit Today, May 1977:19).  If ITC is not considered
activist enough by organizations like COPE, at least
one affiliate, the Inuit Cultural Institute, considers the direction of ITC to be too political.
The ICI announced its withdrawal from affiliation

with ITC in January 1977 "to prevent political con-
siderations from interfering with the organization's
work in developing social, cultural, and educational
policies for Inuit" (Inuit Today, March-April 1977:
17).

As tensions mount over the sensitive issue of land
claims, hints of internal problems and potential
factionalism in Inuit Tapirisat become evident.  For
example, the question was raised at the 1977 general
assembly as to whether ITC would become the government of Nunavut if and when a claims settlement is
reached.  Officers responded that this would not be
the case, and the people of the region would have
the right to decide how the new government would be
organized.  Another question raised was whether current procedures for electing the Board of Directors
allowed adequate representation of all Inuit.  Some
individuals expressed the view that restricting voting rights to members of ITC meant that "the majority of Inuit in the North feel they are being neg-
lected by ITC" (Inuit Today, March-April 1977:49-50).
In addition, there has been some cross-fire between
ITC and one of its affiliates, the Northern Québec
Association, which recently ratified the James Bay
and Northern Québec Agreement and has been making
slow headway in negotiating implementation of the
agreement.  NQIA has not had the full support of
the people it has tried to represent; the residents
of Povungnituk disagree with some of the points in
the agreement, and negotiations with the Naskapi of
Schefferville have been necessary.  These problems
have evoked negative comments about the overall
settlement from ITC.  In reply, a representative
of NQIA has written an unusually acerbic letter in
which the following statements appear (Inuit Today,
May 1977:10-11):

> ...I want to point out that the Quebec Inuit
> were never much assisted by ITC in their ef-
> forts to reach a settlement... the N.W.T.
> Inuit would be completely justified in making
> such comments if they had taken a deeper in-
> terest in the progress of the Quebec nego-
> tiations.  Not once do I remember any ITC
> leaders coming to express their support and
> their concern when we were at the height of
> carrying the tremendous burden of negotiating
> this settlement....  This is past now, and

I do not want to dwell on it.... I politely suggest that land claims leaders in the N.W.T. shut up about the Northern Quebec settlement and concentrate their energy on producing an agreement which is even better than ours. When I am shown that the N.W.T. settlement is so much better, and when people such as Tagak Curley again make critical comments about the Northern Quebec agreement, it will then be my turn to shut up. But only then.

Editorial statements by ITC leaders asking for unity within the organization and good relations with other organizations are increasing in the newsletter. John Amagoalik, for example, writes (Inuit Today, May 1977:54):

It disturbs me a great deal to hear about native organizations squabbling with other native organizations. If we are to achieve anything, we must not fight among ourselves. We can agree to disagree, but we must sort out our problems together. We must be of one mind and of one voice. This is not always possible among human beings. But we must not let petty disagreements divide us.

The tensions over land claims and political action are not only internal. Perhaps the most serious controversy to date concerns cancellation of a local government training workshop scheduled to have been held in Baker Lake in March 1977. The actual reasons for the initial government decision to cancel the workshop are not known to the ITC staff, but it has been suggested that "some unidentified person was worried about the so-called 'radical' or 'revolutionary' material to be used in the workshop" (Inuit Today, May 1977:15). Initial protest against the cancellation led to reconsideration by N.W.T. officials and the decision was reversed. But then the delegates decided to boycott the workshop. The settlement council of Baker Lake followed their charge with this challenging statement:

...we believe the overriding factor is that cancellation of the workshop is a deliberate political attempt by the executive of the N.W.T. government, namely the commissioner,

271

to ensure that native people learn and are
taught, only what the government wants to
teach them.  This completely rules out the
right to self-determination of the native
peoples of the N.W.T.

According to the Inuit Today account of the controversy, there is conflict within the N.W.T. government
concerning the proper functions of such workshops.
The article states (Inuit Today, May 1977:17) that
one official,

gave "fear of too much political involvement
by training officers" as the reason for the
cancellation.  He remarked that it is the
role of local government to teach the settlements how to deal with day to day affairs,
not how to deal with political concerns such
as native organizations or higher forms of
government.

The dynamics of this controversy are particularly
interesting because it is one of the first examples
of unified opposition and retaliation by Inuit against
the government.  Whether the boycott will have a positive effect or simply create an impasse in relations
is not certain, but it does introduce a hint of militancy and assertiveness contrasting with the general
stance of Inuit less than a decade ago.


THE ISSUE OF MILITANCY

When Inuit Tapirisat was first established in 1971,
the tone of public statements explaining the purpose
of the new organization was decidedly non-militant.
While not fully pro-development, certain statements
suggested that northern development was accepted as
inevitable and that Inuit simply wanted involvement
and partial control in the process.  For example,
Tagak Curley stated (IEA Bulletin, March 17, 1971:1):

... We don't want to blame the white man
25 years from now for destroying our environment.  If the government continues to introduce programs without consulting the people,
it will not be able to meet its own goals.
To be successful in development of the north,
it needs to involve the people, and to enable

them to have control over their lives.

Another officer commented (Eastern Arctic Star, January 3, 1972:14): "We are a liaison between the government and a native people. We intend to work with the government, not fight it."

The original leaders of the organization were probably correct at the time in their assessment that militancy would receive little support. There are several reasons for ambivalence about activism. First, a number of local leaders who had attained a fairly secure position in their communities were uncertain about opposing development. As harsh as their private criticism might be of certain Eurocanadians, they tended to be cautiously positive toward each new southerner they encountered, expecting some benefit from each new policy. One informant, for example, stated:

> ... You know, some people say that the government should leave us alone, just pull out and let us keep the old way of life. But my wife says who would run the hospital? What if the kids get sick? I don't know, what I figure is that the government is pretty good for us right now. The only thing is I can't always understand what the government wants, what those people are trying to tell us.

It was precisely this need for explanation and education which ITC initially proposed to serve by informing Inuit in the Native language "so that they may understand the changes being introduced by the government" (IEA Bulletin, March 17, 1971:5).

A second reason for uncertainty about organized, committed opposition is that some Inuit and Eurocanadians develop genuine and enduring friendships. This bond is particularly true of the few Eurocanadian families who have decided to stay indefinitely in the North. Inuit who continue to deal with each individual on a personal, one-to-one basis are able to discriminate in their level of trust in dealing with Eurocanadians. A statement by an Inuk writing to Inuit Today (June 1975:72-73) exemplifies this attitude:

273

We have always welcomed the white people
to our land as friends, but many Inuit
are beginning to get edgy about the white
man's exploitation of the land and the
Inuit in the North.  White people will
remain our friends, and we will continue
to consider them good neighbours when they
come to live with us.  It is when people
like oilmen, anthropologists, zoologists,
and countless numbers of government researchers start combing the land and disturbing the environment, the animals, and
the people, that we Inuit get upset.

In coping with the intrusion of whalers, traders, and
missionaries, as well as all the government personnel
of the modern era, Inuit have shown great flexibility.
This quality of adaptability is evident in two principal spheres.  First, Inuit tolerate great diversity
in acculturation among themselves, perhaps because
kinship ties take priority over socioeconomic differences and divergence in life-styles, although the
primacy of kinship is beginning to decline in the
larger settlements.  This toleration reflects a number of traditional sociopsychological traits which
continue to be maintained in the town setting.  According to Honigmann and Honigmann (1971:69-70),
these traits include:

> ... a considerable measure of traditional
> atomism, weak and informal leadership,
> patience of people with one another, and
> a reluctance to press too closely on one
> another in expecting conformity.  Behind
> their disinclination to press one another
> is a reluctance to idealize the world, to
> see it as the blue-print says it should be,
> and to measure people and situations by
> whether they come up to standards.

The latter quality, the disinclination to judge
people by ideal standards, serves to inhibit polarization and active antagonism between whites and Inuit
in the communities.

Flexibility also means many Inuit have not sharply
questioned or challenged the innovations and advice
of Eurocanadians.  It is possible that Inuit are
cautious about challenge because they do not wish to
lose possible advantages.  But Willmott (1968:156)
suggests a deeper dynamic is operating:

274

The Eskimo's attitude toward the environment is summed up in the word "arunamut,"
which literally means, "because nothing
can be done," and implies "therefore we
must face the situation without regret."
Ever since the white man entered the
Arctic, the Eskimo has said "arunamut"
to all his incomprehensible antics.
White economy, then white religion, and
finally white political authority have
penetrated Eskimo society, wrought far-
reaching and irrevocable changes on it --
often without the understanding of the
Eskimos involved. Yet these changes have
not been overtly opposed by the Eskimos.
Rather, the social organization has adapted
to the changes as it would adapt to a
natural disaster or an environmental change.

## CONCLUSIONS

In the early stages of Inuit Tapirisat development,
members generally concurred about the appropriate
goals: communication between Inuit and government
agencies, the transmission of information, heighten-
ing of ethnic awareness and pride, and ensuring that
Inuit had representation in the inevitable land
claims processes. These functions may be categor-
ized as "negotiations" analogous in style to the
kinds of interpersonal politics which have characterized interethnic relations in the last few decades.

As long as Inuit Tapirisat and its affiliates negotiated in this style, little conflict arose between
government and the private agencies supporting these
organizations. The very nature of the original goals
precluded the risk of impasse and breakdown ensuing
from hard bargaining and rigid opposition. Militancy
was avoided not only because it did not concur with
the charter of the organization, but also because
it would not be supported at the "grass-roots" level.
In this context, impasse was as much an internal
threat as an external risk; too militant or rigid
a stance might bring conflict within the organization
and a breakdown of consensus.

The Nunavut proposal, with its separatist overtones,
represented a definite step toward action. While

not overtly militant, the document did represent some real decisions about the political identity of Inuit. Thus it was threatening, not so much to the Federal Government, which is probably ready to examine the issue of aboriginal title, but to Inuit themselves. Possibly, any kind of proposal, no matter how carefully developed and representative of local concerns, would have created the kinds of tension and emerging factionalism which Inuit Tapirisat now faces. As the time for actual submission of a new proposal and the beginning of negotiations with the government approaches, the Inuit will need to consider the threat of change on their internal political processes. They may also have to evaluate the history of their relations with Eurocanadians.

This history has been one in which personalistic relations have predominated and Native leadership has been situationally defined in part by white patronage. In the contact and early modernization periods, for example, one Inuk might become a leader in the church, another in organizing the whale hunting and processing teams employed by the Hudson's Bay Company, and yet another as a manager of a housing co-op. Inuit have been treated as a "people under tutelage" to use the Honigmanns' characterization (1971:55). The process is not necessarily oppression or exploitation in the usual sense of the word, but the particular dynamic of interaction has inhibited the development of an independent political structure. Until recently, no one individual or group has been able to speak legitimately for an entire community or regional population. Formal political relations between Inuit and Eurocanadians have been impeded as much by the dynamics of contact as by the individualism of the Native society. The consequences of these dynamics are becoming apparent as Inuit leaders unify their people and actualize their goal of self-determination for actic peoples.

The stakes of development are high for all parties concerned. For the Northwest Territories, the tapping of natural resources may mean a step toward economic self-sufficiency and implementation of the goal of provincial status. For Canada, development promises a stronger position vis-a-vis the United States and other nations. To the Native peoples, development poses the highest stakes of all. A

suitable settlement could bring the respect and ac-
knowledgment of their basic rights and ethnic autonomy,
thus easing the pressures for assimilation which dominate the present educational system.  An unacceptable
settlement could bring increased conflict and destroy
the foundation of consensus and unification which
Inuit Tapirisat of Canada has created.

One other issue has been heightened by the land
claims issue: one that concerns the effect of political tensions on basic Inuit values and identity.  More
than one leader has spoken out on this issue affirming
that political success at the cost of losing an Inummarrit identity is no success at all.  Perhaps the
most eloquent statement has been provided by John
Amagoalik, and sections from his essay serve to conclude this paper (Inuit Today, May 1977:53-54).

> ...  It may be true that the physical part
> of our culture has been eroded to the point
> where it can never return to its full poten-
> tial.  But the non-physical part of our cul-
> ture -- our attitude towards life, our re-
> spect for nature, our realization that others
> will follow who deserve the respect and con-
> cern of present generations -- are deeply
> entrenched within ourselves.  The presence
> of our ancestors within ourselves is very
> strong.  The will to survive is there.  If
> we are to survive as a race, we must have
> the understanding and patience of the domin-
> ant cultures of this country.  We do not
> need the pity, the welfare, the paternalism
> and the colonialism which has been heaped
> upon us over the years....
>
> ...  In a world which becomes more compli-
> cated with each passing year, we must rely
> on the simple, gentle ways of our people to
> guide us.  In a world so full of greed, we
> must share.  We must remember that, of all
> the things in this world, nothing belongs
> to us.  Of what we take, we must share....
>
> ...  I have become more and more concerned
> about the angry words which some of our
> people are starting to use.  I cannot really
> blame them for their feelings.  Their feelings

toward the white man are easy to understand.
It is very easy to blame the white man for
the predicament we find ourselves in today.
But anger and hate are not the answers.  We
need the patience and understanding of our
white brothers.  If we are to expect that
from them, we must offer the same in return.
The Inuit, by nature, are not a violent
people.  This is one of our virtues which
we must not lose.

## REFERENCES CITED

Balikci, A.
    1970    The Netsilik Eskimo.  Garden City, New
            York:  The Natural History Press.

Boas, F.
    1964    The Central Eskimo.  Lincoln:  University
            of Nebraska Press.

Cumming, P. A. and N. H. Mickenberg
    1972    Native Rights in Canada.  2nd edition.
            Toronto:  The Indian-Eskimo Association
            of Canada, General Publishing Co., Ltd.

Eastern Arctic Star
            Frobisher Bay, N.W.T. weekly newspaper,
            R. E. Jackson, Ed.

Fleming, A. L.
    1932    Perils of the Polar Pack.  London:
            Missionary Society of the Church of
            England.

Freeman, M.
    1971    "A Social and Ecological Analysis of
            Systematic Female Infanticide among the
            Netsilik Eskimo."  American Anthropolo-
            gist 73:1011-1019.

Graburn, N.
    1969    Eskimos without Igloos.  Boston:
            Little, Brown & Co.

Graburn, N. and B. S. Strong
    1973    Circumpolar Peoples:  An Anthropological
            Perspective.  Pacific Palisades, Ca.:
            Goodyear Publishing Co., Inc.

Hall, C. F.
    1970    Life with the Esquimaux.  Rutland, Vt.:
            Charles E. Tuttle Co.

Haller, A. A.
    1966    A Human Geographical Study of the
            Hunting Economy of Cumberland Sound.
            M. A. Thesis, Department of Geography,
            McGill University, Montreal.

Higgins, G. M.
    1967    South Coast - Baffin Island.  An Area
            Economic Survey.  Ottawa:  Industrial
            Division, Northern Administration Branch,
            Department of Indian Affairs and Northern
            Development.

Hobart, C. W.
    1975    "Socioeconomic Correlates of Mortality
            and Morbidity among Inuit Infants."
            Arctic Anthropology 12:37-48.

Honigmann, J. J.
    1975    Five Northern Towns.  Anthropological
            Papers of the University of Alaska
            17(1).

Honigmann, J. J. and I. Honigmann
    1965    Eskimo Townsmen.  Ottawa:  Canadian
            Research Centre for Anthropology,
            University of St. Paul.

    1968    "People under Tutelage."  In V. F.
            Valentine and F. G. Vallee (Eds.),
            Eskimo of the Canadian Arctic.  Toronto:
            McClelland & Steward Ltd., Carleton
            Library 41:173-185.

    1970    Arctic Townsmen.  Ottawa:  Canadian
            Research Centre for Anthropology,
            University of St. Paul.

    1971    "The Eskimo of Frobisher Bay."  In J.L.
            Elliott (Ed.), Native Peoples.  Scar-
            borough, Ont.:  Prentice-Hall of Canada,
            Ltd.
279

Indian-Eskimo Association of Canada
          Association Bulletin.  G. Kaegi, Ed.
          Toronto.

Inuit Tapirisat of Canada
     1976     Annual Report.   Ottawa.

Inuit Today
          Inuit Tapirisat of Canada newsmagazine
          (formerly Inuit Monthly).  L. d'Argen-
          court, Ed.  Ottawa.

Jenness, D.
     1964     Eskimo Administration II:  Canada.
              Montreal:  Arctic Institute of North
              America Technical Paper 14.

Lantis, M.
     1966     "The Administration of Northern Peoples:
              Canada and Alaska."  In R. St. J.
              MacDonald (Ed.), The Arctic Frontier.
              Toronto:  University of Toronto Press.

Lewis, A.
     1905     The Life and Work of E. J. Peck among
              the Eskimos.  London:  Hodder and
              Stoughton.

Lurie, N. O.
     1971     "The Contemporary American Indian
              Scene."  In E. O. Leacock and N. O.
              Lurie (Eds.), North American Indians
              in Historical Perspective.  New York:
              Random House.

MacBain, S. K.
     1970     The Evolution of Frobisher Bay as a
              Major Settlement in the Canadian Eastern
              Arctic.  M.A. Thesis, Department of
              Geography, McGill University, Montreal.

Matthiasson, John S.
     1979     "Northern Baffin Island Women in Three
              Cultural Periods."  In A. McElroy and
              C. Matthiasson (Eds.), Sex-Roles in
              Changing Cultures.  SUNY Buffalo, Occa-
              sional Papers in Anthropology No. 1.

McElroy, A. P.
    1972    "The Origins and Development of Inuit
            (Eskimo) Alliance Movements in the
            Eastern Canadian Arctic." Genoa:
            Proceedings of the XL International
            Congress of Americanists 2:603-611.

    1975    "Canadian Arctic Modernization and
            Change in Female Inuit Role Identifica-
            tion." American Ethnologist 2:662-686.

    1977    Alternatives in Modernization: A Study
            of Styles and Strategies in the Accul-
            turative Behavior of Baffin Island
            Inuit. New Haven: HRAFlex Books.

Northern Economic Development Branch
            Canada North of '60. Ottawa: Depart-
            ment of Indian Affairs and Northern
            Development.

Rea, K. J.
    1968    The Political Economy of the Canadian
            North. Toronto: University of Toronto
            Press.

Vallee, F. G.
    1968    "Differentiation among the Eskimo in
            some Canadian Arctic Settlements."
            In V. F. Valentine and F. G. Vallee
            (Eds.), Eskimo of the Canadian Arctic.
            Toronto: McClelland & Steward, Ltd.,
            Carleton Library 41.

Van den Steenhoven, G.
    1959    Legal Concepts among the Netsilik
            Eskimos of Pelly Bay, N.W.T. Ottawa:
            Northern Coordination and Research
            Centre, Department of Northern Affairs
            and National Resources.

Van Stone, J. W. and W. Oswalt
    1959    The Caribou Eskimos of Eskimo Point.
            Ottawa: Northern Coordination and
            Research Centre, Department of Northern
            Affairs and National Resources.

Willmott, W. E.
    1968    "The Flexibility of Eskimo Social Organ-
            ization."  In V. F. Valentine and F. G.
            Vallee (Eds.), Eskimo of the Canadian
            Arctic.  Toronto:  McClelland & Steward,
            Ltd., Carleton Library 41.

Yatsushiro, T.
    1960    "The Changing Eskimo Economy:  Wage
            Employment and Its Consequences among
            the Eskimos of Frobisher Bay, Baffin
            Island."  Paper presented to the
            American Anthropological Association,
            Minneapolis, 1960.

CHAPTER 11

The Politics of Power:
Indian-White Relations in a Changing World

Fred Eggan, The University of Chicago


During the long period of Indian-white relationships
in North America there has been both conflict and
accommodation as the various Indian groups were dispossessed of their land and moved to new locations.
The major political instrument involved in this process, in addition to the military, was the treaty.
An analysis of the treaty terms over time, along
with the relevant court decisions, provides one in-
dex to the changing relations between the Indian and
white worlds.  While the U. S. Congress ended further
treaty-making with Indians in 1871, they recognized
the validity of the 371 existing Indian treaties, and
as Ernest Schusky notes, much of the current conflict
between Indians and whites centers on the interpretation of treaty relations.  In Canada treaty-making
was less usual and treaties are still being made with
Indian groups, though on a more modest scale, and a
comparison of the results will be illuminating.

Much of Schusky's paper is devoted to Indian-white
relationships in the colonial period and through the
American Revolution.  He documents the shift from
"independent foreign nations" to "dependent domestic
nations," as the position of the Indians vis-a-vis
the colonists changed.  In the colonial period both
the British and French made treaties with Indian
tribes as independent foreign nations, in the European tradition, but once the colonists had achieved
their independence from Britain, the Indians were
no longer foreign nor were they altogether independent.

The process is illustrated by the Wabanaki Confederacy which developed in the northern New England
states, the Maritime Provinces, and eastern Quebec
in the seventeenth and eighteenth centuries, when
this region was part of New France.  Willard Walker
and his associates provide a fascinating account of
these tribes who developed an alliance lasting until
the expulsion of the French in 1759.  They then
played an important role in the Revolution.  The

283

French missionaries had a strategic role in the
French colonial period, and aided in the arranging
of the Treaty of 1700, which ended the long series
of Iroquois-Algonkian wars and brought about an alliance with the Catholic Mohawks at Caughnawaga, near
Montreal.  The Wabanaki Confederacy has interesting
parallels with the League of the Iroquois, but the
precise relationships have not yet been worked out.

During the period of British control the Penobscots
and other tribes had a difficult time, but the Revolution provided a possible escape.  They joined the
colonists in 1775 and participated in the siege of
Quebec.  France's entry into the war in 1778 ensured
the continued loyalty of the Wabanaki tribes to the
American cause, but they were badly treated in terms
of supplies near the end of the war.  The Treaty of
Paris ignored their claims to land.

During the post-revolutionary period the confederacy
was divided by the international boundary, and political factions made difficulties for several tribes.
By the end of the nineteenth century the Passamaquoddy
were without an effective tribal organization and completely subject to the State of Maine.  The Penobscots
were not much better off.  In 1920, representatives
of the two tribes petitioned the Governor of Maine
not to extend the franchise to Indians.  "We are
wards of the State of Maine," they said, and "we are
satisfied with our lot as Indians."

In 1950, however, after the Indians had lost much of
their remaining lands, a federal judge held that the
"Indian Non-Intercourse Act of 1790" was applicable
to the Maine tribes, and ordered the Justice Department to file suit against the State of Maine on their
behalf.  Currently, the Indians are claiming the
eastern half of Maine--some ten million acres--and
the tribes involved are showing a new vitality and
confidence.

The Wabanaki were, at least, spared the effects of
intense assimilation pressure in the late nineteenth
century.  But elsewhere assimilation was combined
with pressures to divide tribal lands among the individual Indians and thus make portions of the reservation available to white settlement.  Senator Dawes
of Massachusetts visited the Western Cherokee in the
late 1880s and reported on their general prosperity,

but he noted they had gotten as far as they could go while owning their land in common: "There is no selfishness, which is at the bottom of civilization. Till the people consent to give up their lands and divide them among the citizens so that each can own the land he cultivates they will not make much more progress." The supporters of the General Allotment Act of 1887 often meant well but the results were disastrous. Tribal landholdings fell from approximately 138,000,000 acres in 1887 to some 48,000,000 in 1934, when the process of allotting lands was stopped, but Indians were left impoverished and with shattered morale.

Sharlotte Neely provides a picture of what happened to the Eastern Band of Cherokee who lived on a federal reservation in North Carolina during this period, in terms of the imposed educational system. This group of Cherokee escaped removal to Indian Territory in 1838. Initially, they were under Quaker tutelage, but when the Bureau of Indian Affairs took control of the Cherokee schools, they instituted a "harsh system of forced culture change" lasting until John Collier became Commissioner of Indian Affairs in 1933. What Dr. Neely states for the Eastern Cherokee was standard practice for most Indian reservations in the United States and Canada as well. She recounts John Collier's eyewitness report when he visited one of the Cherokee schools in the 1920s, and its influence on his later efforts to change Indian education when he became Commissioner.

The Indian Reorganization Act of 1934 endeavored to repair the damage done during the preceding decades by recognizing the importance of Indian communal life as an agency for preserving and encouraging social controls and values. It sought to restore initiative and self-government to the Indian tribes. D'Arcy McNickle, himself an Indian and a participant in this process, provides an inside view of the difficulties that Collier encountered, both with Congress and the Bureau of Indian Affairs bureaucracy, in his efforts to restore Indian lands and raise their morale. Collier's attempts to provide Indians with a viable future were bitterly opposed by many whites and even by educated Indians, who saw his policies as a backward step. But much of his program prevailed and today Indians are in a much better position in almost all respects. As McNickle concludes,

"Indians were not held back by Collier's efforts to
build upon the tribal past.  Instead they have plunged
affirmatively into the twentieth century, asserting
their identity, and acquiring the skills that will
enable them to survive as Indians and as members of
an Indian community."

During World War II all government resources were
directed toward the war effort and progress on most
reservations was at a standstill.  Many Indians served
in the armed forces and returned as veterans with new
skills and a widened horizon.  Other families moved
to neighboring cities to work in factories or army
depots.  They returned to the reservations with hopes
to improve life with labor-saving devices and with
better schools.

In the early decades of the post-war period, Congress
set out to reverse most Indian Reorganization Act
principles.  House Concurrent Resolution 108, passed
by Congress in 1953, was the keystone to new policy
designed to free Indians from federal control, and
their wardship, and make them subject to the same
laws as other citizens.  But Indians by this time
were citizens, with most of the rights possessed by
their white neighbors, and the federal government
could not abandon their trust responsibilities set
up under law.

An initial program of Indian relocation in selected
cities had some initial success but ultimately failed,
as many families returned to the reservation.  Relocation was followed by a policy of termination of
government control over reservations as soon as practical.  The Klamath and Menominee, each possessing
large stands of commercial timber, were prepared
for handling their own affairs.  The outcry against
termination was strong, however, and those tribes
that were terminated have been given an opportunity
to return to federal control.  Notably, the Menominee
have so decided.

When John Kennedy was elected President, he appointed
a task force on Indian Affairs which proposed the
following objectives:  (1) maximum Indian economic
self-sufficiency, (2) full participation in American
life, and (3) equal citizenship privileges and responsibilities.  The task force recognized that the
support of the Indian communities was vital to attain

these objectives and believed Indians could retain
their tribal identities and much of their culture
while actively participating in American society.
The educational program was enhanced and a survey
of tribal reservation resources was undertaken pre-
paratory to greater exploitation.

At the same time that the task force was reporting,
the American Indian Chicago Conference convened,
with some 460 Indians from 90 tribes in attendance; but
their recommendations were radically different.  They
asked for the return of Indian lands and the enlarge-
ment of their reservations as well as protection of
their rights and privileges against the encroachment
of both state and federal governments.  They were
particularly concerned with their treaty rights as
self-governing, though dependent groups.

Not all Native Americans have agreed to these objectives.  Almost half of the Indian populations are
no longer on reservations.  In the city, they do not
have some privileges of reservation living--federal
education and medical services, and freedom from
taxation on lands used for farming or housing--which
make many Indians still prefer to reside on reservations, despite other difficulties.  On the reservation
the Indian is surrounded by kinsmen and friends, and
patterns of sharing remove some of the hazards of
existence.  The Indian who ventures into the cities
meets with good will, but also with race and class
prejudice, and the government has been reluctant to
extend special services to urban Indians.

As Indian communities form in the cities, however,
they recreate a society in which to survive.  The
Narragansetts, who once occupied most of Rhode
Island, have lost most of their distinguishing features and their aboriginal culture but have been
able to maintain their group identity and unity
through a tribal organization, an annual pow-wow
and other social activities, and the Indian church
and its management.

On a national scale the growing Pan-Indian movement
provides a similar integration through the pow-wow
circuit, July 4th ceremonies, and the rituals of
the Native American Church.  At the political level
the National Congress of American Indians, composed
of official tribal representatives, has had some

success, but sometimes it has been eclipsed in publicity by the American Indian Movement, a more aggressive and militant group appealing to many young urban Indians. With the "Trail of Broken Treaties," the occupation of the Bureau of Indian Affairs building in Washington, D.C., and their dramatization of the events at Wounded Knee a century and more ago, the American Indian Movement has called the plight of the Indians to the attention of a large segment of the American public, enlisting the support of important individuals in all walks of life.

Against this background, Margot Liberty provides a first-hand account of the events which took place at the celebration of the 100th anniversary of the defeat of General Custer by the combined forces of the Sioux and Northern Cheyenne, which occurred at the same time the American nation celebrated its first centennial. The defeat of Custer and his 7th Cavalry was the high point in Indian resistance on the Plains, and while it may have hastened the day when all Indians were established on reservations, the victory has become "a major symbol in movements demanding Indian independence."

It also had the effect of ending President Grant's Peace Policy and beginning a half-century of attempted assimilation of Indians into American life with eradication of traditional Indian culture. But a century later, the victory is being utilized by Indians as evidence of their one-time superiority over whites, while providing a new confidence in efforts to utilize their reservation resources. With the current energy crisis, the reservation resources in oil, gas, uranium and coal have become crucial to future developments for the nation as a whole. Indians face a difficult task in getting an adequate return in the face of national needs. Tribes like the Northern Cheyenne are making a conscious comparison between the onslaughts of General Custer and the coal companies. Already they have forced the Secretary of the Interior to cancel leases with inadequate returns and protection for the environment. They are convinced of the necessity to ban strip mining on the reservation for the present.

The frequent changes in government policy with regard to Indians have left them confused and apathetic. Each administration begins anew to solve the Indian problem, with little or no reference to the past.

Congress has repeatedly demonstrated that politics comes before justice, so far as the Indians are concerned. I have said elsewhere that there is not one "Indian problem" but many--as many as there are Indian tribes or groups. Each is different in important respects, though there are also common features. In the past we have attempted to solve these problems by a single formula, where a flexible program is required. But the basic conflict between the goal of full participation in American life and maintenance of Indian identity is a difficult problem to solve in the American scene. We find it hard to treat societies as different but equal.

The logic of House Concurrent Resolution 108, which dominated post-war policy regarding the American Indian is the logic of the "melting pot." The political leaders of this country, beginning with the colonists and the founding fathers, have never been willing to contemplate a country made up of different nations, nor to give more than lip service to the possibility of plural cultures. While it is possible for some individuals to retain their tribal identities and much of their culture while actively participating in American society, it is impossible for whole groups to do so in any real sense.

Lewis Henry Morgan was one of the first American scientists who saw the "Indian problem" in a realistic perspective; his recommendations were largely ignored though many of his predictions have come to pass. The Merriam Survey Report, in 1928, under the auspices of the Institute for Government Research, had an important effect, and provided part of the policy for the Indian Reorganization Act in 1934, but many of its recommendations were ignored. The Indian Declaration of Purpose does not seem to have been read by the Congressional committees turning out legislation to mold the Indian to their image of what the red American should be. Even the Report of the Commission on the Rights, Liberties, and Responsibilities of the American Indian in 1966 has never made any impression on Congress or the Executive Branch, despite its distinguished membership and its important conclusions. Currently the Report of the American Indian Policy Review Commission is under consideration, but it is not likely to have much more input than its predecessors.

In the last analysis, it is the Indians themselves who will solve their problems. There is currently a great ferment on many reservations and increased communication between different Indian groups and between Indians and whites. Out of this dialogue will come a greater realization that the future of the Indians is in their hands and that they need to make the basic decisions. If their dependent status is their greatest problem, they need to work toward interdependence rather than independence, if they are to create a viable future for themselves and their children.

The papers in the second half of this volume are more varied and deal with contemporary political problems, though many have a historical background. They are divided between United States and Canadian examples, and the latter are particularly interesting since the Canadian government has taken a somewhat different approach to the problems of Indian-white relationships. Here we can only indicate some of the important conclusions, but the details are interesting in providing the framework for interaction.

The Seminole Indians are well known to visitors to Florida but few are aware of their origins and their long fight against removel to Indian Territory. Merwyn Garbarino sketches their origins in the eighteenth century, as small groups fled the Southeast and its wars to seek refuge in Spanish Florida, where they gradually formed a new "tribe," which came to speak dialects of Muskogean. When the United States purchased Florida from Spain in 1819, the new white settlers began agitating for the removal of the Seminoles. The Second Seminole War resulted, which lasted some seven years, and a majority of the Seminoles were forced to relocate in Indian Territory, but a small group retreated southward to the region of the Everglades where their descendants still reside on several reservations.

Secretary of the Interior Harold Ickes, in his <u>Secret Diary</u> (1953) reports on his trip with John Collier to visit the Seminoles in 1935. He was sympathetic to their requests for more land to carry on their hunting practices, and he noted that they were never conquered: "Though they are still savages, they still distrust the white man, and they still live in primitive conditions."

A tribal government was set up, following their be-
lated acceptance of the Indian Reorganization Act in
1957, and Garbarino outlines the practices by which
the Bureau of Indian Affairs has brought the independent Seminole to the verge of dependence. For
several generations, she notes, "the bureaucracy has
treated Indians like children," with expectable results. Many Seminoles have come to believe in their
own dependence and to behave on that basis.

The problem of making the bureaucracy a servant
rather than a master is a difficult one in the American system. John Collier had great difficulty in
trying to implement the New Deal policies, despite
the fact that he was in office for a dozen years,
and his successors can seldom accomplish anything
important in four-year terms. Even where the Bureau
is willing to experiment with self-government on the
reservation, as in the case of Zuni, the Governor of
the tribe still finds that he has great difficulties.
The dissatisfaction with the Bureau of Indian Affairs
on the part of Indian groups is real, and the more
than three-fourths of all tribes operating under the
Indian Reorganization Act want community responsibility and self-determination. The Bureau has many
tasks assigned to it by law and these it cannot escape. But self-government is one task Indian groups
must learn for themselves, and they must be given an
opportunity to manage their own affairs and make the
decisions affecting their future.

The Crow Indians of Montana, now living adjacent to
the Northern Cheyenne, have had a somewhat different
history than their fellow plains tribes. They early
established friendly relations with the invading
whites, and a treaty in 1868 established a reservation which they occupied after the buffalo disappeared.
They prospered as middlemen in the fur-trade during
the nineteenth century, and were able to transform
their institutions and values so as to adjust to the
new reservation conditions.

Fred Voget's account of traditional institutions of
the Crow and their remodelling on the reservation
shows how the Crow have been able "to achieve a sense
of historic identity, direction, and cultural continuity," despite strong pressures for acculturation,
and demonstrates that a viable life is possible under favorable circumstances. He thinks five factors

are important: (1) possession of a homeland, (2) a local economy which permits the maintenance of social exchanges and traditional statuses, (3) Native-based religious ceremonies, (4) a world view which brings meaning to religious forms, and (5) a living language. The Crow have all of these, and Voget notes there has been no great interest in the American Indian Movement or other types of political action on the Crow reservation.

Developments in Indian-white relations in the Canadian North in the post-war period illustrate many of the same problems we have mentioned so far, and the Canadian solutions will be interesting. We have recently concluded an agreement with the Alaskan Native populations, both Eskimo and Indian, but the implementation of the provisions will be complicated and difficult. This agreement will be in the forefront as the Canadian Eskimo (Inuit) and the various tribal groups in the North organize politically. Treaties have been made with most of the Indians in the Canadian provinces, except for British Columbia, but the northern territories have been governed more directly, and treaties or other agreements are still to come, for the most part.

W. K. Barger provides a comparative account of Inuit and Cree adaptation to town life in the Canadian North, and the political developments which have taken place in both groups. Barger concentrates his attention on Great Whale River, Québec, and details the changes in community life and structure in the post-war period, as radar bases and mineral development expanded white influence and attracted Indians and Inuit as laborers.

Barger thinks western culture has had a different impact on the Native peoples of the Canadian North than in the United States and southern Canada, and orients his discussion in terms of internal colonialism, a now fashionable but pejorative term which seems out of place. He notes that "recent developments have stimulated many changes in the traditional cultures of the northern Indians and Inuit. New constraints and new opportunities have impinged upon their independence and guided their alternatives in the modern world." But this is true for all migrant groups into the cities--whether white, black or

Indian--and Canadian Indians are still able to return to the "bush."

Terminology aside, Barger gives an excellent account of the differences in Inuit and Cree residence patterns and social status in the new environment, and the varied reactions encountered in contacts with government officials, teachers, traders, and missionaries. Here the patterns of political, social, and economic domination are clear but the class system has not hardened into a caste system and there is still mobility. As Barger notes, the Inuit and Cree have "responded to this colonialistic system with initiative and innovation, and made functional changes in their social structures and world views."

In addition to the changes in social structure from local groups to communities, the Inuit in the 1970s were joining the newly-formed Northern Québec Inuit Association and aiding in the formation of the national Inuit Tapirisat--the Eskimo Brotherhood modeled after the Indian Brotherhoods--and were developing clear positions on aboriginal rights, which included self-determination, claims to land, and preservation of their ethnic heritage. They want to live in their own territory and control their own affairs: "Once we get the land, in time we will be able to manage it. Then we won't need an outside government." Whether the Inuit can be full citizens of the national society, and still maintain their special status and unique heritage is a problem they share with the Indian groups.

The Cree groups were formerly organized on the basis of family and kinship groups and leadership was based on consensus, but when Band Councils were organized the chiefs were elected. Within the Cree community traditional patterns were maintained, but the elected leaders represented the community in external affairs. Like the Inuit, the Cree joined the Québec Indians Association, and later the Grand Council of the Crees of Québec in the 1970s, and are also demanding self-determination, claims to land, and preservation of their ethnic heritage.

The Inuit and Cree cooperated mainly when they were opposed to particular governmental policies--otherwise they emphasized their own interests and individual goals. Thus they objected strongly to the

293

move to transfer federal services and control to the Province of Québec, fearing that the latter was mainly interested in natural resources. The James Bay hydroelectric project, which would flood much of their lands to provide power for southern Canada and New York State, was likewise jointly opposed, and they were able to stop the project until their rights were clarified. The Québec Court of Appeals reversed the ruling on the grounds of "general public interest," and the Crees and Inuit were forced to negotiate a settlement in 1975, giving up their land claims for a financial settlement and use rights to traditional areas. Barger concludes that the two groups have achieved some of their political goals and their future, while not clear, is a promising ·one.

June Helm reports on a related problem concerning the social, environmental, and economic impact of a proposed energy corridor along the Mackenzie River to bring natural gas to southern Canada, with other development to follow. Here some 30,000 people live in a vast area making up the western portion of the Northwest Territories. About half are whites in three settlements and the rest Natives, mostly Dene, and Metis, the mixed-blood population which here has a distinctive identity and cultural heritage.

Dr. Helm is primarily concerned with the Athabaskan-speaking Dene, and she provides a brief but excellent account of their history and relations with whites, and in particular the processes by which the Dene became dependent on European goods and technology, particularly since World War II. The Family Allowance (1944) and Old Age Security Pension (1951) provided an economic floor under family living, and encouraged a retreat from independent life in the "bush" to a resettlement around the trading post or mission station.

In the 1960s the federal government began to transfer some activities to the Northwest Territorial government, a move which was interpreted as a "termination policy" and vigorously opposed. Earlier there had been treaties in which Native rights to land were given up in return for definite band reserves, but these were never established. By 1970 the Dene were beginning to organize on the basis of

294

the "Indian Brotherhood" model in order to deal with
the national and territorial governments.  A first
task was to develop a base for negotiation of Indian
land claims and the Indian Brotherhood of the Northwest Territories took an active part in assembling
the necessary information, with financial aid from
the federal government.

Mr. Justice Berger, as Commissioner for the Mackenzie
Valley Pipeline Inquiry, took extensive testimony
from a variety of sources, and Dr. Helm provides a
sample from the informal Community Hearings in which
Dene experiences, values, concerns, and fears are
voiced, and which reveal better than anything else
their perceptions of their loss of a self-sufficient
structure for action.  The themes of life on the
land, the loss of resources, relations with whites,
worries over social problems, and concern with aboriginal rights recur repeatedly, and they affirm the
Indian Brotherhood position:  "No development without
settlement of Indian land claims."

In 1976 the Dene Brotherhood of the Northwest Territories submitted a position paper to the federal
government with regard to their claims, which rejected the tradition in Canada that Native rights
should be extinguished, and advocated their right
to recognition, self-determination, and self-definition as Dene, with jurisdiction over their own territory.  Dr. Helm notes that this is a proposal that
is unparalleled in the history of Indian "claims
settlements," and if obtained will require major
adjustments and sophisticated leadership.  The Dene
are aware of the problems involved but the Brotherhood leaders believe they can be solved.  The only
parallels are the efforts of the Navajo Dene to set
up a similar autonomous "nation."

The final paper, by Ann McElroy, is devoted to the
"Politics of Inuit Alliance Movements in the Canadian
Arctic," and she provides a broad picture of the activities and policies of the Inuit Tapirisat, or
Eskimo Brotherhoods, in the Eastern Canadian Arctic.
Her research was centered on Baffin Land, and particularly the community of Frobisher Bay, and she outlines
the early history of Eskimo-white contacts, including
the explorers, traders, missionaries, and government
officials.

The rapid growth of northern communities in the 1960s, and its effects on Native Inuit life, is presented in considerable detail. The initial impression is one of diversity and complexity, and interpersonal relations run a wide gamut. The Inuit Tapirisat dates from 1971, and was organized by the Eskimo themselves, with the assistance of the Canadian Association in support of Native Peoples, and has begun to formulate some guidelines for their own organization and objectives. Their formal objectives include the preservation of Inuit culture and language, the uniting of all Inuit in Canadian regions, protection of hunting and trapping rights, improvement of communication among Inuit communities, information on history and relations with whites, and assistance in achieving full participation in Canadian society.

The Inuit Tapirisat has tackled all these--and more--problems in the 1970s with great determination and skill. Their leaders are mostly young, with a wide range of experience, and the leadership is mostly male. The first major task was to prepare a position paper on land claims and northern development, and this has threatened the unity of the organization since it has proved difficult to achieve consensus, particularly at the community level. Initially, also the Inuit Tapirisat was non-militant, but some controversies with the government have led to threats to use boycotts as a weapon. As Dr. McElroy notes, "the stakes of development are high" on both sides, and have international repercussion, as well.

I have presented the Canadian papers in some detail because they will be less familiar to most readers. The Native response to white pressures in terms of "Indian Brotherhoods" represents an important difference from that found south of the border, and offers the possibility of an united front which may be able to gain important concessions. The demographic balance is different, as well, and in many areas it may be possible to allow different patterns of utilization and exploitation to exist side by side, for a period at least. The question of land is the key question on both sides of the border. The bold claim of the Dene for sovereignty over their own territory and self-government within it, and the parallel claims of the Inuit, are not likely to be

realized in full.  As Dr. Helm notes, the Indians
active in the Brotherhoods "are not unaware of the
paradox that achievement of a substantial degree of
Indian economic and political self-determination
threatens the socio-political autonomy, self-sufficiency, and consensuality in Dene life that traditionally was lodged in the local group and local
community."  But as a young Dene leader has put it,
"A true government would be people themselves deciding what they want and then helping each other get
what they want."  It is a goal worth striving for.

Kutchin

Hare
Dogrib
Metis
Slave
Yellowknife
Beaver
Chipewyan

Inuit

Inuit

Inuit

Cree

Micmac
Maliseet

Abenaki
Penobscot
Passamaquaddy

Blackfeet
Crow
N.Cheyenne

Santee

Iroquois

Sioux

Shawnee

PACIFIC
OCEAN

Hupa

Navajo

Kiowa
Commanche

Cherokee
Chicasaw
Creek
Choctaw

ATLANTIC
OCEAN

Location of Tribes

Described in Text

·dwc·

0                    500
MILES

N